RUSSIA RE-EXAMINED

The Land, the People and How They Live

ALSO BY WILLIAM MANDEL

The Soviet Far East and Central Asia
A Guide to the Soviet Union
Soviet Source Materials on USSR Relations with East Asia, 1945–
1950 (*a compilation of documents*)

RUSSIA RE-EXAMINED

The Land, the People and How They Live

By

WILLIAM MANDEL

HILL AND WANG • NEW YORK

Manufactured in the United States of America by
The Colonial Press Inc., Clinton, Massachusetts

1234567890

For
Neal Burroughs (1922–1963)
friend, translator, and unique product
of two societies

A Note on Sources

To make this book short and readable, citations of sources are as few as possible: chiefly English-language newspapers and books available in most libraries and Soviet sources when not available in translation. A considerable portion of the information presented has never appeared in book form, Russian or English. This material is largely from Soviet scholarly journals published in English in quarterlies of which I am the translator: *Soviet Anthropology and Archeology, Soviet Law and Government, Soviet Psychology and Psychiatry, Soviet Sociology, Soviet Studies in History,* and *Soviet Studies in Philosophy.* The translation monthlies, *Soviet Education, Soviet Economics,* and *Soviet Review,* have also been employed. The selection of articles for translation in all these journals is by leading American academic authorities. My own evaluation of material used is based on visits to the U.S.S.R. in 1931–32, 1959, and 1962, upon which I have also drawn for many illustrative conversations and observations. But fundamentally this book is the end product of my twenty-five years in the field of Soviet affairs, ranging from a research fellowship at Hoover Institute, Stanford University, and publication in scholarly journals, to wartime service with the United Press and my present radio program reviewing the Soviet press, now in its seventh year. The vast number of questions asked me by listeners have, I think, been a reliable guide to what Americans of all backgrounds and ages want to know about Russia.

All photographs were selected by me from the collection of the American Russian Institute, Inc., San Francisco, and are used with their permission.

W.M.

Jacket and cover photographs—Front, top: (left) Larissa Latynina, Olympic gymnastics champion and daughter; (right) construction at Bukhtarand-on-Irtysh; bottom (left to right): city beach on Don River at Rostov; tape recorder, television, good clothes, good apartment— signs of high-income work in Soviet Union; 250,000-acre farm in "virgin land" program. Back, top: atomic icebreaker *Lenin*; middle: (left) oil town east of Volga; (right) kindergarten; bottom: (left) Moscow fashion show; (right) amateur dancers of Perm, industrial city in Ural Mountains.

Contents

Illustrations

RUSSIA RE-EXAMINED

The Land, the People and How They Live

Union of Soviet Socialist Republics

1: The Land, Its Population, Essentials of the System

> Summer reigned with an intense thundery heat over the vastness of Siberia that year. From the moment the searing orange sun rose above the horizon, it flayed the earth with a pitiless, unlivable heat. Toward the end of the day the air was so heavy that people simply gave up. Defeated, they took refuge in the lakes and rivers or crawled into the cobwebs in the darkest corner of barn or storehouse. Only the thunderstorms saved the grass from withering, the trees from shedding their leaves, and the earth from cracking, contracting, and turning to ash.
> —Georgi Markov, *Salt of the Earth*

Siberia is not always cold. Russia is not far from the United States at all points. In the Bering Straits, the Soviet Union is closer to Alaska than Cuba is to Florida. Russia is also the direct neighbor of six countries in Europe, reaches to within nine miles of India, touches Afghanistan, Iran, and Turkey, and has a very long common border with China. It is centrally located relative to most countries. The airline distance from Siberia to Australia is only half as great as from Australia to the United States.

The area of the Union of Soviet Socialist Republics—the country we commonly call Russia—is 8.6 million square miles, more than twice the size of the second largest country, China. The

3

Typical spring scene of European Russia and Siberia

United States is 3.6 million square miles, including its territories and possessions.

Most of the Soviet Union lies in exactly the same latitudes as Canada and has the same range of climate from cool temperate to frigid. It has the same problem of ice-clogged ports in winter, even in the south. But the U.S.S.R. is much larger and bulges farther south than Canada. At the southern end of the Caspian Sea, bordering Iran, is a terribly hot desert area. A 560-mile irri- gation-and-inland-waterway canal, claimed to be the world's largest, has made possible a manifold increase in the planting of cotton, orchards, vineyards, and even dates. Another hot seacoast area, at the east end of the Black Sea, has been made useful in the opposite way—by draining its humid swamps.

But these hot areas are unusual. The U.S.S.R. is chiefly a cold country, and because man has only recently learned to prosper in cold areas with poor farming conditions, the Soviet Union ranks lower in population than in size. In 1963 it had 223 million people, which is only one-third the population of China and one-half of India. The United States, with 188 million, is much closer to the U.S.S.R. in numbers of people than in area. The Soviet population increases by approximately 3.3 million per year and the United States by 2.8 million.

The people of the U.S.S.R. live under a single socioeconomic and political system, but within it there are some extraordinary differences. Ultramodern eleven-story apartment houses are to be built on shoals in open water seventy-five miles from the shore of the Caspian Sea to house workers who are tapping an immense pool of oil three miles beneath its floor. Twenty minutes away by jet, still within the Soviet Union, is a mountain fastness where the people of one valley speak a language incomprehensible in the next.

The U.S.S.R. is a country of new frontiers. In Siberia and the Kazakh Republic to its south, 350,000 youthful pioneers under the leadership of very few experienced adults, have broken the prairie sod to put as many acres under crop in three years as the entire farmland of Canada from ocean to ocean. An additional 600,000 youths have built thirty major plants and railroads through the virgin forests, shadeless plains, and mountain gorges of Siberia. On the remote sub-Arctic Angara and Yenisei rivers three thousand miles from Moscow, they have put up dams, each of which is to yield two and one-half times the power of Grand Coulee. Two earlier postwar dams on the Volga were already outproducing the largest in the United States. The youngest Ph.D. in the Soviet Union, mathematician Alexander Kirillov of Moscow University, proudly wears a gold medal awarded for several summers' work as a volunteer farmhand in Siberia.

These Khrushchev-era projects have had their full quota of problems, but the farms and new industries function, and enough of the youthful builders remain to populate the dozen brand-new permanent towns every year. More than five hundred have been founded in the thirty-five years since planned industrialization was begun. Karaganda, for example, is now a city approaching a population of half a million. Many are past the hundred-thousand mark.

In this century of scientific advancement one of the most popular forms of pioneering for Soviet young people is prospecting—not with the sourdough's pan but with the modern tools of the geologist. Despite the fact that much can now be done with magnetic and gravity instruments from the air, the final work, exciting and physically challenging, must still be done by tramping through the wilderness. No secret is made of the dangers, but the rewards of discovery are there, and although ownership does not accrue to the finder, the government gives handsome bonuses in cash and public honor. It was in the mid-1950's that the Soviet's first commercial diamond deposits were discovered 150 miles from the nearest riverboat landing in Yakutia, the coldest territory on earth outside the Antarctic. The finders were treated as public benefactors, as indeed they are.

To compile a list of the known resources of the U.S.S.R. would be to name every kind of natural wealth known to man except for some products of tropical agriculture: coffee, cocoa, pineapples, bananas, certain nuts. Russians even grow their own tea, as well as dates, figs, and oranges in limited areas.

Agriculture is not easy in most of the country. Four-fifths of the farmlands suffer periodic droughts. The opening of the Virgin Soil Territory (that's the official name) would probably have been impossible without modern equipment. Harvesting must be done in the few days between the maturing of the crop and the first frosts. Planting must follow hard on the heels of the retreating snow, which is plowed to slow the rate of melting and give the water a chance to soak into the ground, for there is little rain in summer. Yet this territory is in the *southern* half of the Asian portion of the U.S.S.R., mainly south of the original Trans-Siberian Railroad.

From satellites to safety pins, there is almost nothing the Soviet Union does not produce other than luxury items. But she tries to buy abroad whatever is more cheaply available in that way. While she was building steel mills for India and a number of other countries in 1963, she contracted for Austria to build a mill employing a process the Austrians had developed that is particularly suited to Russian ores and coals. On the other hand, when, that same year, the West German government forbade its steel mills to supply the U.S.S.R. with 200,000 tons of oil pipeline, Moscow channeled extra funds and equipment into that industry. Although she had just begun production of "Big Inch" pipe in 1962, she built four immense mills that year and the next, which made the Soviet Union independent in this field by 1964.

Forty years ago, it was easy to indicate the few centers of Soviet industry. Machinery came from Leningrad in the northwest; textiles and a variety of general merchandise from Moscow; coal, iron ore, steel, and aluminum from the Ukraine in the European south; petroleum from Baku on the west shore of the Caspian Sea. Under Joseph Stalin, a second center of steel production was built in the Ural Mountains, which divide Europe from Asia, and a second center of coal mining was established in Siberia.

Today, it would take a textbook in economic geography to show the distribution of mineral extraction, power production, and manufacturing. The Ukrainian Donbass region is still the largest single producer of the basic materials of industry, but nearly one-half the iron and steel now comes from east of the Volga.

Power plants along the Volga and eastward through Siberia will be producing 46 per cent of the electricity by 1965. This means that Russia's "wide open spaces" will have become as important industrially as the long-developed areas west of that river. Even so, the U.S.S.R. is still overwhelmingly a European rather than an Asian country, for there is still a much denser concentration of people, industry, transport facilities, and agriculture west of the Volga.

POPULATION: ONLY HALF RUSSIAN

The U(nion) of S(oviet) S(ocialist) R(epublics), or the Soviet Union, does not consist of Russians alone. Russians are a Slavic people and if we add the other Slavs—Ukrainians, Belorussians, and small numbers of Poles and Bulgarians—to the Russians, the total number of Slavs is more than three-quarters of the population of the U.S.S.R. But Ukrainians and Belorussians aren't Russians any more than Spaniards and Italians are Frenchmen, or Norwegians and Danes are Swedes. The Slavs are related to each other, but their languages and customs differ. "Krahsnee Pahhar" in Russian means the same as "Cheervunnee Hlibahrub" in Ukrainian—the Red Plowman (the name of a collective farm)—but they are very different words indeed.

The U.S.S.R. is the successor state to the Russian Empire of the tsars, a nation of many different peoples. In a struggle of eat or be eaten, the Russian Empire expanded in all directions over a huge, mainly flat territory, in which there were no real natural boundaries. Native peoples were subjected and left where they were, particularly if their territories were swampy, sandy, excessively cold, or otherwise unappealing to the Russians. Only in its farthest southern expansion into the Caucasus, and westernmost into the Baltic, did the Russian Empire encounter folk with more advanced agriculture and urban crafts. By that time, however—the eighteenth and nineteenth centuries—these small, progressive peoples could not hold out against the overwhelming number of Russians.

When the Communists came to power in 1917, they offered independence to the subjected peoples of the Empire, simultaneously urged their working classes to make revolutions against the wealthy, and offered the help of the Red Army. The result of a struggle in which fourteen foreign governments did their best to destroy the Soviets or pull territories away from them is that the U.S.S.R. today is somewhat smaller than the old Empire. Finland and Poland, which were part of the Russian Empire, are not part of the U.S.S.R.

School is taught in the U.S.S.R. in sixty-one languages. The culture of each ethnic group, except in part that of the Jews (see pp. 65–70), is respected and developed. Many tribes of only a few thousand people have their own newspapers and schools. Fifty-three nations and tribes have territorial recognition and direct representation in the parliament of the U.S.S.R., called the Supreme Soviet. Fifteen areas are "sovereign," and it is they that constitute the Union of Soviet Socialist Republics. They range in population from Russia's 122 million to Estonia's million and a quarter. They are listed here with their populations as of January 1, 1962:

Slavic		Central Asian	
Russia	122,084,000	Kazakh	10,934,000
Ukraine	43,527,000	Uzbek	9,986,000
Belorussia	8,316,000	Kirghiz	2,318,000
		Tadzhik	2,188,000
Slavic–Romance		Turkmen	1,683,000
Moldavia	3,106,000		
Baltic		Caucasus	
Lithuania	2,852,000	Georgia	4,271,000
Latvia	2,170,000	Azerbaijan	4,117,000
Estonia	1,235,000	Armenia	1,958,000

The Central Asians and the Azerbaijanis are chiefly Moslem in religious tradition. The Georgians and Armenians have two of the oldest Christian denominations on earth. The Slavs and Moldavians are Orthodox Christian in background. The Estonians are Lutheran. So are most of the Latvians, a large minority of whom are Roman Catholic. The Lithuanians are Catholic, historically. In addition to Christianity and Mohammedanism, Judaism and other major religions are practiced in the U.S.S.R., as are many forms of primitive worship. But 90 per cent of the people are atheists.

Opera and ballet conductor in Kirghizia. He and all his people
were nomads thirty-five years ago

SOVIET SOCIALISM ("COMMUNISM"): HOW IT WORKS

Until the Russian Revolution every modern country lived under
a system in which factories, mills, mines, and banks were almost
all privately owned. People talked about socialism—public ownership of all enterprise—but it had never been tried. Some claimed
that it would never be. Others said that if it did come about that
it wouldn't work.

The Soviets were the first people to try socialism. Being the
pioneers, they have gone through a great deal of trial and error.

But after forty-five years they are still in business. And for nearly thirty-five years they have made no compromise with the principle that all industry, transportation, communications, banking, wholesale trade, foreign commerce, education, and science must be in public hands.

The world today accepts the fact that the Soviet Union has had great successes in these fields. This is why Asian, African, and Latin countries which are trying to leapfrog into the twentieth century wonder whether to follow the Soviet example or that of the United States and Western Europe, or to seek to combine elements from each system suited to their own traditions. This is why some have adopted Moscow's principles. Almost all countries that were colonies until recently have chosen a hybrid system in which large, expensive undertakings are chiefly publicly owned, while small business and farming are mainly in private hands.

Russia's present leaders are, almost without exception, former manual laborers and peasants, people whose families had no property whatever. This helps to explain why, in Italy, France, and Finland, which are modern Western countries, tens of millions believe that communism would provide their children with the opportunities people such as they do have in Russia. These are the challenges posed by the existence of the U.S.S.R.

How does this system work? From the viewpoint of the consumer, differences from what Americans are used to are not great. In the Soviet Union, work is paid for in wages or a salary, and the money is used to buy the goods one wants. Higher education and medical care are free. Other services cost very little, because of government subsidy or lack of bonded indebtedness. This is true of rent, public transportation, vacation accommodations, and child care in nurseries or kindergartens.

Stores, factories, and publishing houses have managers who tell the employees what to do, and organize and arrange matters, as in Western countries. Enterprises pay for the products and services used, and money is paid to them by customers.

One difference is that sales and advertising staffs are small, except in stores, of course. This is because there is little problem in marketing. Since all businesses are publicly owned, the government knows almost exactly how much of each item will be produced, because its agencies plan and direct production. It knows what prices will be because it sets them. It knows what the total purchasing power will be, except in farming, because its planning agencies, jointly with the business management agencies and the labor unions,

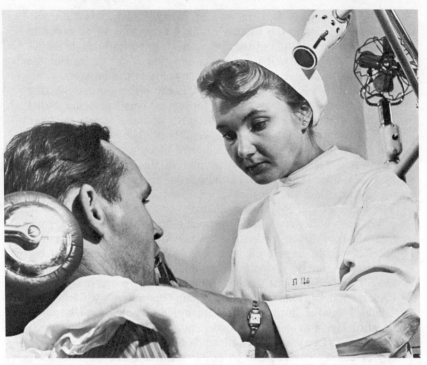

Free dental care at clinic

set wage and salary scales. It sets wages high enough to absorb each year's growth in production and to leave enough over for savings to buy expensive items such as cars or pianos. The over-all retail price level has shown virtually no change since 1958, although meat and dairy products have gone up and certain manufactured consumer goods have gone down.

Under this system, the government may decide, for example, that it is more important to produce farm machinery than private cars at a time when the country can't yet make enough of both at the same time. If so, it sets automobile prices so high that the public can't afford to buy more than the number offered for sale.

This brings us to the major difference between the Soviet economic system and that of the West. In the case just described, the Russian automobile industry makes an extremely high profit because of the difference between costs (including wages) and selling price. In the United States, the profit is used by the owners of the industry as they see fit: to increase dividends to stock-holders, to change the models of their cars, to save in order to strengthen the position of the company, or to go into new branches of business. Usually, it is some combination of all these. But the use of the profit is entirely up to the owners of the business.

In the U.S.S.R., the government sets the prices on cars. As the owner it takes the profits, except for a fixed small percentage that the manager may distribute as incentive bonuses or use to make additional improvements in labor conditions. The government may use its profit to expand another branch of industry, such as farm machinery. Or it may use all or part of this money for general purposes: space exploration, atom bombs, schools, hospitals, hous-ing construction, the opening of new farmlands, or building ferti-lizer factories and irrigation projects.

We have used the word "government" in a manner that suggests that Moscow directly manages the individual enterprises through-out the world's largest single country. At present, almost all big business is run by regional "economic councils," of which there are forty-seven—about the same number as there are states in the United States. There are also chain operations within these "states." Smaller businesses are run by city, county, and borough or ward levels of government, depending on the area each busi-ness serves. Local stores of all kinds are owned and operated by city or county government. In large cities there are neighborhood ("borough," "ward") governments for about each quarter-million people. Neighborhood governments run whatever does not have to be operated on a city-wide scale.

The federal government now directly controls only a very small percentage of the country's business. Its primary economic func-tion today is to make plans for industry, agriculture, transport, construction, and communications, to lay out lines of new develop-ment to finance and launch them, and to co-ordinate local plans where the pieces don't fit. The arrangement is practical econom-ically, and constant changes are made as production rises and the technological revolution advances. However, plans issued by the government have the force of law. Managers must obey them as strictly as a citizen is required to obey traffic lights.

Although managers have very broad powers and final responsi-bility, employees and consumers have a good deal to say. The employees elect production committees that suggest nominations for management. They draft output and improvement plans jointly with management, and management must report to these committees. The system of volunteer citizens' committees functioning alongside and as part of local government bureaus in charge of each branch of business is very important. There are 2.3 million citizens who are members of these committees. They take part in planning and day-to-day supervision and report to city, county, or neighborhood government council meetings, which are open to the public.

The Soviets claim that the economic system described above explains their very rapid rate of progress. That progress, and what remains to be done, was very well described by *The New York Times* critic and correspondent Brooks Atkinson, who was stationed in the U.S.S.R. in 1945 and revisited it eighteen years later: *

Although the Russians face serious problems, they have solved serious problems before.

The problems range all the way from agriculture and honest administration to the Wall, the Chinese Communists, and America. When these problems are discussed in America there is sometimes a disposition to imply that they indicate that Russian socialism is failing. Nothing could be further from reality. Whatever kind of socialism it is (no one is quite sure), it has survived two world wars, an explosive political revolution, counter resistance, and the bloody scourge of Stalinism.

When I see the Russians hurrying along the streets in their warm, good clothing or seated politely in the theaters, I cannot help wondering how they have survived all this privation and violence and emerged strong and confident. For I remember when they looked tired, when their clothing was pathetic, the food scarce and the housing appalling.

They are not likely to question a system of government that has given them the status of a great world power, that made them first in space exploration, that is providing good apartments that cost only $9 or $12 a month, free medical and hospital services, livable pensions for cripples and aged people, and other benefits of the modern welfare state.

Since a rise in the standard of living of any people is good for all people, Americans should rejoice in the great progress in Russia. To put the matter on the lowest plane of self-interest, Russians have a lot more to lose now than they had before and are just as anxious as we are to avoid the calamity of war.

* *The New York Times,* March 8, 1963.

2: History

A thousand years ago a principality called Rus, its capital the city of Kiev, ruled more than half of European Russia. Its princes adopted Christianity, which had filtered in through trade contacts. Christianity brought Russia its alphabet and other cultural traditions from Byzantium.

In 1237, the Tatars, under a grandson of Genghis Khan swept across Russia and smashed what was left of Kiev Rus, which had already been weakened by internal troubles. The Tatars ruled for almost 250 years.

The Russian princes who finally defeated the Tatars by a combination of passive resistance and military might were from Moscow, far to the northeast of Kiev. Moscow became the center of Russia until 1712, when the capital was shifted to St. Petersburg by Peter the Great. Lenin restored Moscow to its position as capital more than two hundred years later.

After the last remnants of Tatar rule were eliminated in 1480, unification under a central government finally came a hundred years later. It was completed by the tsar who has come down in history as Ivan the Terrible (1530–1584). He slaughtered the old nobility, and, after he had broken up its lands into smaller divisions, gave them to loyal soldiers in his forces.

The peasants were forced into serfdom. In 1497, tenant farmers were forbidden to leave or change masters except during a two-week period each year. About one hundred years later, a fugitive-serf law was enacted, and serfs were deprived of all right to change masters, thus becoming lifetime serfs. In 1649, serfdom was made hereditary. In 1718, under Peter the Great, peasants who had been freed by their own masters were returned to the status of serfdom. Unlike slaves, serfs (except household servants) could not be sold away from the land they tilled. Later, the serfs were reduced to what amounted to slavery: they could be gambled away in card games, bought and sold away from their homes; children could be taken from mothers in such sales, husbands from wives.

But 1917 was foreshadowed in various uprisings. In 1606, a peasant army marched 350 miles to Moscow and laid siege to it for more than a month. It took a government army of 150,000 men and a four-month siege of the rebel capital, Tula, to break the rebellion and capture its leader, Bolotnikov. But this was possible only after the government had undercut the uprising by edicts that eased the position of the serfs for some years.

On the southern frontier, runaway serfs, who came to be known as Cossacks, built up a free society of their own. They combined farming with raiding Russian as well as Turkish and Persian territories. They were finally bought out, by the offer of special privileges, to serve as frontier troops and as an internal emergency police force for the tsars. But in the seventeenth century their hatred of tsarist oppression and their kinship with the serfs was still dominant. In 1670–1671, Stenka Razin, who is still sung of by folk singers in many lands, led the entire Volga valley in a great rebellion. The uprising was finally drowned in blood; eleven thousand Cossacks were slaughtered in one small town alone.

The greatest of the revolts occurred in 1773–1775, in the very years when, five thousand miles away, the conflict over American independence was coming to a head. This uprising, headed by a Cossack named Pugachev, took on some of the aspects of a political revolution. Overthrown tsarist authorities were replaced by chieftains chosen by election, manifestoes were issued, a general staff was organized. In the preceding years the tsars had begun to exploit the mineral resources of the Ural Mountains at the boundary between Europe and Asia, and had set up a large number of small factories. Pugachev controlled the enormous territory along the southeastern frontier from the Volga into Siberia, and gained the support of the native peoples as well as of the Russian serf workers of ninety-two mines and factories: three-quarters of the Urals industry of that day.

Although numerous economic, political, military, and personality factors played a role, all these uprisings were defeated fundamentally because the rebels offered only to replace a bad tsar by a good one and to ease the burden of feudal obligations upon the peasantry. They did not propose the abolition of either tsarism or feudalism. Revolutionary leaders usually proclaimed themselves tsars, and thus helped to strengthen the tradition of one-man rule that has so strongly influenced Russian government down to our day.

Peter the Great, who ruled at the beginning of the eighteenth century, combined extraordinary height and strength, personal vice, scintillating intellect, insuperable will power, vast organizing ability, diplomatic shrewdness, and complete disregard for the established rules of tsarist conduct. His capacities were so overwhelming as to make him a perfect example of the inability of even the greatest of men to do more than their time and place and the circumstances of their country permit.

At twenty-three, Peter led a war against Turkey for an outlet to the Black Sea. At twenty-four he founded the Russian fleet; at twenty-five, he went to Western Europe incognito to build an alliance against Turkey and did the manual labor of the shipbuilder in England and Holland to learn how good ships should be built. After he returned to Russia, he developed an educated government personnel from the best people available regardless of rank or race, established an iron and steel industry, a textile industry, and built overland canals. He planned and erected an entirely new, beautiful capital city, St. Petersburg, in a desolate swamp; established an Academy of Sciences; instituted an educational system; simplified the alphabet; introduced a calendar more in accord with the progress of astronomical knowledge; founded the first printed newspaper; and won for Russia a firm hold on the Baltic and Caspian seas. He also tried to change the psychology of the nobility by compelling them to exchange traditional Russian dress for the breeches and wigs of the West.

But the money for his achievements was found by squeezing the serfs even more mercilessly than previous tsars. In his time and country there was no other way to get money. Most of Peter's reforms survived his death at the age of fifty-three, but Russia continued to be a semifeudal absolute monarchy based on serfdom.

In 1812, Russia was attacked by Napoleon. Cautious Russian generals skillfully retreated and waited while the peasants harassed the French invaders by guerrilla action on their own initiative. This

Guerrillas harass Napoleon's army

cost Napoleon 100,000 men before the stand-off battle of Borodino. The partisan operations reflected the tremendous patriotism without which so huge a state could never have been built and survived, and the initiative that would revolutionize it socially and industrially a century later. Napoleon, although a dictator, brought with him the ideas and the legal code of the most advanced revolution the world had yet seen. When he was defeated, by Kutuzov's worrying tactics, and the tsarist and other armies swept into Paris in 1814, intelligent young Russian officers aware of their country's stagnation seized upon the ideas of the French Revolution.

In December, 1825, a group of these officers made the first attempt at a truly political revolution in Russian history: not merely the replacement of one tsar by another, but the institution of a new system of government. One of them drafted a proposed constitution, which was based on what he liked most in the constitutions of each of the states then constituting the United States. These young noblemen were crushed very easily and quickly but they are revered and their goals never faded from memory. Russia's first writer of world stature, the poet Pushkin, was associated with them. They are known as the Decembrists from the month of the rebellion.

The freeing of the serfs occurred at the same time as the Civil War in the United States. Emancipation in Russia came partly because one class of landowners had become involved in the growth of commerce and the beginnings of industry and wanted a system that would produce cash income. Serfs did not pay cash to their owners, but surrendered to them much of their crops and produce and performed unpaid forced labor. In addition to the problem of the serfs, Russia's defeat in the Crimean War, 1853–1856, made its hopeless backwardness clear to all. It could not even properly supply or arm its own troops on its own soil against the English and French, who had to come by ship via the Mediterranean and the Black Seas. In 1861, Tsar Alexander II decided to abolish serfdom. He said: "It is much better that this be done from above than from below."

The freed peasant families found themselves with less land than they had when serfs. They were not given the land they tilled outright but were compelled to buy it at a total cost 30 per cent higher than the market value of that day. Consequently, more than half of them refused to sign the deeds and there were more than a thousand peasant disturbances in the two years following the reform. Afterward, the thirty thousand landowners still owned as much as the ten million peasant families. The average landowner's holding was 5,700 acres, the average peasant's seventeen. Half of them had only two to five acres, and a third of the peasantry did not even have horses to pull their wooden plows. And so they were forced into sharecropping dependence upon the landowners and later also upon the wealthier peasantry called *kulaks*—"tightfists."

Because the freed peasants had so little land, they could not accumulate enough capital to improve their methods of farming. Unable to read and write, they were ignorant of progressive farming practices and knew no way to soften the results of even slightly bad turns of the weather. This meant repeated crop failures and famines. While a minority of peasants began to accumulate land and wealth at the expense of their fellows, others sank to the position of farm laborers, and millions gave up trying to meet land redemption payments and taxes in addition to paying 50 per cent of the crop as rent. They fled to the cities, where they constituted a supply of cheap labor, and this helped the growth of industry.

The families that moved to town were housed in barracks in wide double-decker bunks, one family per bunk or, if lucky, two families to a room. Wages averaged under four dollars per week.

Labor learned it had common interests and discovered the weapon of the strike. In 1897, it forced the first limitation of the working day by a law that provided that hours of work would be 11½ on weekdays and ten on Saturdays. At the time of the revolution in 1917, the workday was generally still ten hours. In the United States, the eight-hour day had generally been gained thirty years earlier.

Because of the system of absolute monarchy, which permitted no freedom of expression or organization whatever, labor saw no great chance to better itself through unions, which are agencies of reform, and must be legal to be of regular benefit. Instead, working people supported revolutionary parties pledged to overthrow both the autocracy and the capitalist system and to replace it by socialism.

In 1904, Russia's industrial backwardness and general inefficiency was demonstrated once again by her defeat at the hands of Japan, which had modernized rapidly in a short period. The war brought great hardships, and political parties representing capital, the peasantry, and labor, sprang into being and became influential. On January 9, 1905, more than a thousand St. Petersburg working people were killed and several thousand wounded when troops were ordered to fire on an unarmed procession. Headed by a priest, Gapon, the workers sought to present a petition to Tsar Nicholas II. This date has gone down in history as "Bloody Sunday." In May, the sailors of the cruiser *Potemkin* mutinied, an event that was immortalized years later in a great motion picture. In October, a general strike began, and soviets (the word *soviet* simply means "council") of delegates of working people were set up in all the major cities. The soviets exercised the functions of government. Meanwhile, police agents organized massacres of Jews ("pogroms") in an unsuccessful effort to divert popular wrath from tsarism. But in December, an armed uprising took place in the major cities of European Russia, Siberia, and the Ukraine. It was suppressed. The suppression was successful partly because the tsar had issued a manifesto promising political liberties and convocation of a legislature. The revolutionary forces were divided and confused by the promise. This series of events constitutes what is known as the Revolution of 1905.

Thereafter the monarchy, thoroughly frightened, undertook two sets of measures to preserve its rule. One was a land reform deliberately designed to enlarge the rich kulak group at the expense of the rest of the peasantry, in order to increase rural support for tsarism. The other was the institution of fearful political repression by field courts-martial established in July, 1906, and by storm troopers called the Black Hundreds. Executions were in the thousands: punitive expeditions exterminated with ruthless cruelty what remained of the revolutionary movement in Russia and Siberia. An assembly called the Duma was instituted in 1906, which in reality could do no more than talk, because the tsar had an absolute veto. It was elected on a basis of class representation, with the propertied classes guaranteed a majority. Despite these handicaps, a large revolutionary socialist minority was elected to the Second Duma in 1907. Many socialists were exiled to Siberia, the Duma was dissolved, and the election rules were changed to disfranchise the common people more fully. Although further elections to the Duma were held, it had no power, and, with only a dozen years of life before the Revolution, constituted Russia's only experience with an elected legislature. Efforts by the common people to improve their conditions were met by terror. Police bullets killed 270 in a single unarmed procession of striking miners at the Lena River goldfields in 1912. Similar methods, and mass exile to Siberia, were used to deal with the thirteen thousand separate peasant "outbreaks" officially reported in 1910–1914.

The Russian catastrophe in World War I precipitated the revolution. Russia's involvement in the war was due partly to the greed of her rulers and those of Germany, and partly to the fact that she had declined to a position of dependence on the West. The Russian railroads had been built with French loans, a debt doubly repaid by an alliance that made Russia a tail to the French kite. Seventy-two per cent of the iron and steel industry was owned by foreigners and a similar percentage of the coal industry. Half the oil output of Baku was in British and French hands. Russia's industrial ability to fight a modern war was so poor that 30 per cent of her troops were without any arms at all by mid-1915, the second year of the war. Soldiers often had to wait for a man with a gun to be killed or wounded before they could obtain a rifle.

The government was sitting on a volcano: 57 per cent of the people were non-Russian, and all of these suffered handicaps or repressions. Fourteen million men were drafted into the armed forces. In 1916 the government, which did not dare to put guns into the hands of Central Asians, tried to draft them for labor service. A widespread uprising occurred that was the harbinger of the history-making events of the following year.

Industrial conflict, rural disorganization, colonialism, and a disastrous war caused a unique combination of events: a peace movement without precedent (the soldiers just went home, and working women demonstrated for bread and peace), a workers' revolution for socialism, a peasant demand for land, and movements for independence or equality on the part of the subject nationalities.

A man of profound intellect, Vladimir Ilyich Lenin, succeeded in co-ordinating and gaining the leadership of these movements through the disciplined party he had organized. This was an organization of selfless men and women with a clear understanding of what they wanted, where they could get mass support, and how they could accomplish their ends. The party was the Russian Social-Democratic Labor Party (Bolsheviks). After the Revolution, it changed its name to the Communist Party. The slogan that rallied the people to the Revolution was "Peace, Bread, and Land."

Tsar Nicholas was ousted in March, 1917. Moderate parties set up a Provisional Government that held power for the next eight months. It failed to end the war, feed the starving people, or distribute the land of the landlords to the peasants, who were suppressed whenever they tried to seize it. Most of these steps would have violated private property rights, and this the moderates proved unwilling to do. One of the moderate groups, the wing of the Socialists called Mensheviks, hoped to progress by reforms and was theoretically in favor of such steps at some time in the future. As a consequence of the unwillingness of the moderates to institute necessary but radical changes, Lenin's revolutionary Bolsheviks gained a majority in the soviets of workers', soldiers', and peasants' representatives that sprang up all over the country.

Lenin had very little faith that the ruling classes would surrender power peacefully. However, he was not pledged to violence in principle. He wrote in 1917:

> To obtain the power of the state the class-conscious workers must win the majority to their side. As long as no violence is used against the masses, there is no other road to power. We are not Blanquists, we are not in favor of the seizure of power by a minority.*

He proposed that the soviets oust the self-appointed Provisional Government. In September, Lenin wrote a final appeal for a peaceful solution to the country's political crisis:

> By seizing power now—and this is probably their last chance—the soviets could still secure a peaceful development of the revolution, the peaceful election of representatives by the people, the peaceful struggle of parties within the soviets, the testing of the programs of

* Vladimir I. Lenin, *Selected Works,* New York: International Publishers, Vol. VI, p. 26.

the various parties in practice, and the peaceful transfer of power from party to party.*

There was no peaceful transfer. When Lenin's party gained a majority in the new Congress of Soviets (390 seats out of 650), he had the cruiser *Aurora* fire one shot across the building where the Provisional Government, headed by Alexander Kerensky, was meeting. This was on the night of November 6–7, 1917. A force of armed workingmen and soldiers charged across the square. There was some machine-gun and rifle fire on both sides, and the building and its occupants were captured. That was the revolution. The most exciting eyewitness account is *Ten Days That Shook the World,* by an American, John Reed. In the next three months, the local soviets took power clear across Siberia to the Pacific Ocean —without armed action. In European Russia there was minor fighting in several places.

The Soviet Congress urged a three-month truce in the war to end it by negotiation. The Congress nationalized the land and divided it among the peasants. It set up a government that introduced the eight-hour work day, abolished all privileges enjoyed by the Russians over other nationalities and by the Russian Orthodox Church over other faiths. It did away with all ranks and class privileges; legalized civil marriage (religious marriage had been compulsory); proclaimed equal rights for women in all respects, and declared that children were entitled to government protection whether or not their parents had been legally married.

Walter Duranty, *The New York Times* correspondent in Moscow for nearly twenty years following the Revolution, and a universally respected observer of the Soviets during his lifetime, believed that Lenin was willing to compromise with the capitalists as a matter of practical politics, but that they would not give him the chance:†

At the outset, indeed, Lenin seems to have wished or at least been willing to co-operate with the bourgeoisie [capitalists, in Marxist terminology—W.M.] in the urgent tasks of starting his administrative machine and of buttressing the shattered structure of Russia's national life. His overtures were generally cold-shouldered. . . . The attitude of the bourgeoisie soon developed into a regular boycott. . . . When the banks and financiers held aloof, he decreed nationalization of the banks. . . . Actually, it was not until May, 1918, that any one industry was fully nationalized. . . . In my opinion they were acts of self-protection . . . to prevent "sabotage" from stopping the wheels of industry and trade.

* *Ibid.,* p. 241.
† Walter Duranty, *U.S.S.R.,* New York: Lippincott, 1944, pp. 43–44.

Foreign intervention soon made it impossible ever to answer the question of what might have happened if Lenin had been able to apply his ideas under peaceful conditions. The Intervention was a three-year war. In the first months of 1918, the invading Germans seized almost as much territory as they did under Hitler twenty-four years later. The Western Allies invaded Central Asia in the south, and Murmansk and Archangel in the north, with American troops playing the main role in the last two cities. Monarchist and other rebel forces sprang up, the most important of which were under Admiral Kolchak in Siberia. President Wilson, along with Premier Clemenceau of France, and the British, Japanese, and Italian prime ministers, signed a declaration reading:

The Allied and Associated Governments are . . . disposed to assist the government of Admiral Kolchak and his associates with munitions, supplies, and food to establish themselves as the government of all Russia. . . .

In his two-volume study, *The Cold War and Its Origins,* Professor D. F. Fleming writes: *

Until the Nazis made wholesale murder a scientific business, the campaign of Admiral Kolchak in Siberia resulted in the most gigantic tragedy in all recent times.

Winston Churchill, then Britain's War Minister, was the originator and organizer of the Intervention. He later reported that one single anti-Communist general in the Ukraine, Denikin, received 250,000 British rifles, two hundred pieces of artillery, thirty tanks, and hundreds of British officers, advisers, and fliers.

At one point in the three-year struggle, the Soviet government had lost *all* of Siberia, Central Asia, the Caucasus, and the grain-, coal-, and steel-producing Ukraine. Lenin held only central European Russia, and was even cut off from the breadbasket of its southern steppes. To win out, the Communists put the country on strict rationing, established a militarized form of government, and reinstituted the draft. The peasants accepted it because this government had given them the land. It was at this time that the psychology of siege first gripped the country ("capitalist encirclement" was the Communist phrase). This our-backs-are-to-the-wall psychology was a major factor among those who permitted dictatorship to operate so harshly for over thirty years.

By 1920, the major armies on Soviet territory, foreign and

* D. F. Fleming, *The Cold War and Its Origins,* New York: Doubleday, 1961, Vol. I, p. 20.

Soldiers' rally at front, 1919

native, were defeated or evacuated. However, the Japanese remained in Vladivostok another two years, and on northern Sakhalin Island until eight years after the Revolution. German talk of revenge never ceased. The fact that the United States did not recognize the Soviet government for sixteen years was regarded in Moscow as meaning that Washington had not completely given up the idea of intervention, in which United States forces had taken active part in northern Russia and Siberia, suffering 2,845 casualties around Murmansk and Archangel fighting against the Soviets. A year after the Revolution (December 13, 1918), *The New York Times* still urged editorially that the American forces be reinforced "to drive the Bolsheviki [Communists] out of Petrograd and Moscow."

After the Intervention, the country was in a state of devastation and exhaustion. Eight-ninths of its territory had been in the hands of opposing forces at one time or another during the fighting. Industry was at one-seventh of the pre-World War I level. Fifty million acres of farmland had not been planted. Commerce between city and country had been completely disrupted: a rail journey south from Moscow that had taken a single day now took eight to ten. The next year, 1921, there was famine affecting thirty or forty million people. Millions died of hunger and millions more, weakened by starvation, of deadly epidemics. The American Relief Administration, headed by a future President, Herbert Hoover, and a Quaker relief effort, helped many, and were remembered with gratitude until World War II and later.

During the Intervention the country was run under a system of emergency measures called War Communism. Peasants had to sell to the government, at fixed prices, all produce above rock-bottom minimum subsistence needs. Grain trade and small manufacturing were nationalized. There was compulsory labor service for all.

The peasants had accepted these measures because the war was being fought to prevent the landowners from coming back to take away their land. When the fighting was over, this incentive was gone. All successful politicians are realists, and Lenin was no exception. To get the country back on its feet, he introduced his New Economic Policy (NEP). Nearly half the total number of industrial enterprises in the country were rented to private capitalists, domestic and foreign. The more important remained in government hands. Government made steel; private enterprise converted it into hammers and plows. The peasants were now required to pay only a fixed agricultural tax. This restored incentive, as everything but the tax was theirs to dispose of as they saw fit.

The famine year of 1921 was followed by one with good weather and a good crop. Industry began to meet the pent-up needs of the peasants. Labor had its eight-hour day, paid vacations for all, paid sick and pregnancy leave, strict safety and health regulations by the standards of that day, and compulsory collective bargaining in private industry, with government frankly on the side of the unions. But the private industrialists were prospering, for industry had doubled its annual output from its civil-war low.

Even at the height of the fighting, the new government and local initiative that it encouraged brought 25 per cent more children into schoolrooms than in peacetime years under the tsars. The teaching profession was enthusiastic. Working people were moved from their cellars and barracks into the apartments of the well-to-do. There, even one room per family represented luxury when compared to their former conditions. Mansions of the former ruling classes were converted to hospitals, dispensaries, and children's day nurseries.

Lenin was shot by a would-be assassin in 1918, and his health declined thereafter until his death in 1924 at the age of fifty-four. However, in this period he not only effected the New Economic Policy but outlined the directions he believed the country should follow to attain a socialistic society, in which no property used for production would be privately owned. He believed in economic planning and that only public ownership could make that possible, since it eliminates unknown factors that exist when private firms in competition do their best to keep production and market secrets from one another.

BUILDING A NEW SOCIAL SYSTEM

The revolution had taken place in a land with very little industry. Therefore, the problem had to be faced of how to establish socialism in a country that consisted chiefly of peasants who tilled their own very small farms. Lenin offered a two-part answer: industrialize, and bring the peasants to socialism through co-operatives. The problems were interrelated. Unless farming became efficient, it could neither spare the labor force nor provide the capital needed for major industrialization. Nor could it produce food for the industrial workers or raw materials for the factories.

In the field of government, Lenin taught that "every cook must learn to rule the state." Although his Communist Party was highly disciplined and would not permit organized factions, it held annual conventions so long as he lived. At these, opposing viewpoints were thrashed out openly after having been published in newspapers and magazines for all to read. Matters were settled by majority vote both at the conventions and at the meetings of the Central Committee that made policy between conventions. During Lenin's lifetime, no Communist leader was imprisoned or shot. Opponents of the regime, however, were executed in reprisal for the attempted assassination of Lenin and successful assassinations of others.

Timing was of vast importance in both the industrialization and the later farm collectivization programs. No government in the world was friendly to Soviet Russia and few were neutral. Therefore, loss of popular support would mean its overthrow. These questions of timing were basic to the debate that raged in the Communist Party for some years before and after Lenin's death.

Soon, two chief opponents appeared in the debate: Joseph Stalin and Leon Trotsky. Among their many differences was Stalin's belief that socialism could be made to work in one country, which led him to a foreign policy he called "peaceful coexistence."

In an interview in 1929, Walter Duranty asked him: "You see,

Lenin describes his vision of an industrialized Russia, 1920

then, no reason why capitalist and communist systems should not exist side by side without fighting?"

"They have not fought for ten years," said Stalin dryly, "which means they can coexist." *

Trotsky thought the Russian Revolution had to have the support of some industrialized country and therefore urged efforts to stir up revolution elsewhere. Stalin won out in the inner-party struggle through a combination of persuading, joining forces with and against others, and placing his supporters in key positions. He was aided by the general improvement in the country. Once in power, he brooked no opposition. The official rules of the Communist Party provided for democratic discussions and elections in that organization, but Stalin got around them in several ways. He stretched the intervals between conventions until, finally, thirteen years elapsed between one held in 1939 and the next one in 1952. He used the Russian tradition of an all-wise tsar to make his influence greater than the Party's. He framed his opponents as traitors so that he could deal with them through agencies of repression

* Walter Duranty, *Stalin and Co.*, New York: William Sloane Associates, 1949, p. 59.

rather than by debate and vote. Finally, he and his secret police became a law unto themselves. Trotsky, exiled, was murdered in Mexico by a man who was almost certainly an agent of Stalin.

Three-quarters of the Party Central Committee elected in 1934 was executed in subsequent years. So were 90 per cent of the Soviet generals of that day. But Stalin and Molotov, his closest associate, were able to retain the support of the bulk of the people because the country did progress mightily, and because everything was done in the name of the Party, which enjoys a prestige that one must talk to ordinary Russians to appreciate. It must be remembered that the half-million Communist victims of Stalin's purges executed and jailed, and the much larger number of recalcitrant peasants shipped to camps in Siberia and the Arctic, were only a small percentage in a population of 170 million at that time. The people at large, and even most of the Party members who remained after the purge, believed that Stalin was infallible and that those he did away with were truly guilty of treason. Some of the very men he shot, including his closest associates, wrote heart-rending last-minute letters to him indicating their belief that he had nothing to do with this, and would have justice done if only he knew what his secret police were up to. But few of them seem to have realized that it was the very existence of a system of "justice" by secret police that was at fault. The truth both about the purge and the secret-police system only began to be generally known inside the U.S.S.R. after Khrushchev made his famous "secret speech" in 1956, three years after Stalin died. Yet virtually all of Khrushchev's revelations had been published in the West seven years earlier by Isaac Deutscher in his scholarly biography, *Stalin*.

When all this repression began—very cautiously at first—it was against the background of the need to industrialize, to collectivize farming, teach the ignorant, heal the sick, and provide equality and advancement for the most downtrodden sections of the population: women and the formerly colonial peoples of Soviet Central Asia and the other border lands.

The decision to convert Russia from an agricultural to an industrial country was made in 1925, and that for collectivization of agriculture in 1927. The first effect of planned industrialization (building of government-owned industries under a Five-Year Plan) was to abolish unemployment. This was accomplished by the end of 1930. Labor was more than grateful. It was an enthusiastic participant, as I was able to see during a year in Moscow, 1931–1932, where my father had gone on contract as did many other American engineers at the time. After some months of private tutoring in the Russian language, I enrolled at the University to study biochemistry. My fellow students were, with one exception, the children of laboring people and peasants who would never have dreamed of this opportunity under the empire. They remembered the old days, for they were much older than American freshmen. They had almost all worked for years before being sent to special prep schools to prepare them for college.

After a long, hard day at the University they would pile into open trucks, go to construction sites, and teach illiterate workingmen and women how to read and write. The working people were grateful for this. They would put in extra hours, quite voluntarily, because to them socialism was not a theory but a very practical thing: steady jobs, education, opportunity for advancement, free doctors, open doors for women and minorities. Thirty years later, I visited one of the plants that had been under construction in 1932 and found that the management consisted of some of the very same people my fellow students had taught their alphabet. Today these ex-peasant boys and girls are running an enterprise of five thousand workers making lines of automated machinery good enough to command a market in England and Japan. With immense modesty, and the enormous psychological burden of their knowledge of Russia's age-old backwardness, they said to me: "And so we are beginning to have some respect for ourselves."

The situation Stalin faced in agriculture was different from that in industry. The banding together of peasants into co-operatives ("collective farms") was originally a voluntary matter in which people were persuaded to join by the demonstration of the benefits of farm machinery, which they could not afford to own individually. Later, collectivization was proclaimed a revolution in which the poorest peasants were frankly set against those who had become employing farmers, moneylenders, millers, and village merchants. The great battle was for the loyalty of the middle group that had neither sunk into dependence upon others nor risen to dominance. The government used its powers against the prosperous opponents of collectivization as well as against others who could not see surrendering to impersonal control the farm animals they had worked to raise.

The world-wide Great Depression that began in 1929 made matters worse. Alone in the world, Soviet industry continued to grow. However, Stalin's plans to buy equipment abroad with money gained by selling farm produce were disorganized by the tremendous drop in agricultural prices on the world market. To carry on with his plans, he had to extract additional grain from the peasants at very low prices. They replied by refusing to plant more than enough for their own needs, and by hiding their grain from government buyers. What followed was described in a letter to Stalin, April 16, 1933, from the Communist novelist Mikhail Sholokhov, who lived in the heart of the Cossack farming country:*

Disappearance has been the fate of tens of thousands of collective farmers. . . . Send to Veshenskaya County real Communists who will have enough courage to expose . . . the mortal blow delivered to the collective farms of the district, who will investigate properly and show up not only all those who have applied loathsome "methods" of torture, beating up, and humiliation to collective farmers, but also those who inspired them.

This was before the blood purge in the Communist Party itself, and Sholokhov could still safely write such a letter. His own exciting novel, *Seeds of Tomorrow* (also published under the title *Virgin Soil Upturned*) is the best description of collectivization.

This revolution in farming worked. In 1934 and 1935, the government was able to abolish food rationing in the cities. In 1937, using tractors and harvester combines instead of horses and scythes, Russia's farmers brought in what was far and away the largest crop in its history, with the highest yield per acre. When the Germans occupied large Soviet agricultural areas in 1941 and 1942, they found the collective farms so well established they did not attempt to break them up. American intelligence interrogators questioning Russian peasant displaced persons in Germany after World War II found that one of the reforms they did *not* want was breakup of the collective farms.

When Stalin believed the agricultural situation had been sufficiently improved, he turned to getting rid of those who disagreed with him in the cities. The year 1937 was probably the bloodiest of his rule for Communists and intellectuals. But the ten years before that had been something of a golden age in culture. These were the years when the first generation of intellectuals given opportunity by the Revolution came to the fore. The motion picture became an art with Eisenstein's *Potemkin*. Shostakovich was acclaimed for his First Symphony. Numerous fine novels, plays, and short stories were written. The poet Mayakovsky was as newsworthy throughout the world as Yevtushenko is today. Recordings of the excellent Red Army Chorus were popular in the United States as elsewhere. The sculptural group atop the Soviet Pavilion

* *Soviet News,* Soviet Embassy, London, March 13, 1963.

Moscow, 1934. Russian cities looked like this
until the mid-1930's

at the Paris World's Fair was popular with its millions of visitors
(it now stands outside Moscow's permanent Exhibition of Economic Achievement). The Moscow Art Theatre was generally regarded as the finest such company anywhere.

In 1937, young Soviet violinists won five out of six prizes in an
international competition in Belgium, and pianists did equally well
at the Chopin Festival in Poland. A survey in December, 1936,
showed twenty-eight opera houses and legitimate theaters being
built across the U.S.S.R. Nearly sixty million children's books were
published in 1938. Newspaper reading increased vastly: *Pravda's*
circulation trebled in three years and acceptance of new subscrip-
tions was halted because there was not enough paper to satisfy
the demand.

Out of its meager resources of that day the Soviet government
was giving extraordinary support to all branches of science. Pavlov,
the physiologist, was won over to the government by this. The
International Geological Congress held its 1937 meeting in Mos-

cow in recognition of the achievements of Soviet scientists. Four twenty-five-ton Soviet transport planes landed on the ice at the North Pole in 1937 to deposit a scientific wintering party and then took off for a safe return. This unprecedented feat was regarded as no less remarkable in its day than the orbiting of the first space man in 1961.

On the world scene, the rise of Adolf Hitler in Germany brought a change in foreign attitudes toward the Soviet Union. In 1931, when Hitler had already piled up a tremendous vote, Stalin made an accurate appraisal of the time Russia had left: "We are fifty to a hundred years behind the advanced countries. We must make good this distance in ten years. Either we do this, or they crush us. . . ." In 1933, Hitler came to power in Germany with a frank program of conquering Russia to the Urals. That year, after sixteen years in which there had been no diplomatic relations between the United States and the Soviet Union, Washington extended recognition. President Franklin D. Roosevelt said:

"I believe sincerely that the most impelling motive that has lain behind the conversations which were successfully concluded yesterday between Russia and the United States was the desire of both countries for peace and for strengthening the peaceful purpose of the civilized world."

In 1934, the U.S.S.R. was admitted to the League of Nations after having been barred for fourteen years. In 1936, Hitler and Mussolini backed Franco's rebellion against the Spanish Republic, describing themselves as the world's saviors against communism. This was reinforced by titling the Japanese–German–Italian alliance of 1936 the "Anti-Comintern (Communist International) Pact." Stalin, however, believed Hitler's true objectives were more frankly stated at a public rally in September, 1936, when he said that Germany would "swim in plenty" if it had the Urals, Ukraine, and Siberia. It was against the background of fear created by these developments that Stalin was able to convince the Soviet people that many of their former top leaders were traitors and should be shot.

In 1938, England and France appeased Hitler at Munich by compelling Czechoslovakia to surrender to Germany without resistance. They believed that Hitler's only ambitions were in the East. (The details of this and subsequent events are best set forth in D. F. Fleming's *The Cold War and Its Origins*.) The Soviet Foreign Minister, Maxim Litvinov, hinted broadly that his country would move to save itself if it could. Speaking at the League of Nations he said: "At a moment when there is being drawn up a further list of sacrifices to the god of aggression . . . I must plainly declare here that the Soviet Government bears no responsibility whatsoever . . . for the fatal consequences which may inexorably ensue."

The Soviet Union decided that it was not going to be left holding the bag, and signed a nonaggression pact with Germany. The former U.S. Ambassador to Moscow, Joseph E. Davies, offered the following judgment to the Acting Secretary of State: "As my previous reports . . . to you . . . would indicate, the development of this nonaggression pact between Russia and Germany to me was not unexpected. . . . [In Moscow] The suspicion continued to grow that Britain and France were playing a diplomatic game to place the Soviets in the position where Russia would have to fight Germany alone." *

Hitler launched World War II in September, 1939. Upon the collapse of the Polish government, the Red Army marched into the western Ukraine and western Belorussia, which had been in Polish possession. Winston Churchill commented in a radio broadcast of October 1, 1939: "That the Russian armies should stand on this line was clearly necessary for the safety of Russia against the Nazi menace. . . . Hitler, and all that Hitler stands for, have been and are being warned off the east and southeast of Europe."

Stalin further strengthened his borders by retaking the Baltic states of Estonia, Lithuania, and Latvia, as well as the territory of Bessarabia then in Rumanian possession. He also made war on Finland to push back the Finnish border from Leningrad. The Soviet attack on Finland completely destroyed the good will for Russia in the West that had painstakingly been built up when Litvinov was Foreign Minister. Twenty years later a Russian engaged in the successful effort to rebuild good Soviet relations with Finland said to me: "If [Foreign Minister] Molotov hadn't been so bullheaded, maybe we could have protected Leningrad without a war." But Professor Fleming puts it most simply: "[The Russians] *could not say* that they were seizing strategic territory against a war with Hitler," because they had a nonaggression pact with Germany.

Although Stalin regarded these actions as necessary insurance, he was convinced that Hitler would not dare attack the Soviet Union. This became clear to careful observers in February, 1941. At that time his chief economic planner announced at a national Communist Party conference that expansion of industry in Lenin-

* J. E. Davies, *Mission to Moscow*, New York: Simon and Schuster, 1941, pp. 453–455.

grad would be resumed. It had been suspended since the eve of the war because of that city's exposed position. Stalin also refused to believe direct warnings both from the West and from his own intelligence service that Hitler was preparing an assault on the U.S.S.R. Many Western sources reported this blindness, and Khrushchev later confirmed it in detail in his "de-Stalinizing" speech in 1956, citing specific messages from the British Ambassador to the U.S.S.R., Sir Stafford Cripps, Soviet citizens in Berlin, and a German defector.

Hitler thus had the advantage of surprise when he struck on June 22, 1941, the very date Cripps had given Stalin. Consequently, vast masses of Soviet troops were encircled and isolated behind Nazi lines. On February 22, 1963, the Soviet military was finally allowed to offer its view of what happened. Marshal Malinovsky, Minister of Defense, who had been one of the successful leaders at the battle of Stalingrad and later, said:

A major cause of our setbacks at the beginning of the war was the harsh conditions of the Stalin personality cult. In the years before the war, the commanding and political personnel of our armed forces had —on his orders—been subjected to unwarranted mass purges. Stalin's arbitrary actions resulted in the death of many thousands of Soviet officers devoted to the Party and the people. Stalin made a grave miscalculation in appraising the military and political situation on the eve of the war, for he held that Hitler Germany would not risk attacking the Soviet Union and fighting on two fronts.*

But the Soviet troops fought so well that, on July 26, 1941, Hitler said the Russians did not know when they were defeated. After the war, German General von Halder wrote that the Russian troops who were pushed back fought to the last man. Leningrad, surrounded by the Germans on the south and their Finnish ally on the north, would not surrender through two years of siege, although librarians were reduced to eating their glue, and 600,000 persons starved to death in that city. The Germans were stopped outside Moscow, and on December 6, 1941, the day before Pearl Harbor, the Soviets launched the first successful counteroffensive by any country against the Nazis, routing fifty-one divisions.

The next summer, even before the Soviet counteroffensive at Stalingrad, British Prime Minister Winston Churchill said: "Russia has already inflicted injuries upon the German military organism which will, I believe, prove ultimately fatal." Afterward, General

---

* *Soviet News,* London: U.S.S.R. Embassy, February 25, 1963, p. 119.

von Halder reported that his side had by this time lost half its invasion army of 3.4 million. General Marshall, U.S. Chief of Staff, reported officially at the close of the war: "There can be no doubt that the greed and mistakes of the warmaking nations as well as the heroic stand of the British and Soviet peoples saved the United States a war on her own soil."

The British Minister of Economic Warfare, Lord Selborne, estimated that nine-tenths of Germany's losses had been in Russia.

By the end of 1942, American and British tanks, planes, and artillery had replaced 20 per cent of the Soviet losses in the battles from Leningrad to Stalingrad. The Russians themselves had manufactured the replacements for the other 80 per cent. The United States also provided one-twentieth of total Soviet food consumption during the war. As the late President Kennedy put it:

> . . . no nation in the history of battle ever suffered more than the Soviet Union in the Second World War. At least twenty million lost their lives. Countless millions of homes of families were burned or sacked. A third of the nation's territory, including two-thirds of its industrial base, was turned into a wasteland—a loss equivalent to the destruction of this country east of Chicago.*

Railroads were destroyed tie by tie and track by track as the Germans retreated, so that, at the war's end, food could not reach the cities or manufactures the countryside. Cattle had been eaten by the occupation forces, driven off with the retreating enemy, or had died from disease or lack of care.

U.S. Supreme Court Justice Jackson, serving as one of the prosecutors at the Nuremberg Trial of war criminals in 1945, submitted evidence from the Germans' own records showing that fifteen million civilians had been exterminated throughout Europe in an effort directed by no means solely against Jews: 60 per cent of this number were non-Jewish.

The Potsdam Agreement of July, 1945, signed by President Truman, Attlee (the new British Prime Minister), and Stalin, found the German people guilty of "the terrible crimes committed under the leadership of those whom, in the hour of their success, they openly approved and blindly obeyed." They were, therefore, to "atone" by reparations and the reduction of their standard of living to a level not higher than that of the people they plundered. Further production of any implements of war was prohibited. In point of fact, the Soviet Union has never allowed East Germany to make

---

* *The New York Times,* June 11, 1963.

Returning village women seek their men among civilians
killed by Germans during World War II

anything but small arms, according to the West German Defense
Ministry.*

The Potsdam Agreement also provided that "the German economy shall be decentralized for the purpose of eliminating the present excessive concentration of power as exemplified in particular
by cartels, syndicates, trusts, and other monopolistic arrange-
ments." The Soviet Union was also to get one-fourth of the industrial equipment in western Germany not needed for the German
peace economy. It did not.

Soviet policy in Europe since the war has been protection against
the possibility of a third invasion in this century across the open
plains from the west. Soviet forces are maintained in Germany, in
Poland along the supply line to Germany, and in Hungary. In the
years immediately after the war, chiefly in 1946, the U.S.S.R. with-
drew its forces from Norway, Finland, Denmark, Czechoslovakia,
Yugoslavia, Rumania, Bulgaria, Iran, Manchuria, and Korea.

* *The New York Times,* April 26, 1963.

American G.I. and Soviet soldier meet in Germany, 1945

United States Lend-Lease aid to Russia was stopped as soon as the fighting ended. The U.S.S.R. was not given a reconstruction loan such as the United States granted to all its non-Communist allies. The Russians believe the reason for this lay in the attitude expressed by President Truman when he was still a Senator, the day after Germany attacked the Soviet Union: "If we see that Germany is winning the war we ought to help Russia, and if Russia is winning we ought to help Germany, and in that way let them kill as many as possible." *

The United Nations Relief and Rehabilitation Administration (UNRRA), financed by the United States, gave twice as much money to a former enemy, Italy, as to the Soviet Ukraine, with equal population, which had been utterly devastated. The U.S.S.R. regards these policies as the beginning of the Cold War. Disagreements over Germany and the city of Berlin, over nuclear weapons

* *The New York Times,* July 24, 1941.

and foreign bases, and over disarmament, later piled up and created an impasse that still exists. But the 1963 nuclear test ban treaty and the U.S.–Soviet pledge not to orbit atomic weapons are regarded as opening the way to solution of these problems.

In 1949, the world balance of power changed, becoming approximately even, for in that year the U.S.S.R. tested its first atom bomb (the U.S. had had the bomb for four years) and the Chinese Communists, having driven Chiang Kai-shek from the mainland, signed a military alliance with the U.S.S.R. This world stalemate was vividly demonstrated by a number of events from the inconclusive Korean War of 1950–1953 to the Cuban confrontation of 1962 ending with Soviet withdrawal of missiles and a U.S. pledge not to invade Cuba.

The late President Kennedy expressed this reality as follows: "We must deal with the world as it is, and not as it might have been had the history of the last eighteen years been different." *

Stalin died in March, 1953, after devoting the postwar years chiefly to internal reconstruction. We now know that his heirs were divided in their judgment of every problem, foreign and domestic. But the public mood made it clear that no sudden change was possible. The United Press reported from Moscow: "Hundreds of men and women wept in the streets," and all sources agreed that millions of people lined up in the ten-degree cold for hours to pay their respects at the casket. Doubtless there were cheers out in the concentration camps, but the populace in general regarded the tremendous advance of their country in the years of Stalin's rule as his personal accomplishment.

At Stalin's death there were plenty of obvious problems. In agriculture, there were dangerous tensions produced by Stalin's policy of squeezing the peasantry in order to finance reconstruction and industrial and scientific expansion. In 1952, there had actually been a drop in the country's cattle population after a steady rise since the war. But this happened again in 1963, under Khrushchev.

The first Premier after Stalin was Georgi Malenkov. He was hardly in office before riots broke out in East Berlin, which were caused basically by the hardships of life. Frightened, Malenkov instituted throughout the Soviet bloc a program to boost the living standard sharply in two or three years at the most. This would have meant a sharp cut in the funds allocated to expanding heavy or basic industry.

Although Khrushchev and Molotov had deep differences, they agreed that Malenkov's program would make it impossible for the

* Speech at the American University, June 10, 1963.

U.S.S.R. to catch up to the U.S. economically. They ousted him by vote of the Party Presidium, which was endorsed by the larger Central Committee. Nikita Khrushchev became the acknowledged leader. This was partly because he had specific plans to solve the farm, foreign policy, and other problems. Another reason was that Molotov (and Mikoyan, who shared Khrushchev's views) was too closely associated with Stalin's methods and policies. Unlike them, Khrushchev was not tainted by having been a policymaker: his name is not even mentioned in Deutscher's 1949 biography of Stalin.

The leadership was agreed that Stalin's policeman and executioner, Beria, had to go. He was executed in 1953, but that act seems to have ended violence as the means of settling control of power in the U.S.S.R. Over a decade has passed, during which there was a major struggle for power in 1957, but no one has lost his life, gone to jail, or faced a court for losing a political argument.

In internal affairs, two policies were pushed from 1953 to 1956. One was to boost agriculture. The prices paid to the farmers were raised; also, a tremendous program was undertaken to cultivate 100 million acres of virgin and idle lands in Siberia, Central Asia, and in Europe east of the Volga. That is equal to the entire cropland of all the Pacific Coast and Mountain states, plus Texas, Oklahoma, Arkansas, and Kansas. Almost 100 million acres were actually planted within three years.

The other policy concerned many other aspects of Soviet endeavor. It consisted of loosening the bonds placed on the country by Stalin. The drumhead courts of the internal security police were abolished. (In 1962, as we left the Kremlin after a stroll, a Soviet friend said to me: "And to think that ten years ago we couldn't set foot in here." His wife added: "And when we had to go past the gates, we hurried our steps to pass as quickly as possible." He is a decorated, wounded veteran of World War II; she had been the nurse who brought him back to health. He had been arrested.)

Planning began to be decentralized both in industry and agriculture. People with technical training found themselves reassigned from comfortable bureau jobs to the factories and farms where their skills were needed. In 1954 and 1955, staffs of government offices were cut by 750,000 persons.

The Korean War was ended by a compromise between the Khrushchev and Eisenhower administrations. Likewise, the U.S.A. and U.S.S.R., with Communist China, brought an end to the seven-

year war between the French and the Vietnamese. Another compromise, chiefly on Khrushchev's part, finally made possible the
signing of a peace treaty with Austria. Also, Khrushchev went to
Yugoslavia to apologize to Tito for Stalin's having read him out
of the Communist camp, and began to woo him back. On another
trip, Khrushchev visited India, made clear that he valued her neutrality, and began to give her economic aid. (Stalin's attitude had
been: if you're not for us, you're against us.) The Soviet armed
forces were cut by two million men in 1955 as a result of the general easing of international tensions.

At the beginning of his term in office, Khrushchev was called
"Nikita the Corn Man" by Soviet farmers for his belief in Amer-
ican-style corn-and-hog agriculture. But by 1956 he had won solid
popularity and was ready to disclose Stalin's mistakes and crimes.
That year, in a secret speech to a Communist Party Congress,
Khrushchev exposed Stalin's misdeeds as perhaps no ruler in history has attacked a predecessor representing the same party and
political system. He recalled Karl Marx's basic idea that it is the
people, not individual heroes, who are the real makers of history.
He said that Stalin's one-man rule had damaged Russia and held
her back by limiting the people's initiative. Fear of doing anything
without orders from above had hampered even technological progress. Khrushchev specifically cleared the names of a great many
individuals the Soviet people had been told were traitors and
criminals. He made it clear that Leon Trotsky had been a political
opponent, not an "enemy of the people."

This lifting of the lid was followed by a strike in Poland and a
long general strike in Hungary accompanied by an armed uprising,
which the Russians crushed. But in 1963 the Hungarian government released the leaders of the 1956 rebellion, and the United
States State Department issued a statement saying:

> Present conditions in Hungary are a decided improvement over the
> Rakosi era from 1947 to 1956 and over the 1958–1959 period of
> repression that followed Soviet armed suppression of the Hungarian
> revolt. The situation of the Hungarian people is comparatively better
> than that of peoples in the Soviet-bloc countries other than Poland.
> . . . Further developments include the curbing of arbitrary police
> power.*

Stalin's death in 1953 broadened the seat of real authority in
the U.S.S.R. from one man to a committee of about a dozen, the
Party Presidium, in which both the Khrushchev and Molotov fac-

* The New York Times, May 13, 1963.

tions were represented, and decision was by majority vote. In 1957, authority was further extended to the Party's Central Committee, a body not much smaller than the U.S. Congress. In that year, Molotov, a former Premier and Foreign Minister, challenged Khrushchev's leadership. Of the 309 persons present at the Central Committee meeting, 215 participated in the eight-day discussion. Khrushchev's policies of internal reform and peaceful coexistence won. The losers were not punished in the manner of previous years, but were given less influential positions in industrial management, college teaching, and the diplomatic corps. The older ones were soon retired on pension.

Sputnik in 1957 shocked the world into realizing that the U.S.S.R. was abreast of—and in some ways ahead of—the times. Then in 1959, a Soviet rocket hit the moon; another circled the moon, aimed a camera, and televised pictures of the never-seen half back to earth. In 1961, Russia put the first human being into space. In 1962, the Russians conducted the Nikolayev-Popovich twin capsule flight, with two capsules maneuvering within four miles of each other. In 1963, the first woman astronaut, Valentina Tereshkova, was sent into space.

Within the country, major reforms, such as an improved pension law, big changes in the educational system, sale of the government's farm machinery stations to the collective farms, and decentralization of economic management, were opened to public discussion in the press before adoption. So was the new Program of the Communist Party: its blueprint for communism, which was to be achieved in about twenty years. As a result, newspaper circulation doubled from forty to eighty million in the first ten years after Stalin. But basic opposition was still not allowed to be heard: Molotov and his friends could not get one minute of air time, one inch of newspaper space, or a hall for a single public meeting.

At the 1961 Party Congress, a Khrushchev supporter said: "According to Molotov, it is precisely by war that we should win hundreds of millions of people to communism." This idea was completely defeated. Khrushchev is deeply convinced that the whole world will some day go communist because the U.S.S.R. will eventually have the highest standard of living. But, as he told a group of American manufacturers, he doesn't think the American people will be interested in communism until the Russians live better. And according to Russian expectations, that's many years off.

Khrushchev believes with Lenin that capitalism needs war and that socialist economies do not. He told the 1956 Party Congress,

Khrushchev and his space champions: Valentina Tereshkova
has married Major Nikolayev, on her right

however, that capitalists don't want to commit suicide by nuclear
warfare but to win. He said then, and has since repeated it many
times, that the U.S.S.R. and her allies were clearly undefeatable,
that the West could see this, and that war had therefore ceased to
be inevitable. He also put forth the idea that revolutionary change
toward socialism should be sought by peaceful means. To avoid
civil wars in countries whose working people want to introduce
socialism, the new Communist Party Program adopted in 1961
proposed that the property of capitalists be bought out instead of
confiscated. From the communist point of view this is a major
concession and compromise because, under Marxist theory, all
wealth is produced by working people and employers aren't entitled
to any profit at all.

Mr. Khrushchev's devotion to compromise was tested most
sharply by the Sino-Indian border conflict and by the Cuban crisis
of October, 1962. With respect to the former, he refused to back
his Chinese allies, on the ground that India's neutrality was worth
more than some square miles of uninhabitable territory. He urged
a negotiated solution. And in his speech of December 12, 1962,
after the Cuban crisis, he compared the Chinese Communists with
the West Germans:

What do they want, these people who call themselves Marxist–
Leninists? Why are they pressing for the same thing, in fact, as [former
West German Premier] Adenauer? . . . They obviously would prefer
to sit it out. . . . Can it be that they want the blood of the peoples of

the Soviet Union, Cuba, and other socialist countries to flow? . . .
They are clearly disappointed that a thermonuclear war wasn't touched
off. . . . On the one hand, war is eagerly desired by the aggressive
adventurist forces of imperialism . . . on the other hand, attempts
are being made to push events in the same direction by people who
call themselves Marxist–Leninists. . . . Both the former and the latter
want to prod history on to a new war. . . . We reject not only world
thermonuclear war, but all wars between states in general, with the
exception of a just war of liberation and a defensive war which has
to be waged by a people which is the victim of aggression. . . . To
preserve peace . . . we are ready to agree, and do agree, to reasonable
political compromise.

On the other hand, he had kind words for leaders of any type
who work to keep the world on an even keel. Asked by an Italian
publisher his opinion of Pope John's "Peace on Earth" encyclical,
Khrushchev replied, April 20, 1963:

We welcome the Pope's statement for peace. In the recent encyclical,
Pope John has pronounced himself in favor of the ending of the arms
race, the prohibition of nuclear weapons and the stopping of nuclear
tests, in favor of disarmament under effective international control,
the peaceful coexistence of countries, equal relations among countries
and peoples, and elimination of war hysteria. One cannot fail to see
that these statements are based on a realistic understanding of all the
dangers of war.

I am no theologian, but if I remember rightly, according to the
Gospel, Christ preached peace and not war. . . . People of good will
should be able to discard all prejudices in order to pool their efforts in
the struggle for universal and lasting peace, for general disarmament.

A new period in Soviet history began with a meeting of the
Communist Party Central Committee in November, 1962. Special
steps were taken to improve the output of consumer goods, and
investments in agriculture were raised 30 per cent over the existing
plan for 1963. This meant that, for the first time, enough money
would be made available to modernize farming, with ample fertilizer, weed-killers, and machinery in the barns and chicken coops,
and not only in the fields. A complete reorganization of the Party
and the government was undertaken. Each would henceforth have
separate pyramids of organization, one for farm country, and one
for industrial cities. This is an entirely new concept of government,
never tried elsewhere. A new system of elected workers' committees
to advise management was established.

Also in November, 1962, cultural freedom reached its highest
level in nearly thirty years. Yevgeni Yevtushenko's poem "Stalin's
Heirs" was published in *Pravda,* warning against the unrecon-

Moving day

structed hard-liners waiting in the wings to take over if they can. Alexander Solzhenitsyn's novel of Stalinist concentration camp life, *One Day in the Life of Ivan Denisovich,* was brought out. Shostakovich's opera, *Lady Macbeth of Mtsensk,* suppressed for many years, was staged anew, along with his oratorio based on Yevtushenko's poems, including "Babi Yar," against anti-Semitism. Abstract sculptors and artists showed their work in public for the first time. This brought severe official criticism in all the arts, but no artist lost his livelihood.

One aspect of the post-Stalin decade was an effort to return to revolutionary first principles. Khrushchev, cautious and wily, did this step by step. So long as he had not removed the threat of defeat by the old-line Molotov group, he did not strike out at the entrenched Party machinery, whose support he needed. But early in 1963, a very bold step was taken to clean out graft, corruption, nepotism, and deep-rooted bureaucracy. The courts, the government's systems of inspectors, and the Party itself were bypassed by the setting up of an enormous system of citizen monitors, responsible directly to the Central Committee of the Party and the government Cabinet. These monitors were given the right to demand the books of any enterprise or undertaking, stop the execution of orders they believed to be against the public interest, demote or fire executives, demand that they repay funds used in their personal interest, and publicize these things through radio, newspapers, movies, television, and meetings.

On March 5, 1963, ten years after Stalin's death, a *New York Times* editorial summarized the changes during those years:

A decade after Joseph Stalin's death, the Soviet Union is still very much a nation in transition. A remarkable revolution from above, led by Premier Khrushchev, has removed many of the barbarous customs and practices whose totality we call Stalinism. The old tyrant is no longer worshiped as an infallible near-God. The power of the secret police has been sharply curbed. Most of the slave labor camps have been closed down and their inmates freed. The iron curtain has been partially lifted. Substantial economic advance has permitted a significantly improved standard of living.

The most important fact about Stalin's successors is that they have not plunged the world into thermonuclear disaster.

Perhaps the Khrushchev administration will be remembered best, in the long view of history, for the fact that its policies enabled President Kennedy to say, on June 10, 1963:

Every thoughtful citizen who despairs of war and wishes to bring peace should begin . . . by examining his own attitude . . . toward the Soviet Union.

Among the many traits the peoples of our two countries have in common, none is stronger than our mutual abhorrence of war.

Today, should total war ever break out again—no matter how— our two countries will be the primary targets. It is an ironic but accurate fact that the two strongest powers are the two in the most danger of devastation. All we have built, all we have worked for, would be destroyed in the first twenty-four hours. And even in the cold war— which brings burdens and dangers to so many countries, including this nation's closest allies—our two countries bear the heaviest burdens. For we are both devoting massive sums of money to weapons that could be better devoted to combat ignorance, poverty, and disease.

We are both caught up in a vicious and dangerous cycle with suspicion on one side breeding suspicion on the other, and new weapons begetting counterweapons.

Agreements . . . are in the interests of the Soviet Union as well as ours—and even the most hostile nations can be relied upon to accept and keep those treaty obligations, and only those treaty obligations, which are in their own interest.

We can still hail the Russian people for their many achievements— in science and space, in economic and industrial growth, in culture, in acts of courage.

The nuclear-test-ban treaty negotiated the following month was widely regarded as marking the beginning of the end—perhaps the very end—of the eighteen-year-old Cold War.

3: Nationalities and Republics of the U.S.S.R.

Russia (the Russian Soviet Federated Socialist Republic—R.S.F.S.R.) occupies the northern half of the U.S.S.R. from the Gulf of Finland to the Pacific Ocean. In Europe it is flat or gently rolling, with much woodland and swamp. Asian Russia is called Siberia, and is mountainous in the east. The geography of the two together is almost exactly like that of Canada, but with the location of the mountains and plains reversed east for west. The climate, too, is like Canada's.

All men are created equal, but some men and some peoples make more use of their endowments than others. In that sense, the Russians are surely one of the world's great modern peoples. The 120 million Russians are fewer by far than the number of Americans or Chinese in this world. Like the people of the United States, and like the Chinese much earlier in history, the Russians under the tsars grew in numbers and territory essentially because they were able to get a better living from nature for a larger number of human beings than those with whom they competed for the same land.

The Russians have their roots in Europe, and their population is still densest west of the Volga River. Siberia has only 25 million people, one-fifth of the population of the R.S.F.S.R.; 90 per cent of the Siberians are Russians.

The process of Russian expansion within the U.S.S.R. is still continuing. The difference from pre-Revolutionary times is that the native people are invited to participate rather than being pushed out. Because of the evacuation of industry and people eastward during World War II, and the plowing up of the prairies starting in 1954, there are today many more Russians and Ukrainians than Kazakhs in the immense Kazakh Republic south of Siberia. Most of the Russians are in the northern part of Kazakhstan, bordering Siberia.

There are regional differences within the Russian nationality, as among Americans. The tall-story tellers of the American north woods have their direct counterpart in the Pomory, the Russian fishermen and lumbermen of the European Arctic coast.

The Siberians are the Texans of Russia. They think in terms of endless spaces and have boundless self-confidence. This is personified, perhaps, by the best-known of all Siberians today, the young poet Yevtushenko. I have heard a visiting Siberian song-and-dance troupe in Leningrad put into song a biting challenge and invitation to city folk to come out and help build up a vast new country.

The peasantry of European Russia, on the other hand, used to have such a sense of inferiority that it sang in a folk song of the smart Englishman who invented machines to do everything for him, while the Russian *"muzhik"* relied on his trusty oaken club. But the gunsmiths and samovar-makers of Tula, south of Moscow, are so proud of their traditional skills that they sing they can shoe a flea. And the miners and smiths of the old hand-industries of the Urals have created a beautiful folklore based on their craft and their cave-laced mountains, translated in recent years into a lovely color movie, *The Stone Flower*.

Russians are a singing people and can harmonize wonderfully. Among the Russians the Cossacks are perhaps the best singers. Their distinctive squatting dance is known throughout the world. Among Russian decorative crafts, lacquered, hand-carved wood-ware is the best known, although every other type of handicraft, including fine lacemaking, is found in Russia.

Because the Russians are the most numerous people in the U.S.S.R. and have played the major role in its history, everything in this book is about them in one way or another. And so let us turn to some people who are less known.

THE UKRAINE

The Ukraine, occupying most of the southwestern corner of the
U.S.S.R. in Europe, is not a province. Bordering Poland, Czechoslovakia, Hungary, and Rumania, it is a distinct country, with a
language, culture, and history of its own, although these are closely
related to the Russian. Its 44 million people give it about the same
population as France, and it is a member of the UN in its own
right. Three-quarters of the inhabitants are Ukrainians. Most of
the rest are Russians, but there are nearly a million Jews, and
substantial numbers of Poles, Bulgarians, Hungarians, Greeks, and
Rumanians.

The Ukraine, which is somewhat larger in size than France, has
a warm vacation coast in the south, on the Black Sea. It is a flat
country except for the cliffs of the Crimean coastal range and the
Carpathians in the extreme west. The country near the capital city
of Kiev is very pleasantly rolling, with geese-filled ponds in the
bottoms and whitewashed clay cottages set against the green of
woods and fields.

The Ukraine has become a world leader in industry. In 1962, it
produced as much as the entire U.S.S.R. in 1940. West Germany
has 40 per cent more people than the Ukraine, but barely exceeds
it in steel production, and lags behind it in pig iron and coal. No
other country comes close in the output of its basic industry except,
of course, the U.S.A. and the U.S.S.R. as a whole.

In agriculture, the Ukraine has more livestock and hogs than
West Germany despite the fact that animal husbandry—like industry—was virtually wiped out during the two years of Nazi occupation and the fighting that preceded and followed it. To us,
World War II is long past. To a Ukrainian, as to every Soviet
citizen, it crops up in every conversation with a foreigner. The fact
that Ukrainian industry today produces four times as much as
before that holocaust is a measure of the fundamental nature of
the Soviet challenge.

West Germany, with universities dating back to the Middle Ages,
and a world reputation for the degree of education of its people,
now has 140,000 college students, which is more than ever in its
history. But the Ukraine has 380,000 students, nearly three times
as many as West Germany, although the Ukraine was largely
illiterate fifty years ago. At that time, instruction in the native
language of its people was forbidden by the tsar in an attempt to
Russianize the Ukraine.

Kiev main avenue. All buildings were erected after war,
reproducing Ukrainian style

The Ukraine today also has more doctors than Germany. Their
number has increased twelvefold since the last peacetime year before the Revolution, when typhus, typhoid, malaria, diphtheria, and
cholera were epidemic. Today, there is only an occasional case
of diphtheria and malaria. The others are gone.

There is something that makes southerly peoples more lively
than their northern neighbors. Ukrainian and Russian dancing are
essentially similar, but often in a Ukrainian *hopak* a man will
leap over the heads of others, stretching his legs out in front and
touching hands to toes. Ukrainians and Russians both wear pull-
over shirts buttoning at the side of the neck, but the Ukrainian
collar and the buttoned foot-long slit are brightly embroidered.
When a girl dancer wears multicolored ribbons streaming down
from a garland in her hair, she's Ukrainian. The Russians wear a
headdress that doesn't move. The Russian countryman decorates
his cottage with wood-carvings, the Ukrainian with brightly painted
designs over the whitewash.

The greatest of Ukrainian writers—and patriots—was the poet

Taras Shevchenko, also talented as an artist. Poetry is hard to translate, and so he is not known very well outside the U.S.S.R. Nikolai Gogol, famous for his satirical play *The Inspector General,* was Ukrainian and did much writing on Ukrainian themes, but he wrote in Russian.

Since the early 1950's the Ukraine has made more use than any other Soviet republic of the right of self-government. The Soviet Union takes pride in the fact that its educational system is fairly uniform. Children graduating in any part of the country may go on elsewhere with little disadvantage. However, the present eleven-year system of public-school-through-high-school education was originated in the Ukraine. It pioneered an agricultural reform in which many collective farmers get regular salaries instead of depending on a co-operative income-sharing arrangement. It broke with U.S.S.R. divorce procedure by requiring couples to go through only one court instead of two, and even then only if the divorce is contested. It also has made its own laws on such matters as the storage and use of arms and munitions by civilians, the operation of power installations and utilization of electricity, the protection of major oil and gas pipelines.

MOLDAVIA

Right between the Ukraine and Rumania is the Moldavian Republic of the U.S.S.R., a pleasant fruit-growing region most of whose three million people speak a language that is essentially Rumanian. The Moldavian culture is a mixture of Rumanian and Ukrainian. A typical mixed borderland, Moldavia has changed hands twelve times in its history.

BELORUSSIA (WHITE RUSSIA)

Every invasion of Russia from the west has been through Belorussia, because it is on the direct line from Moscow to Berlin and Paris. It is very flat, and the south is an endless swamp. The soil is very rich, however, and drainage is the key to its progress. Today it has 8.4 million people, which is half a million less than before World War II. This provides some idea of the extraordinary suffering caused by the invasion, for of the five Soviet republics wholly occupied by Germany, only Belorussia has not yet fully recovered its human losses. Eighty per cent of the people are Belorussians. Their language is similar to Russian, Ukrainian, and Polish. The rest of the inhabitants are Russians, Poles, Jews, and Ukrainians.

Before the Revolution, the distinction between rich and poor was probably sharper in Belorussia than anywhere else in the European part of the Empire. A few thousand landowners held 40 per cent of the land. The working day for the wage earner was thirteen or fourteen hours and there was no machinery to ease the burden of physical drudgery. Nor was there labor legislation to give the worker any kind of protection.

The average life span was only thirty-two years. There was one doctor per ten thousand people, which meant that most White Russians went through life without ever seeing a physician. Today there is a doctor for every 820 inhabitants. She (Soviet doctors are chiefly women) has roads and mechanical transportation to bring her patients within reach, and a medical air service that brings emergency cases from the remotest corner of the swamps to the capital city in a maximum of two hours. As a consequence of this and other factors, the life span is now exactly twice what it used to be.

Where four out of five Belorussians used to be unable to write their own names, school attendance today in relation to population is higher than in Britain or France. School is taught in Belorussian.

Nowadays, labor puts in a forty-hour week, but Belorussian industry produces as much every two weeks as it did in a year in tsarist times. It makes forty-ton trucks, completely automated production lines of machine tools for the manufacturing industries, pianos, electrical instruments, and is a major center of the tractor, bicycle, and motorcycle industries. And yet, every single one of the ten thousand enterprises in operation in 1940, large and small, was destroyed in the war. They had to be completely rebuilt.

Of 270 cities and towns in Belorussia before World War II, 209 were wiped off the face of the earth. Every second farmhouse in Belorussia was destroyed in the war, and has had to be replaced. The new ones are not modern by American standards. Belorussia is cold and snowy in winter, and the job was to put houses up as fast as possible with the materials, knowledge, and methods at hand.

The Belorussian farmer was so poor in the past that, like Ireland, his country's chief export was emigrants. Like the Irish, the Belorussians came mainly to the United States. A large part of the Jewish immigration to the United States was also from Belorussia. Today the Belorussian farmer produces more milk per head of population than the American, more meat per person than the English or Norwegian, more flax than the Belgian. But the farmers

Forty-five-ton earth mover made in Belorussia

(chiefly women: most of the 2.2 million war dead were men) work very hard for this. Cows are still milked chiefly by hand. As in most of Europe, even about half the water for the animals is still carried in buckets.

The great objective in the Belorussian countryside at present is rural electrification. Ten times as much power is to be available for farm consumption by 1965 as in 1958, and most of the milking, shearing, and water haulage will by then be by mechanical means; 2.5 million acres of peat bogs are to be drained.

Belorussia is the only member republic of the U.S.S.R., other than the Ukraine, independently represented in the UN. Like all the Soviet republics, it also has a permanent delegation in Moscow, representing its interests before the federal government. With the expansion of the rights of these republics in recent years, the number of matters handled by that delegation rose from 20–25 annually up to 1953, to seven hundred per year since 1959. For example, Belorussia is in contact with foreign firms through the U.S.S.R. Ministry of Foreign Trade, and, through the U.S.S.R.

State Planning Commission, keeps track of the delivery of Belorussian manufactures to the other republics.

THE NON-SLAVIC REPUBLICS

There are nearly fifty million Soviet citizens whose languages have nothing in common with Russian. Over twenty million have a religious history of Mohammedanism, and their languages and cultures are chiefly related to Turkish, but also to Iranian and Chinese. Most of the non-Slavs live in Central Asia—the Uzbeks, Kazakhs, Kirghiz, Tadzhiks, Turkmens. However, the three million Azerbaijanis, of Moslem tradition, dwell in the Caucasus. The five million Tatars, also of Islamic background, have their major center on the upper Volga River only a few hundred miles from Moscow.

THE CAUCASUS

The Caucasus includes in its population two of the most ancient of Christian peoples: the Armenians and the Georgians (Mikoyan's and Stalin's countrymen, respectively). Their languages are very unusual. Although there are fewer than three million people in each of these nations, the Armenians speak forty dialects and the Georgians fourteen, because both peoples live in isolated mountain valleys, or on plains or highland plateaus divided by ridges. The fragmentation of peoples in the Caucasus brought a rocklike hardening of national characteristics. This has resulted in a particularly overdeveloped national pride, among the Georgians and the mountaineers above all.

The Georgian in his soul is a man of the soil or the saddle, although his country is today very highly advanced by world standards, in science, medicine, and the arts of industry.

Armenians have a very long and world-wide tradition in commerce, and it is perhaps no accident that Anastas Mikoyan has been for a quarter century the major Soviet name in the consumer-goods field and in foreign trade. This field requires great negotiating skill, and he may yet be remembered in history as a great peacemaker because of his talks in Washington during the Cuban crisis of 1962.

The Georgians have produced the world's most thrilling folk dances. Toe-dancing seems to come naturally to every man. Their Chabukiani is the greatest of Soviet male ballet stars, and their classical ballet company is the only one I have seen in which the women are outshone by the men. The neighboring Armenians, whose dance steps are pedestrian, have produced composers and

Amateur dance troupe in Georgia livens up lunch break

vocalists of world stature (Khachaturian, Dolukhanova). Perhaps
it is because folk dancing is the creation of the countryman, and
orchestral music and concert singing are urban arts.

The third Caucasian Republic, Azerbaijan, has a tail that wags
the dog, the small Apsheron Peninsula, which projects into the
Caspian Sea. It was one of the first centers of the world petroleum
industry. The oil city on that peninsula, Baku, is the capital of
the republic and, with a million people, has a fourth of its population. The farmlands grow cotton, tobacco, green tea, grapes,
and vegetables. Thanks to irrigation and drainage the cotton yield
per acre is six times as high as in 1920. Natural silk is another
rural product. Industry, which used to consist solely of the oil wells,
now includes the manufacture of steel tubing and machinery for
the wells and refineries, and the production of silk fabrics, knit-
goods, leather footwear, and processed foods. Azerbaijan has a
ballet company and an academy of sciences with numerous research institutes. A leading crystallographer is the son of an illiter-

ate peasant. The entire native Azerbaijani medical and engineering professions could have been entertained in someone's home before the Revolution: a dozen engineers and forty-five doctors. Now there are eighteen thousand engineers and nine thousand doctors, of whom one-half are Azerbaijani. Because of the mistrust of non-Moslems in Central Asia, Azerbaijani rather than Russian Communist professional people and cultural figures played a major role in the modernization of the Central Asian republics thirty years ago.

While Russian cities, usually inland and on flat plains, look much alike, the three capitals in the Caucasus differ greatly because of physical setting and ethnic tradition. Baku is on the sea, has ancient round towers and a backdrop of oil wells. The Georgian capital, Tbilisi, straddles a river hemmed in by mountains, and has an impressive walled medieval fortress. A striking colonnaded dining pavilion on one of the surrounding mountains is reached by funicular and aerial tramway and provides a magnificent view of the city in its valley. Tbilisi bustles in a Near-Eastern way, although the architecture is Western except for the churches. The Armenian capital, Erivan, is dominated by the seventeen thousand- and thirteen thousand-foot peaks of Mount Ararat, just across the border in Turkey.

THE BALTIC STATES

Far to the northwest, on the shores of the Baltic Sea, are three other peoples, speaking languages quite different from Russian: the Latvians or Letts, the Estonians, and the Lithuanians. They include the only substantial Roman Catholic population in the U.S.S.R.

The Baltic peoples, like many other small peoples throughout the world who live on the fringes of great states, have had a long history of subordination to one great neighbor or another: Germany, Sweden, Poland, and Russia have ruled them at various times. Except for Lithuania, the Baltic states have not been independent for seven hundred years, except for a twenty-year break from 1920 to 1940. The first Russian town in this area was established in 1030. Russian rule over the eastern shore of the Baltic dates from 1721.

It is very difficult to judge the true state of feeling of these peoples toward the Soviet Union. Reality is not as simple as either Moscow or the Baltic emigrants in the West would have us believe. The official stand of the U.S.S.R. is that these lands have a long

background of being part of the Russian Empire, and that their
people (particularly those of Latvia) were among the most determined initial supporters of Lenin's revolution. Early books on the
Russian Revolution uniformly refer to the Lettish (Latvian) Rifles
as Lenin's most loyal forces. A former American Ambassador to
the Soviet Union, Joseph E. Davies, has written about the Baltic
period of independence from 1920 to 1940: "It should be remembered that the Baltic States were all carved out of, and taken
away from Russia, after the last war." *

Baltic emigrants to the United States and elsewhere hold that
these nations were forcibly reincorporated by the Soviet Union on
the eve of and again at the end of World War II. There is truth
in both positions. The U.S.S.R. has now had nearly two decades
of peace in which to try to win over a younger generation that
has never lived in any other way, and to placate their elders by
material benefits. Latvia's entire prewar fishing fleet had a capacity
no larger than that of three of the big trawlers it has today.
Lithuania now produces more machine tools in proportion to
population than any country in the West. In Estonia there are
three times as many doctors as a generation ago. Perhaps the
true state of morale is suggested by the fact that in 1962 Latvian
industrial growth was two years ahead of schedule. Lithuanian
industrial output increased 60 per cent in the four years 1959–
1962, twice as fast as planned.

A *New York Times* correspondent reported from Riga, Latvia,
April 17, 1961:

Latvians and Russians have learned to work well together. . . . The
outward impression of this stately 760-year-old city . . . is of notable
industrial growth and rising living standards. . . . Such locally made
products as radio phonographs, furniture and chocolate compare favorably to those in the West. . . . Latvians usually have retained the
best jobs.

The mayor of Riga claimed that bias due to nationality was not
a problem, and "pointed to the aides flanking him. Mr. Baumanis'
deputy was a Russian, his cultural assistant a Latvian, and his administrative assistant a Jew." Jews constitute less than two per
cent of the population of Latvia.

Reporting from Vilnius (also known as Vilna), Lithuania, *The
Times* correspondent, Seymour Topping, wrote:

* *Life*, March 29, 1943.

On the ruins left by the Nazi occupation forces, a modern city . . . has taken shape. New apartment houses . . . and rows of modest suburban one-family houses slowly are replacing the slums of centuries.

Turning to the relationship among ethnic groups, he reported that Lithuanian, Russian, Polish, and Yiddish may be heard in the cafés. The 200,000 Poles

have their own schools, newspapers and magazines. . . . Many of the old antagonisms between Lithuanians and Poles have faded and the two nationalities appear to get on well in Vilna.

Speaking of the impact of the new order of things on the generation that has known no other way of life, Topping quotes an elderly Lithuanian as saying: " 'The Soviets have given them all the advantages, free education, sport and travel everywhere in the Soviet Union.' " On the basic question of the relation between Lithuania and the rest of the U.S.S.R., *The Times* dispatch concluded:

The influx of Russians and the Sovietization of Lithuania has been accepted with less resentment in Vilna than in . . . more purely Lithuanian regions.

The picture is complicated and embittered by the fact that, during World War II, the Baltic peoples sided with both Nazis and Soviets, and no crueler war was ever fought. Wartime and postwar executions for real or suspected opposition to the Soviets, and for collaboration with Hitler, were very numerous.

In general, Americans visiting the Baltic states get the same impressions, good and bad, as of the rest of the Soviet Union. The major exception is that the architecture, from Gothic to modern, looks more familiar, and people dress with more of a flair for current Western style. The capital cities, Riga, Vilnius, and Tallin, are smaller, quieter versions of Copenhagen, with much of the same charm. There are medieval dungeons, Renaissance churches with the imaginative spires characteristic of Scandinavia across the water, and some of the best modern architecture to be found in the U.S.S.R.

CENTRAL ASIA

Asia and Africa—and Latin America—are far more interested in the peoples of Soviet Central Asia than in the other non-Russian areas of the U.S.S.R. This is because Central Asia was the colonial hinterland of the tsar's empire. The American or European is prone to overlook the fact that what has happened there is an inspiration to Asians.

To Asians, the important thing is that, with rare exceptions, Soviet Central Asian women are no longer veiled; people are clothed and no longer in rags; there is milk for children—all children; there are hospitals—good hospitals; there are enough Asian doctors to staff them.

American visitors to Soviet Central Asia see a living standard not to be compared with that of the United States. Asians see that there are no beggars: people have jobs. Americans are depressed by the fact that city people are crowded a whole family to one room, and farm families in two- or three-room cottages. Asians see that there is no one sleeping in the streets, no sewage in the gutters, no scooping of drinking or washing water from open ditches.

English is spoken better in Tashkent, Uzbekistan, than in Moscow, I found, perhaps because an Uzbek college student must already be bilingual. He has to know Uzbek and Russian, and a third language often comes easier. In the best restaurant in town, swarthy Uzbek faces under embroidered skullcaps for the men and delicate multiple braids for the women were thoroughly scattered among the Russians—or vice versa. They were so clearly at ease that the concept "integration" didn't even come to mind until I sought a single word to scribble in my notebook as a reminder for later writing.

The next day, wandering through town, it was hard to find "exotic" camera subjects, until we ran across one neighborhood that still had ancient adobe dwellings. As we focused on them, an Uzbek walking by said to me in Russian: "Those houses aren't what they used to be." The glass windows instead of shutters, wood flooring instead of dirt, running water, electric lighting, and, of course, the conspicuous television antennas had made them decently habitable by modern standards until they could be replaced.

One section of Tashkent, the Uzbek capital with a population of a million, is called the Old Town, because it was there when the tsar conquered this territory a century ago. Because of recent reconstruction, it is now more modern than the New Town built by the Russian colonizers at that time. My hotel, in simple modern style set off by classical Mid-Eastern colored tiles, was one of the most attractive buildings of recent construction I saw in the U.S.S.R. in 1959. Its architect is an Uzbek, Bulatov.

Higher education for Uzbeks—in architecture or anything else —is a very exciting story. Back in 1920, when civil war was still raging in the Ukraine and the Caucasus, and the Japanese were occupying the Far East of Siberia, Lenin signed an order founding the University of Central Asia at Tashkent. This was to be the first institution of higher learning in that part of the world. A faculty was assembled in Moscow and shipped out on the single-track railroad across the prairie. Attacked by a troop of hostile cavalry, the professors, complete with wing collars, pince-nez, and Vandykes, fought back from the windows of the chugging train, and made it through.

Today the university has over five thousand students. More important, it has given birth to thirty other colleges throughout Uzbekistan. Education is one field in which the Uzbeks have moved ahead of the best that Europe can show. There are 25 per cent more Swedes than Uzbeks in the world, but there are 29,000 Uzbeks in college as against 26,000 in Sweden.

A rural high school I visited outside Tashkent had a gymnasium that would be laughed at in the United States, but the physics laboratory had equipment that cost thousands of dollars, and magnificent vegetables and grain were growing on an acre out front where the students learned farming.

We were taken to the school by the assistant chairman of the local collective farm, which had built it. The principal's great pride was not in his equipment but in the people the school had produced. From this farm, with a population of four thousand, there had come ninety-six school teachers. The principal and the assistant chairman of the farm both had been graduated from this school and were among those who had gone on to college.

To Americans, industry is no novelty. To the people of the underdeveloped countries it is the most exciting thing on earth, because they see it as the means to entering the twentieth century. But the Tashkent Diversified Textiles Mill is overwhelming even to an American. The exterior is buried in greenery to a degree I have seen in no industrial park here at home. Inside, looms seem to stretch literally to the horizon. If the machinery was impressive, the bulletin boards at various work stations were fascinating: "This is the work place of weaver So-and-So, competing for the title of Shock Worker of Communist Labor." "Let's give the Soviet people beautiful goods, and good quality." "Teach your skill to fifteen others." "He who does not try to improve his education and culture has lost his self-respect." "An advanced worker is not she who is herself ahead, but she who helps others." "Young communist—if you've given your word: keep it."

All of Uzbekistan is not like Tashkent. Samarkand looks nine-teenth-century on the main avenues, and sixteenth-century else-where. El Registan Square is simply magnificent, with symmetrical domes, minarets, and Moslem seminaries with gleaming and fan-tastic tilework. Yet here, too, the revolution is evident. Beneath an ancient arch, three craftsmen in the archaeological service were making adobe bricks by hand to replace those that had crumbled with the centuries. One of the workers was a *woman!* Women bricklayers are rare, if not unknown, even in the West. In Moslem Asia, the woman thirty-five years ago was a family slave. Those who were the first to discard the veil were often kidnaped and tortured to death. Even now, it was news and a blow against con-tinuing prejudice in the countryside when a woman first operated a cotton-picking machine just a few years ago. But to watch these three, and the matter-of-fact glances from passing Uzbeks, one would never know that things had ever been different.

Asked by proud Samarkanders what I thought of their city, I replied that the monuments of antiquity were splendid, but I was surprised at the lack of new construction. They had a practical answer. Tashkent is the capital city, and crowding there is great. In Samarkand the housing situation was not bad. (The idea of putting your best into your capital city seems quite normal to the Soviet nationalities—I noticed that tendency in each of the four republics I visited.) The traffic arteries of Samarkand are asphalt-paved and served by the same noiseless, smokeless trolley-buses one sees everywhere in the U.S.S.R. But on a dirt side street I saw someone digging up the roadway for adobe clay to make bricks, which were piled alongside. Whether this was private or public enterprise I don't know.

Kirghizia, Tadzhikistan, and Turkmenia border Uzbekistan on the east, south and west, respectively. They have only about two million people each. The first is a rugged highland with fine moun-tain meadows and possibly the best horsewomen on earth except for Mongolia. Men are pitted against women—one to one—in a national sport. First, the woman gets a head start on horseback, and if the man catches her, he must be rewarded by a kiss. Then they race in the opposite direction, the man leading off, and if the woman catches him, she may slash him with her riding whip!

Tadzhikistan is in the high Pamirs, the "roof of the world." Above the few and narrow valleys, cultivatable land is so rare and

Kirghiz college graduate reads translation of Theodore Dreiser

precious that it was literally carried on men's backs to build terraces, one heavy load at a time. Mineral riches are great, cotton is grown where possible, and the silkworm is raised. Contact with Afghanistan, to which the U.S.S.R. has made very large development loans, is through this area, and a major highway and tunnel have been built.

Turkmenia may in some ways be the most backward of the fifteen full-fledged Soviet republics. It occupies the earthquake-ridden strip of sandy desert and barren mountains north of Iran. Temperatures go fantastically high in summer, but it is possible to cultivate dates in some places. There is no mountain barrier against the north winds from Siberia, so that open water freezes in winter in most of the country. The raising of sheep and fine horses is the traditional occupation. This is the homeland of the world-famed "Russian" karakul fur. Cotton is grown, and an imagination-boggling project similar to the Central Valley Project now under way in California has put a man-made river five hundred miles across the country. The final goal is to water the entire desert with a canal extending clear to the Caspian Sea. The ultimate consequence will be immense agricultural riches. Sulfur is mined right in the heart of the desert, and the use of airplanes to bring water to the mines goes back to before World War II.

Because these three smaller Central Asian republics are populated largely by recently nomadic peoples, they do not have their own tradition in building large structures, as do the Uzbeks. The cities, therefore, are typically Russian, with ample squares and much planting of trees.

In 1962 a single Economic Council was established for the four Central Asian republics. The republic boundaries follow nationality lines, not geographic or geological ones. The result was that cotton might be transported hundreds of miles to be ginned in the same republic, while a cotton gin might be right next door in a neighboring republic. There is now a joint Central Asian Cotton Board, Construction Board, and Irrigation and Government Farm Construction Board. The Communist Party has also established a supervisory committee for all four of these republics. Industry in them is to rise 25 per cent in the two years 1964–1965, with special emphasis on electricity, chemicals, and fertilizers.

KAZAKHSTAN

Here is the Soviet Wild West. It is a place of nomad Kazakhs, culturally very similar to the Plains Indians of North America before the white man came. The Kazakhs have been catapulted from the twelfth century to the twentieth in thirty-five years. The prairies of Kazakhstan, the site of forced labor camps under Stalin, have now been converted into booming industrial towns. This is a land of superabundant mineral wealth hidden beneath salt marshes and dry plains. Kazakhstan is one-third the size of the United States and, in one enormous corner, there are mountains of stunning beauty. The Kazakh capital, Alma-Ata, "Father of Apples," is framed against eternally snow-capped peaks, much as are Denver and Salt Lake City.

Kazakhstan borders one foreign country—China—and a new railroad starting in this Soviet republic crosses China's vast, underpopulated, and booming western plains.

Russians and Ukrainians in the 1950's planted 69 *million* acres of virgin soil in northern Kazakhstan.

Today, automatic metal-working presses made in Kazakhstan go to equip the industries of India and Afghanistan as well as of communist countries. Nonagricultural employment, which was only twenty thousand in 1913, is now a *hundred* times as large. Kazakhstan now has its own opera company. Most of the girls in the corps de ballet of the company in Alma-Ata are Oriental. The great Moscow star Galina Ulanova herself regards the Kazakh ballet as outstanding among the companies outside Moscow and Leningrad.

These lands in the very heart of Asia show the best and the worst of Soviet society in sharpest relief. The Tadzhik capital, Diushambe, is a European-style city with abundant greenery, and has nearly a quarter million people. In the 1930's it consisted of a few dozen mud houses with blank gray walls on crooked alleys. The tightly disciplined organization needed to work this kind of transformation, and the demand for results at all costs, has had other effects as well. In 1961 both the head of the Tadzhik Communist Party and the prime minister were ousted from office and expelled from the Party for falsifying cotton-crop figures, putting pressure on heads of collective farms and factory managers to cooperate in this, protecting persons who stole from state and collective farms, and favoring relatives and friends in government appointments.

OTHER NATIONALITIES

The fifteen *constituent* republics we have dealt with do not by any means exhaust the list of Soviet nationalities. They are merely those that are largest, or, in some cases, those with the longest tradition of being a nation in their own territories. The Tatars, Mordva, and Bashkirs are the largest of a second group of nineteen peoples, whose territories have the rank of *autonomous* republic in the U.S.S.R. Officially, the fifteen constituent republics have the right to secede, which nobody takes seriously; the nineteen autonomous republics don't, because they are completely surrounded by Soviet territory. But their status is much more than legalistic mumbo-jumbo. The constituent republics frame their own economic plans and budgets, and their representatives are present to support these proposals as they are examined at various levels in the federal government before final adoption. They also pass much legislation of the type that states in the United States do. And, as in the United States, lawyers argue over what should be the province of the federal government, and what of the republics.

The autonomous republics have much more limited powers. Most of them are located within the immense Russian constituent republic. They consist of peoples overrun three or four hundred years ago when the Russians expanded eastward, first to the Volga

River, then to the Ural Mountains, and then eastward across Siberia to the Pacific. Some of these nationalities are outnumbered by Russians within their own home territories, yet they, their languages, and their customs persist. Much assimilation has taken place, however.

The most interesting and by far the most numerous are the Tatars. They are the descendants of the hordes of Genghis Khan, and ruled all of Russia seven hundred years ago. They are the only people besides the Russians who had the chance to enter modern history as the rulers of what is now the U.S.S.R., but their sun set when Ivan the Terrible conquered their capital at Kazan on the Volga east of Moscow in 1552. Russian literature is full of references to the Tatars. Pushkin's "The Fountains of Bakhchisarai" is a classic example, and a ballet in the standard repertory has been written on that story.

I encountered many Tatars in Samarkand and was amazed to find them blond, slender, and tallish. As a consequence of racial mixing they cannot, in most instances, be distinguished from Russians or Ukrainians in appearance. But they retain their own language.

Below the category of autonomous republic in the complicated Soviet structure is the *autonomous region,* for smaller and less unified peoples, and at the bottom is the *national area.* This last is for people who have had a very primitive, tribal structure, such as the American Indians. One of the most commendable aspects of Soviet "nationality policy," as they call it, is what has been done for these people. One night in Moscow I ran into a doctor taking the sixty-six-day vacation he is entitled to for working in the Arctic, at Magadan, west of the Aleutian Islands. Magadan is a modern city of sixty thousand built over permanently frozen soil to exploit the gold and other minerals of the interior. Four months of the year it is accessible only by air, and the other eight only with the aid of icebreakers. There is no railroad within a thousand miles, but the doctor said Magadan had its own theatre company doing both musical comedy and drama. He and everyone else there receives a 50 per cent salary bonus for service in the Far North.

The doctor had the enthusiasm of a pioneer, but he was most excited about what had been done for and by the native Chukchi of the area in which Magadan was built. To win them to a settled way of life they are given houses built for them free of charge, free veterinary care for their reindeer and dogs, and generous loans to buy hunting equipment. Among the eleven thousand Chukchi

Eskimo-like Chukchis and Russians in high school
near Magadan, across North Pacific
from Alaska

there are now physicians, engineers, and a writer whose work has been published in Russian translation throughout the U.S.S.R.

The Soviet Union also includes minorities of the Central European peoples. There are, for example, 1.6 million Germans descended from colonists who settled in Russia in the eighteenth and nineteenth centuries at the invitation of the tsars. They have a central weekly newspaper in Moscow and a local paper in Siberia. Written chiefly in standard German, the papers also carry occasional humorous pieces in the Alamannic dialect used in daily speech. German-language schools exist for children of this minority. There are radio broadcasts in German in two cities in Kazakhstan, and elsewhere.*

THE JEWS

All told, there are 108 nations, nationalities, peoples, and tribes in the U.S.S.R., ranging in population from well over one hundred million Russians down to four hundred Aleuts. The situation of

* *The New York Times,* March 6, 1963.

no group has commanded as much interest in the West as that of
the Jews, who are officially regarded, and who regard themselves
in the U.S.S.R. as a nationality, not as a religious group. Nor
could this be otherwise, because the vast majority of Soviet Jews,
like other Soviet citizens, are not religious. But most of them are
interested in, and aware of, their common history, literary culture,
and traditions, and think of themselves as a people.

There are more Jews in the U.S.S.R. (two and a quarter million) than in Israel. The great majority speak only, or mainly, the
language of the country. However, 20 per cent, or 450,000, regard
Yiddish as their native tongue, and it is frequently heard in the
streets in Vilna, Minsk, Odessa, and Kishinev.

Before the Revolution the Jews were, in general, miserably
poor; 30 per cent of them were sustained by philanthropic relief.*
Their poverty was a result of job and housing discrimination as a
policy of the monarchy. They were compelled to live in the
western borderlands, called the Pale of Settlement. They were
barred by law from holding most public offices. At one time, they
had to serve in the army for longer terms and under more rigorous
conditions than other subjects of the tsar. The number of Jews
admitted to high schools and colleges was restricted by quota.

The tsarist government, through its agents, turned popular dis-
content against the Jews in the form of mob violence, called
pogroms. During the Civil War following the Revolution, "the
anti-Bolshevik soldiery . . . having inscribed anti-Semitism on its
banners, massacred and pillaged the Jewish communities in their
path." † As a result, 100,000 noncombatant Jews were killed and
300,000 children were orphaned. The Bolsheviks, on the other
hand, "denounced anti-Semitism as incompatible with the socialist
tenet of the brotherhood of all nations." ‡ Four top Communist
leaders were Jewish: Trotsky, Sverdlov (the first President of Soviet Russia, after whom the large industrial city of Sverdlovsk is
named), Kamenev, and Zinoviev.

Under the Soviets all residence limitations and employment re-
strictions were abolished, and the ghetto disappeared. One hundred
thousand Jews were assisted in entering agriculture. By 1939, 70
per cent of all gainfully employed members of this nationality were
wage or salary earners. Schools were opened in the Yiddish lan-

---

* *McGraw-Hill Encyclopedia of Russia and the Soviet Union,* New York:
McGraw-Hill, 1961, p. 258.
   † *Ibid.*
   ‡ *Ibid.*

guage for those who wished to attend them. Daily newspapers existed, a Moscow Yiddish-language theatre company was subsidized by the government, and literature was encouraged. A number of talented writers appeared in this language, who won recognition among Jews throughout the world.

The lowering of the bars against Jews caused most of them to assimilate culturally. In 1897, under the tsar, 97 per cent regarded Yiddish as their mother tongue. Three-quarters still did in 1926. But by 1959, only one in five regarded this as his language, although a much larger number understood it.

While the discriminations against Jews were abolished under Lenin, he did not live long enough to put into practice the positive measures that would give them real opportunity, both in the general community and in developing their own culture. This was done under Stalin. In World War II, there were forty-two Jewish generals and two admirals in the Soviet armed forces. At the outbreak of that war in 1939, before the U.S.S.R. was directly involved, it opened its borders to about a million Jewish refugees from Poland, which Hitler was overrunning.

But anti-Semitism had not disappeared in Russia. It had been driven underground, partly by legislation making anti-Semitic acts a punishable crime. It revived during World War II, partly under the influence of Nazi propaganda, particularly among the 83 million inhabitants in the enormous Soviet territory which the Germans occupied.

Stalin's paranoid suspicions, which had been turned against his Party associates in the prewar years, were inflamed against the Jews when an enormous crowd turned out to welcome the first Israeli Ambassador to the Soviet Union. He suspected that the Soviet Jews had transferred their allegiance to Israel. All Jewish cultural institutions were dissolved in 1948, and in 1952 every member of the (Soviet) Jewish Anti-Fascist Committee was executed except for the author Ilya Ehrenburg. The dead included writers, diplomats, and other persons of distinction. In January, 1953, nine prominent physicians, six of them Jews, were arrested and accused of having conspired at the behest of Western powers and Jewish agencies to poison leading Soviet personalities.

Stalin died two months later, the doctors were freed and exonerated, and in 1956 Khrushchev revealed that the "confessions" they had made were beaten out of them. Today the murdered writers of the Stalin era are publicly honored. Their works are published, but not in the Yiddish language in which they were

written, except thus far for those of one man, David Bergelson.
Pre-Revolutionary writers are published in the original Yiddish,
however. A literary magazine in Yiddish resumed publication in
1961. Its circulation of 35,000 (1964) is the largest in that language in the world, and there are 140 Soviet writers in Yiddish.
Since 1956, 187 books by eighty of them have been translated
into fifteen Soviet and four foreign languages, and published in
fourteen million copies, for an extremely high average of 75,000
copies per book. But not one was published in the original
Yiddish! A change in this was publicly promised for 1964.

A professional theatre group was reconstituted in 1962. Very large
numbers of records of Yiddish-language songs have been pressed;
readings and concerts in that language now take place on a large
scale, and posters in the streets announce them in both Yiddish
and the local language. No schools in the language exist, although
400,000 Jews regard it as their native tongue, and many would
presumably wish their children to be educated in it. It is to be remembered that the U.S.S.R. does permit such schools as a general policy, to Germans among others. A Communist Party editor
of a small-town newspaper who permitted a medieval libel of the
Jews to be published was demoted, but neither he nor the writer
of the item was tried under the Soviet law making propagation of
anti-Semitism a crime, and news of this affair was also suppressed.

This confused situation arises from the fact that the men who
today lead the U.S.S.R. are those Stalin allowed to live because
they were efficient executives and managers, not thinkers. The
thinkers and the men of principle were killed. Today's leaders
come from peasant backgrounds in which anti-Semitism was common. As Communists they know they're not supposed to be anti-
Semitic. They refuse to believe they are, and so they deny the
problem exists. But since it does exist, they solve it in the manner
of politicians: they yield under pressure, and bit by bit, while denying that they are doing so. The situation has improved in the ir-
regular fashion we have described. When someone describes the
situation publicly, as did the poet Yevtushenko (who is not Jewish)
in his "Babi Yar" and his autobiography published abroad in
1963, officials became angry, and pressured him to modify the
poem, and refused to publish the autobiography in the U.S.S.R.
But men of conscience like the composer Shostakovich (who is
also not Jewish) incorporate poems like "Babi Yar" into choral
works, and do cycles based on Jewish folk songs, and thus strike
a blow against anti-Semitism.

Forty-five years of educational and job opportunity have had

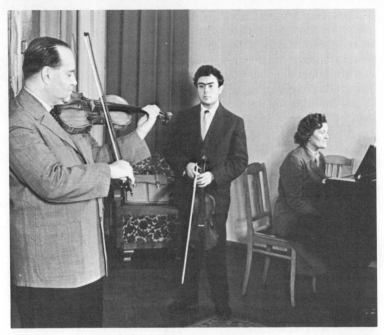

Violinist David Oistrakh teaching

the following effects. Although Jews constitute only 1.1 per cent of the Soviet population, they number 8.5 per cent of the professional writers and newspapermen, 10 per cent of the college professors, 33.3 per cent of the personnel of the film industry, 10 per cent of the scientists, 10.4 per cent of the judges and lawyers, 15.7 per cent of the doctors, and 7 per cent of the musicians, painters, sculptors, and actors. The percentage of Jewish college undergraduates is three times as high as the ratio of Jews in the Soviet population. On the other hand, the percentage of Jews among persons executed for large-scale, long-continued illegal business dealings in a campaign against such practices in 1962 was extremely high. In a dispatch of November 26, 1962, *New York Times* Moscow correspondent Theodore Shabad reported:

Observers differ on whether the heavy involvement of Jews represents an anti-Semitic bias in the Soviet prosecutors or whether it is a natural consequence of the traditional role played by Jews in the business and commercial life of the cities of western Russia. In the absence of indications of overt anti-Semitism on the part of the government, many foreign observers tend to the second view.

Over one hundred Jews are holders of the military decoration corresponding to the Congressional Medal of Honor for heroism in the Soviet forces in World War II, and more than forty have won its counterpart for extraordinary constructive civilian activity. Jewish names are found each year among winners of the Lenin Prizes for creative achievement in the arts and sciences.

On the other hand, Jews constitute only one-half of one per cent of the members of government at all levels, or fill only two out of every five posts to which their numbers would entitle them if posts were allocated according to proportion of population. However, in 1962, the post of Chairman of the State Planning Commission, carrying the title of Vice-Premier of the U.S.S.R. and holding membership in the small inner cabinet, was given to a builder of great construction projects, Benjamin Dymschitz, a Jew.

Every Soviet citizen over sixteen carries an identification card, called a "passport." Among other things, it identifies him by nationality. The official Soviet *Law Dictionary* (1956) says that the nationality recorded must be that of the parents and that it cannot ever be changed. If the marriage is mixed, which is increasingly common in the U.S.S.R., the child may choose the nationality of either parent. The passport system does not apply to most country people, but Jews are almost entirely city folk. In March, 1964, Khrushchev denounced the internal passport system. After its abolition, the citizen's identification document will be his work-record booklet, which does not specify nationality.

About 10 per cent of the people are religious, according to *The New York Times,* March 3, 1964, and there is no reason to believe that the ratio among Jews is any higher. In addition to some 100 synagogues throughout the country, there are small prayer houses. In Leningrad, for example, *The Times* correspondent found sixteen prayer houses in 1961, in addition to the one four-thousand-seat synagogue. There is a seminary in Moscow for the training of rabbis. Enrollment is very small.

Some degree of anti-Semitism (and other prejudices) will remain in the U.S.S.R. until the mass media and the educational system are employed to prove that long-held folk beliefs about other peoples are not true. That has never been done.

4:   People, Their Lives and Their Beliefs

Because the Soviet Union has been changing very rapidly since the Revolution, each age group of Soviet people has greatly differing attitudes.

Once I argued with a Soviet intellectual from late one evening until well into the next morning. We spoke English, a disadvantage for him, but he knew it well enough to quote from *Hamlet* to make a point. He was a well-traveled, erudite man—a literary critic by profession—and he illustrated his argument with stories from his own life.

This man was born in 1910. His earliest memories were of the hardships of a war which Russia lost—and in which it lost ten million men. His next were of a great revolution and bitter years of civil war and intervention in which the daily food ration in his city was cut to an eighth of a pound of bread per day and nothing else. Then came a few short years of respite, followed by the years of his young manhood. This was the time when, by tightening its belt and through Herculean efforts, his country pulled itself from the eighteenth century into the twentieth.

Life had just begun to get better when Hitler struck. The city where this man lived, Leningrad, was encircled by the Germans and one-third of its three million people died—of starvation, of cold, of hardships, and diseases their hunger-weakened bodies

71

could not withstand, and of direct military action. Corpses were stacked against buildings till spring (they would not decompose in the cold): the people didn't have the strength to bury them. But Leningrad would not surrender. The war was followed by five more years of hardship as the country rebuilt—faster, by all reports, than did any other, but this meant even harder work. Then, in this man's view, the hostility of the same forces that intervened against his government when it was just founded, and urged Hitler eastward a generation later, compelled the Soviets to put vast funds into nuclear weapons and missiles that could have gone to make life better faster. Today, he said, life is incomparably better than ever before, and he is immensely proud of this.

This man is *tough*. He is mistrustful of the West, and he is strong. This is typical of the character and attitudes of his generation, particularly of its self-made, educated members. It is they who run the Soviet Union, in government, in production, in the arts. Because of their age, they will continue to be at the highest levels for another dozen years.

Much of his generation is dead. There are 21 million more women than men in the U.S.S.R., and the difference is *entirely* in the age groups older than thirty-five. The men were killed in World War II, in the Civil War, and in World War I. The survivors of his generation have a particular dream. They dream passionately of peace. They know that their country, and a system most of them believe in, survived the war against Hitler by their personal sacrifice, misery, and efforts. The memory of that time brings shudders. A Soviet graduate student at the University of California, a veteran of World War II, who is older than most of his fellow students, said to me: "I know just one thing: another war is *impossible*."

Until they are convinced that you want peace as badly as they do, those who fought up front or suffered in the cities will talk to you of nothing else. A semiliterate unskilled worker visiting the great Exhibition of Economic Achievement in Moscow said to me: "Why should you and I rot in trenches and throw grenades at each other? What did war ever bring people like us but starvation, cold, disease, and death? Isn't it better that we walk, talk in a beautiful place like this?" To him, and to every Russian I have ever spoken to, war is not the unimaginable horrors of World War III; it is foot-slogging, land mines, undernourishment, and suffering of World War II, and he doesn't have to think of anything worse.

Moscow, 1945: the war is over

Almost no Russian over thirty-five seems to think that his government's *basic* policies have ever been wrong, except when the Party itself says so. (I have met only two exceptions to this rule, and I've talked with hundreds of people.) In the lifetime of Soviet citizens, survival for their country and for their system was impossible without the utmost unity and discipline, and they take these requirements for granted. The postwar generation, however, is willing to admit there have been mistakes other than those officially acknowledged, and that matters could sometimes have been handled differently. This is the reason for the abuse heaped upon Yevtushenko for publishing abroad his *Precocious Autobiography,* which could not have been printed in the U.S.S.R.

Today's generation of students and graduate students—the best-educated generation the country has known—not yet bogged down in jobs requiring their thoughts to be concentrated in a single direction, are the most outspoken of all. "Yes," said one to me, "we still have the problem of initiative. Too many of our officials were trained at a time when, if you stepped out of line, whisht," and his hand made a gesture as if knocking over a chessman. Most interesting was that he would say this to a foreigner he had met only once before, and do so in the presence of a Soviet fellow student who frankly disagreed with him.

But there is no doubt in the students' minds about their country's way of life. This was best described by an American law student, George Feifer, who wrote in *The New York Times* of April 27, 1963, after a year spent at Moscow University, where he lived in a dormitory. The average Soviet student:

> . . . scorns his obligatory courses in political economy, dialectical materialism and the history of the Communist Party. . . . He is irritated by corruption and heavy-handedness in high places. . . . Yet . . . it would be the greatest mistake to picture [him] in a state of revolt, or even of anger. . . . [He] feels that the policies and arrangements of his leaders are essentially those needed for the welfare of the nation. . . . On what he considers the fundamental issues, he has no argument with the socialist system or even the Communist Party; he is certain that the advantages of Soviet society far outweigh its disadvantages. . . . However much [he] wants things Western, he does not want what seems to him its essence: capitalism. . . . His patriotism is exceedingly intense by Western standards: "the Russian earth," "the Russian people"—*Rossiya*—have a strong emotional meaning for him.

Yuri Gagarin, the first space traveler, was only twenty-seven when he shot round the earth in 1961. Yet he knows what war

Graduate engineering students

and invasion mean. He had just entered school as a boy of seven when the Germans occupied his village and requisitioned his home. His father had to build a dugout to shelter them through two Russian winters. His little brother was strung up by an ordinary Nazi soldier who occupied their home for being too curious about his job of changing batteries. Fortunately, Yuri and his mother were able to cut the boy down in time. Later, his older brother and sister were driven off to Germany to become slave laborers, but managed to escape en route and join the Soviet forces. When the Germans were driven out, Yuri, aged nine, went to work on the collective farm. He was eleven before it was possible for him to go to school. Even then, in the absence of pencils, paper, ink, chalk, or textbooks, his schooling consisted of learning geography from war communiqués, and learning to read from an infantry field manual the children had found. The childhood of the first spacewoman, Valentina Tereshkova, was equally marred by the war. It widowed her mother at twenty-seven, leaving her with three children to raise alone.

The generation of Gagarin will be prominent in Soviet life for the next forty years. It is not difficult to understand the attitude of these people toward war, military preparedness, and disarmament agreements. While the older generation is still psychologically governed by the prewar feeling of "capitalist encirclement" and needs convincing that another attack by the "imperialist powers" is not inevitable, the younger people have grown up at a time when the U.S.S.R. has had powerful allies, and much of the world is neutral. As a consequence, the rising generation of leaders should be more confident, therefore less touchy, and easier to negotiate with.

CITY AND COUNTRY

The Soviet city dweller comes from the country, or certainly his father did. The 1926 census showed that only one person in five lived in a town. In 1939, the figure was one in three. Today the division is half and half.

The countryman lives in a crude, solid cottage that is his private property. The townsman lives, almost invariably, in a publicly owned apartment house, generally with one bedroom per family, rarely with more than two.

The city family everywhere has electricity. Usually it has gas as well. Radios are universal (and very good in quality). One city family in three had television in 1963. There were enough movie seats for each person in town to go once in two and a half weeks. Of course, some don't care for the movies, and others go very often indeed. Every town has its company of actors (there are over five hundred permanent professional companies).

The villager's chances of having electricity are approaching two out of three. With very few exceptions, he doesn't have gas. If he has electricity, he'll have a radio; if not, there is a loudspeaker in the village square and in the community center. Thus far, television is virtually unknown in the countryside. If the villager's community center works at average efficiency, movies will be shown often enough for him to find a seat once a month. That's a big improvement: there are five country movie houses for every two in 1953. A group of touring players or musicians—or both— may come by once or twice a year when the dirt roads are dry or frozen. The rest of the year, the printed page is his access to culture, through newspapers and magazines—and the public library in every village. In 1956, there were 144,300 public libraries in the Soviet Union; ten thousand in the United States.

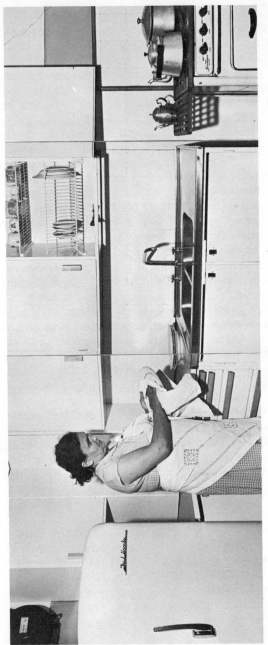

Standard kitchen in new apartment house

In spring and fall the roads are soup and the villages are isolated except for mail deliveries and whatever contact can be maintained on horseback or by tractor. Private telephones are unknown in the countryside, and communication outside one's own village is by mail. In the city, private telephones are few, but pay stations are within easy walking distance, or in one's apartment house.

The city housewife cooks on a stove if she has gas, and on a one-burner kerosene primus stove if she does not. The gas stove often has to be shared with another family, or two, or three, in the apartment. Today, however, about half of all city families enjoy such privacy as is provided by a one-bedroom apartment with its own kitchen and bath.

The peasant woman cooks on her brick-masonry Russian oven. Its heat-retaining top is still used in outlying places as a bed, particularly by the elderly, who are accustomed to this and like it.

City people have indoor running water, usually only cold so they have to heat it themselves. Most apartment houses have baths. Those who live in old apartment buildings go to the public bathhouse in winter, and use the river or beach, to save money, in summer. The peasant woman carries water in buckets hooked to a yoke across her shoulders up from the river bank or from a well, except in a handful of the very best collective and state farms, which provide piped running water. Her family washes in a basin of water poured from a hand ewer. They bathe in the river or in a steam bath made by pouring water on hot stones.

The city person gets where he wants to go by bus, trolley-bus, streetcar, or, in the three largest cities, by excellent subway. Private automobiles are very few (a million in a country of over fifty million families). Motorcycles are not much more common. Bicycles are used widely but chiefly for recreation and sport. The countryman travels locally by horse and wagon, by sleigh in winter, and very often nowadays, if he is going any distance, by hitching a ride in the back of a truck belonging to his collective farm.

The railroad is still far and away the major means of long-distance travel. Intercity bus service is in its early stages. Air transport is fine, cheap, and safe, but departures are not very frequent. The percentage of communities served is low, although very considerable in actual numbers. The planes range from satisfactory to excellent. The total number of passengers carried was 35 million in 1963, and is rising 30 per cent per year. Fares have been cut annually, and the cost of a flight as long as a U.S. coast-to-coast trip was $90 in 1963. Direct air service is maintained to thirty-eight countries.

Country folk make their purchases in co-operative general stores. They look like old-time general stores in the United States. Their stock is limited in variety, with frequent interruptions in supply. City people buy in stores of the presupermarket era, clean as a whistle. I have looked in at all hours, in many cities, and never found one that looked dirty or had any odor at all except that of fresh vegetables or whatever else was on sale. Many foodstuffs are bought at farmers' markets, which are also sanitary.

The city dweller is almost invariably a wage or salary earner. He works short hours (forty hours is the average week), has a steady job, long paid vacations in all occupations, free medical care and hospitalization for himself and his family. The countryman who works on a government-owned farm or in any nonagricultural occupation is in the same situation. On a collective farm—and most farmers belong to these—he may get a monthly advance against a share in the crop, or else a regular wage. The latter is becoming more and more popular. He gets free medical care and hospitalization. He must finance vacation time himself, as do farmers in other countries. Farm pensions were introduced in 1964.

As of the 1959 census, three adult country people out of four had had only four years of schooling, but in the cities two out of four adults were above that level. There is a solid mass of twenty million country dwellers who have had a junior high school or high school education. In the cities, one person in three has completed at least junior high school. In the U.S.S.R., the person who has attended a technical or specialized high school is an "intellectual." In 1964, one-half of the working population, city and country, had a junior high school education or better.

The manual worker in the U.S.S.R., industrial or agricultural, usually does heavy physical labor. Lifting and carrying jobs are not usually mechanized. Hand tools are usually muscle-operated, rather than power-driven, except in factory operations. Because the "intellectual's" and office worker's job is so much easier physically than the manual worker's, and because government has given every kind of incentive, moral and material, to acquire professional skills, there is a great deal of effort to get such jobs, and much disappointment on the part of parents of those who don't get them. Partly because of this, and partly because of European tradition, the snobbishness of some professionals—economists,

Siberian village in winter

radio announcers, or whatever—toward the manual worker is
shocking to an American. One doesn't find this as much among
engineers and other nonmanual personnel whose work brings them
into contact with workingmen on the job. Yet everyone respects
the worker who wears a "Hero of Socialist Labor" or "Order of
Lenin" medal for truly extraordinary performance of any kind of
job.

For the last several years, the government has been trying to
combat this caste feeling by restoring the prestige and privileges
enjoyed by the manual worker after the Revolution. The most
effective measure is doubtless the fact that more and more children

are getting the kind of education associated with the intellectual only ten or fifteen years ago. For example, spaceman Gagarin had not been able to consider going to college because tuition was charged when he reached college age and it would have had to be at his parents' expense. Today there is no tuition charge. In 1962 I spoke to a number of young professionals who had been workers, and they had no feeling of superiority toward working people.

The sharp differences between American and Soviet living and working standards outlined in the last few pages are important to an understanding of the differences between the two countries today. But it would be a great mistake to regard the situation as static or even as likely to last more than a generation into the future. I myself have seen the change from the country of peasants clad in homespun, rag puttees, and birch-bark sandals in 1932. For many of them a tractor was something supernatural because nothing living pulled it. The differences between the U.S.S.R. of 1932 and 1962, both statistically and to my own eye, are far greater than the differences between the Soviet Union and the United States in 1962. One of the most outstanding characteristics of the U.S.S.R. has been the rapidity of change, and it still is, as I was able to observe from the contrasts between what I saw in 1959 and 1962. It is the speed of this change that causes me to place so much emphasis on the differences between Soviet generations.

THE BELIEVERS

The Russian word for one who is religious is "believer." Essentially there are two beliefs in the Soviet Union: belief in communism and belief in God. But while those who believe in communism don't usually believe in God, the religious in the U.S.S.R. usually also believe in communism. This fact was driven home to me in a very unusual conversation.

One day in Moscow in 1962 I ran into a very young man in street clothes with shoulder-length blond hair and a beard that would qualify him to play the Christ in the Oberammergau Passion Play. I knew we had met, and it turned out that I had seen him the previous day at the monastery which is the seat of the Russian Orthodox Church. But there he had been wearing vestments: he was a priest.

We had a long talk. I had never conversed with a clergyman in the U.S.S.R. before, and I was surprised to encounter so young a priest (he was twenty-four) in a country where the congregations consist almost entirely of the middle-aged and elderly. I began,

Ikon corner is still very common in peasant cottages

to be safe, by asking theological questions. I told him I was from a country where most people belong to faiths that have very little outward display, and there is nothing quite like the icons on the outer walls of churches that I had seen Russians kiss as they entered. How did he understand this? He said that if my wife and I had lost a child in infancy many years ago, and had kept no photograph of it, it would be increasingly difficult to recall its appearance, and what it meant to us, as the years went by. But a picture would bring it all back. The icons and other images were therefore a means of recalling Christ and his meaning. There was nothing unctuous or routine in his manner as he spoke.

I then asked how it was that a person so young was a priest in a country where he would probably be the youngest person in church. He answered, quite matter-of-factly, that profound faith is not given to everyone. He did not say this in a way that made him guilty of the sin of pride. But it turned out from further questioning that he, and a majority of the present students at the seminary maintained by the Orthodox Church, are from western

Ukraine and western Belorussia: areas incorporated into the U.S.S.R. at the end of World War II. He came from an area where religion had had no competition from active atheism when he was born, and where it was still much stronger than elsewhere. At this point I suspected that possibly he came from a class in society that had lost by the change, and asked him what his parents had been.

"Peasants," he replied. "And it's better for someone like me in the church nowadays."

"What do you mean?"

"In the past the priesthood almost all came from the wealthy. Today someone like me can be a priest."

I turned to the obvious decline in churchgoing. How would he explain it? He answered:

"In the old days going to church was the thing to do. Today, being a member of the Young Communist League is the thing to do. But we're satisfied. We believe the congregations we have today are the sincerely religious."

He seemed so candid, and so willing to deal even with thorny questions, that I asked him what he thought of the Soviet government's foreign policy. His answer was quite a surprise.

"The Church," and it was obvious he included himself, "thinks Nikita Sergeievich [Khrushchev] is doing Christ's work."

"He's an atheist," I replied; "what do you mean?"

"Our Lord taught us to turn the other cheek; that is why we clergy will never take up arms, although we have always supported our country when it was attacked. But we believe Khrushchev's foreign policy is turning the other cheek."

He then asked me what I thought of the chances of disarmament. I replied that I thought there were forces opposed to it. He took it for granted that I could not be referring to the Soviet Union, and said, in his mild and thoughtful fashion:

"Then perhaps your working people ought to do what ours did in 1917."

If he is typical of the Russian priesthood, there is obviously nothing in their attitude that could antagonize their flock. For he is, at the same time, a religious man, a patriot, and a believer in his country's present social system. Inasmuch as he is aide to the Metropolitan (Archbishop) of Leningrad, in addition to having his own congregation, it is clear that the church fathers look upon him as the kind of young man they would wish to advance rapidly in the hierarchy.

Ninety per cent of Soviet citizens are atheists, according to a *New York Times* estimate.* But the people I met have invariably been tolerant of religious belief. I interpreted from English for an American rabbi in conversations with passers-by in the Kremlin, where one finds Soviet tourists from all over the country, and also in a neighborhood park in Leningrad. Although he identified himself as a clergyman and by his faith, in order to make the conversation as probing as possible, there was not the slightest shading of prejudice against him, either as man of the cloth or as Jew, in the very lively give and take. When the discussion ended, and he gave them his blessing in parting, no one snickered or looked in any way embarrassed. When I was there in 1932, the young people would have been intolerant of him as a clergyman.

The authorities have no doubt that religious people are politically loyal, except for those "who call upon the faithful to refuse service in the Soviet army and to refrain from participating in elections and in civic and cultural life," according to *Komsomolskaya Pravda,* January 5, 1964. On this reasoning, the Jehovah's Witnesses, Reformed Adventists, and Pentecostal Christians were outlawed in 1963. The article admits that "they continue to worship in secret." Says the official *Large Soviet Encyclopedia,*† "There is also a large number of citizens who, while actively participating in the life of the country and honorably performing their duties as citizens, continue to be under the influence of various types of religious beliefs." Another Soviet publication adds: "The religious ideology strives to influence the faithful in terms of morality. . . . It is the task of atheist propaganda to distinguish between popular tradition and superstition, to demonstrate that morality is not dependent upon religion."

There is enough immorality—graft, sanctimonious hypocrisy, pull, power-grabbing—in the "church" of Communism—the Party —to cause a few to look elsewhere for moral guidance. The war, with its terrible inroads into the male population, its starvation and material hardships, brought some loosening of the very high moral standards that the Party had tried to establish since the Revolution. The war also brought uncertainties into the Soviet pattern of secure and predictable existence for the rank-and-file citizen. All this caused many older people to return to religion, and some younger ones to adhere to it. Current Soviet sociological studies of con-

* Theodore Shabad, *The New York Times,* March 3, 1964.
† Vol. 50, p. 642.

vincingly scholarly nature show the present trend in religious belief to be downward. A great many young people who get married in church and have their children baptized to satisfy their own parents never set foot inside the door again. The Party doesn't obstruct such observances, but disapproves on the ground that these are concessions to what it regards as superstition.

Religious bodies face a need to change. When Russia was illiterate, faith was based on tangible beliefs: heaven was above, and hell below. This was so simple that, in the prewar years (and even today in some outlying places), a trip in an airplane provided by the atheist organization was sufficient to win many a peasant away from religion: he had been up in the sky and saw no heaven there.

The theology of the dominant faiths, Christian, Islamic, and Judaic, was highly fundamentalist. This is still true. In general, religion in the U.S.S.R. has hardly adapted itself to the age of education and modern science. Current antireligious propaganda published in the Soviet Union consists largely of efforts to show the uneducated that science offers explanations for phenomena they regard as supernatural. Atheist writings also expose cases of corruption and misbehavior on the part of clergymen. I have seen no attempt to analyze sophisticated modern religious doctrines and to try to demonstrate their errors on philosophical grounds.

Despite the effort to uproot religion by argument and by prohibiting organized religious education for children under sixteen, religious institutions enjoy some rather surprising privileges. Although churches are government property, their congregations use them without rent or other charge. The government itself keeps in repair and restores those churches which it regards as of historical and architectural significance. Church income—from contributions, sale of candles and other religious goods—is tax exempt, the clergy itself being subject to the same extremely low rates of income tax as the rest of the population. In addition to the students at seminaries within the U.S.S.R., Russian Baptist seminarians have gone to England to study in recent years, and Moslems to Cairo. Russian clergymen have exchanged visits with American in the two countries, and some Moslems make the pilgrimage to Mecca each year.

The important Christian churches are the Russian Orthodox, the Roman Catholic, the Lutheran, the Armenian Gregorian, the Georgian Orthodox, the Old Believers (bearing the same conservative relationship to Russian Orthodoxy as it in turn does to Roman

Catholicism), the Reformed (Calvinist), the Methodist, and the Baptist, which is the most important Protestant faith in Russia proper. The Baptists have grown somewhat since the war.

Geographically, Russian Orthodoxy exists wherever there are Russians. Roman Catholicism is centered in Latvia and Lithuania. I happened upon St. Peter's in Odessa one Sunday, and found the attendance to be mainly elderly and female, as is the case with all faiths in the U.S.S.R.

Lutheranism is centered in Estonia and Latvia.

The Moslem faith is second to Orthodox Christianity in membership. Buddhism is practiced in Buriat-Mongolia east of Lake Baikal, Siberia, and in Tuva on the Mongolian frontier, and also in the Kalmyk country in Europe, between the mouth of the Volga and the Caucasus. Most faiths have national centers. Judaism, which exists in individual congregations, and Catholicism, with bishops in Lithuania and a Metropolitan in Latvia, do not have national headquarters. Abandonment of religion has been greatest among people of Jewish and Russian Orthodox background. Among Georgian and Armenian Christians, higher retention of religion is associated with the history and ethnic pride of those nationalities.

5: Education

One of the fields in which the Soviets have made tremendous progress is education. Albert Rhys Williams, an American who observed the Russian Revolution at first hand, told of two peasants staring at a poster shortly afterward. They had tears in their eyes. He asked why. One said: "We can't read a word of it. The tsar only wanted us to plow and fight and pay taxes. He didn't want us to read. He put out our eyes." The other nodded in agreement.

It is only since 1930 that education has been compulsory. Before then there weren't enough teachers, schools, paper, or pencils. In the 1930's, compulsory education meant only four years in school, so that the average person's education ended when he was little more than literate and able to do only the most basic arithmetic. By the beginning of World War II, the city schools were requiring seven years of attendance, but the rural schools only four, and two-thirds of the people lived in the country.

In 1959, the rural system was able to provide seven years of schooling for everyone, but the census that year showed that 35 per cent of Soviet children dropped out of school to go to work before completing that level. Most of these were doubtless in the countryside. An extensive network of continuation schools has been opened for young workers and farmers, and there are incentives and privileges for those who seek to make up the education they failed to take advantage of earlier.

By the late 1950's, there was a new problem. Despite the unparalleled expansion of college enrollment, high schools were turning out more graduates than the colleges could take. A high-school diploma had previously been almost an automatic pass to college education. Because of the tremendous emphasis placed on the development of professionals, those who could not get into college were bitterly disappointed. Their parents were even more so. Worse, the college-preparatory nature of the schooling they had been given did not fit them for any particular kind of job.

The educational system was changed in 1958 to give everyone both a trade for manual or office work and uniform academic schooling, which would permit them to go on to college if they desired and as circumstances permitted. Compulsory schooling (including continuation school for drop-outs) was increased from seven to eight years, and high-school graduation now comes after eleven years of education rather than ten. The extra year at each level eases somewhat the burden of a very intensive education. The year is devoted partly to schooling and partly to work on the job. Today, graduates are not suddenly removed without preparation from complete dependence on their parents to workaday responsibilities. Another reason for the change was to combat a rising snobbishness of the educated (the high-school graduate) toward the rest of the population, by restoring appreciation of physical labor as that which creates the means of life for all. Preference in college entrance is now given to applicants who have had two years of work experience. The first years of college combine work and study, as at Antioch College in the United States. However, the Soviet setup is designed to assure that the work will be in the field one is studying, and not merely a job for employment's sake.

One problem the Soviets share with Americans is that of the double- and even triple-shift school. In the U.S.S.R. this is still necessary, partly because of the consequences of wartime destruction and partly because of continued industrialization, with people flocking into the cities. Urban population has risen 12 million in the last three years. The constant lengthening of the period of education is also a very important factor in preventing the supply of schoolrooms from catching up with the need.

Much has been written about the new Soviet boarding schools. Education at the boarding schools is and will be no different from that in the academic-plus-vocational day schools. But the boarding schools are designed to solve entirely another problem. The Communist leaders are dissatisfied with the degree to which "pre-Communist" personal self-interest continues to govern the life of the Soviet person. In the boarding schools life is co-operative. The psychology of the children is guided from the outset by the idea that the individual benefits most by helping the community. Soviet leaders also advance more standard educational reasons for the emphasis on boarding schools. They say that not everyone is gifted in bringing up children, and that most parents are not trained for it. Therefore, they hold that the job could be done better, and with less conflict and heartache, if it were done by people who have the best personalities for this, and are equipped with the special education required. The children do go home for week ends, holidays, and the summer vacation.

There are now 600,000 children in 2,700 boarding schools. This is one child in fifty. Most boarding-school children at present are orphans, fatherless, or from very large families. Enrollment in the boarding schools is voluntary. It will be a dozen years before there are enough of them for this to begin to be the principal form of education—if Soviet parents accept it.

At present, Soviet schools—day or boarding—educate well. When Ivan gets out of eight-year school at the age of fifteen, he has had 249 hours of physics, 142 hours of chemistry, 465 hours of a foreign language, 286 hours of geography, 71 hours of drafting, and *1,663 hours of mathematics,* plus Russian, literature, history, civics, nature study, physical education, music and singing, freehand drawing, shop, and 180 hours of practice on a real job. However, this heavy curriculum and the fact that peasants still believe that their boys ought to start working on the farm at age fourteen may partly explain why one-third of the students drop out.

I have never met a Soviet schoolchild who could speak a foreign language (except for one linguistic genius who could converse in half a dozen), and I doubt that reading ability in foreign languages is very advanced. A government decision of 1961 proposed to remedy the poor quality of language teaching in seven years. Incompetent teachers were to be fired, others were to be given advanced training, the size of classes was to be reduced to fifteen or fewer (for language classes only), and the teaching of foreign languages was to be permitted in kindergarten and the first four grades where parents request it. Films, records, tapes, radio, and television are to be used widely.

By 1963, there were seven hundred schools in which some courses were being taught in foreign languages. It was then decided to double the number of such schools by 1965. By 1970–1971,

Fourth-grade botany laboratory class (eleven-year-olds)

50 per cent of all schoolchildren are to be learning English, 20 per cent French, 20 per cent German, and 10 per cent Spanish or other languages. A few schools already teach Arabic, Hindi, or Chinese. One may safely guess that the percentage distribution will be modified upward in favor of these last.

All things considered, the Soviet student has, after eight years, an education equivalent to that of an average American high-school graduate after twelve. However, a Soviet educator who made a first-hand study of American schools concluded that classes in this country for intellectually gifted children were approximately on a par with Soviet schools in the demands made upon the students, seriousness of approach, and educational methods.*

The three years of noncompulsory education which follow the eight-year school provide an education rather like the first two years of an American polytechnic institute or technology institute.

* *Soviet Education,* December, 1962, p. 58.

High-school radio station

In addition, the Soviet student learns a specialized trade and gets on-the-job practice in it. Job training and work take up one-third of the additional education. The humanities (literature, history, civics, and foreign languages) get a shade more than one-third of the nonvocational classroom time. The remaining third goes to further study of the sciences learned in the eight-year school, plus a skeletal course in astronomy and economic geography in place of the general geography of the earlier years. Five per cent of the total time, academic and vocational, is reserved for electives.

The ninth through eleventh grades may be taken in one of three ways. There is, in the Soviet Union, (1) the high school as Americans know it, (2) the evening high, and (3) the off-shift high school. The last is usually conducted in conjunction with some major industrial enterprise. The evening and off-shift courses are identical in content with those given in the day schools. The number of hours is much fewer, and so the quality of education can hardly be as good. The purpose of having identical curricula is to qualify these students for college-entrance examinations, in addition to giving them fuller preparation for modern life. The belief is that the student who has given up his evenings for three years during late adolescence to complete high school is going to be a serious and dependable college student. In 1963, 51 per cent of all high-school students also held jobs, six hours a day, or four hours for fifteen-year-olds. As stated earlier, the college applicant with a work record is preferred to one straight from school. The night-school student is let off from work an hour early, with no loss in pay, on the days he has classes.

In 1963, another discussion about educational reform, conducted in the typically heated Russian fashion, got much space in the newspapers. Some leading educators and scientists of great distinction began to propose specialized high schools. They wrote in *Izvestia*:

Unfortunately the view persists that the students must know all subjects equally well. . . . The desire to produce people with a broad education acts as a boomerang and the graduates often do not know anything really well. Failure to give timely support and encouragement to a child's predilection for some branch of knowledge often nips his awakening interest in the bud.

They called for the establishment of a "network of physics–mathematics schools so as to discover and train gifted boys and girls."

A prominent educator defended the existing system of uniform and high-level education for all. Another responded that there actually were a good many special-emphasis schools, for example, seven hundred schools combining music instruction with general education, and one hundred stressing mathematics, to train computer programmers. But the scientists wanted schools that would seek out and develop people with pioneering and creative abilities in mathematics. The Siberian Center of the Academy of Sciences conducted a contest for such talent in all the grade schools in that territory. After the first round, which was conducted by mail, the center sent teachers and scientists to county seats to interview and further test the winners. Those selected in this way were invited to a summer-camp school where vacation relaxation was combined with scientific games, talks, and clubs. On the basis of this personal knowledge of the children, the scientists selected 120 as the entering class of a mathematics boarding school. The results were satisfactory. The next year 240 more were admitted, and other parts of the country began to conduct similar contests and establish similar schools. Schools emphasizing chemistry and other fields have also begun to appear.

The school system is designed to develop co-operativeness. The newspaper *Pravda for the Young Pioneers* (the Young Pioneers is a co-ed Scout-like movement) corresponds to the various junior-level newspapers to which our own schoolchildren are encouraged to subscribe. The following letter, carried prominently at the top of a page, is typical:

Zoya Burakova used to teach in our school. Now she is retired. She lives far away. She is sick, and we learned that red bilberries are good for her. Every year we send her packages of red bilberries from the woods here. But we think that is very little indeed. She lives alone. The latest is that she has to stay in bed. Isn't there a troop in Dnepropetrovsk that will visit No. 20 Belgorod St.?

In another letter in the same paper, a teacher writes from the Ural Mountains:

You know what I like most about our children? Their persistence. We didn't used to have a clubroom. Adult authorities wouldn't do anything about it. But the children persisted, and now we have half of a house. When our classes end, the children disperse to their various villages. How then can we carry out our Young Pioneer affairs? The troop council thought this over and decided that each Pioneer would organize the children of his village. I also set up a combined troop. It has ten children. Here is what we've already done: laid out a ski trail for little children and taught them how to move on skis, flooded an area for ice skating, and sewed dolls for a puppet theatre. We plan to lay out an athletic field in the spring in a birch wood outside the village. We look after the orchard of the state farm. Nobody is bored for want of things to do.

Half a dozen such letters appear in a single issue, plus a page of national news, one of world news, a story or two, and human-interest features. Newspapers for schoolchildren in all countries picture their native land as the best of all possible worlds. The Soviet press is no exception.

CHILDREN AND PARENTS

Because the boarding schools are so few, 98 per cent of the children spend every night at home, and most of their waking hours under the supervision of their parents. All opinion-forming agencies teach a very high level of family morality. Television, radio, and the press carry very little that would suggest to children that any other system of behavior is possible.

Parents associations are regarded as a means of influencing parents away from the attitude of "each for himself" as far as their children are concerned. Soviet citizens also take an active part in government matters through these associations. Thirty million people, it is claimed, participated personally in meetings of one or another type to discuss the educational reform we have described, and to offer their suggestions. This would average one parent per school child.

Parents associations are set up to allow maximum contact with children's classes and to involve the largest number of parents in their activities. One Moscow eleventh-grade school, for example, has a parents committee for each grade (this is standard), a school-wide committee of thirty-four and an executive of fifteen elected at a general meeting. The parents help arrange outings and parties for the children, school entertainments, and discussions of interest to themselves. Members of the committee are on duty each day in the dining room. A room has been assigned to the parents in which to assist children who do poorly in their homework. Daily grades are given in the Soviet school system, and monitors report to the parents on children who have made a poor grade in any subject during the day. The parents committee also investigates home conditions. A Soviet article says:

Sometimes, of course, they [the committee] are told flatly to mind their own business, but in the end most parents are grateful for the help they receive. . . . Parents can make plenty of mistakes in bringing up their children . . . sometimes they forget that the father must bring home love and concern as well as his pay envelope; sometimes they spoil their children.

The committees can do no more than advise, counsel, and give volunteer aid in time, services, or in helping a child with homework if the parent or parents are not equipped to do so. Committees also obtain assistance from government agencies if they find that family conditions require this.

OUT-OF-SCHOOL ACTIVITIES AND ARTS EDUCATION

There are 102 acting companies throughout the U.S.S.R., with their own theatres, serving only children. In addition there are one hundred permanent puppet theatres. Book publishing for children is enormous: three thousand titles in 1960, with enough copies to supply each child with half-a-dozen per year. They are very colorful, entertaining, cheap, and informative.

For boys and girls with a bent for science, there are five hundred Young Technicians and Naturalists centers, and for children at large there are 2,500 centers similar in certain respects to our Y's and settlement houses. However, they also serve as centers for exchange of experience and for training of adult and child leadership for the Young Pioneers. Some of the Pioneer "Palaces" (in certain cases actually occupying former palaces of the old nobility) are unbelievably elaborate in equipment, trained leadership, and even decorations: murals based on favorite books, fairy tales, and so forth.

Thirty-two cities have children's railroads: narrow-gauge lines that children man themselves and that have the latest equipment —radio communication for the engineer, automatic block signals, and the like. A line will have as many as three engines and a dozen cars. It is organized on the same pattern as a regular railway system, and is designed to interest children in entering the railroad industry while giving them pleasure. There is a small number of children's ship lines for the same purpose.

Musical and athletic skills are furthered through special schools. There are 1,800 free after-school-hours music schools giving each child eight hours of instruction per week in playing an instrument, and in theory. A pupil shares a teacher with only three or four others. The course lasts seven years and parallels the school system in age classes. Children who wish to make music a career take competitive examinations upon completion of these schools for admission to high-school-level institutions training professional musicians. These schools have increased to seven hundred in 1963, from 165 just a few years earlier. Musical genius in children is usually recognized at a very early age. For these exceptional individuals there are twenty-two elementary-through-high schools giving a combination of general and musical education, in preparation for entry into an equal number of conservatories. Other musically talented individuals also have access to the twenty-two conservatories, on the basis of competitive examination. The fact that three out of the first four places in the Queen Elisabeth Violin Competition in Belgium in 1963 were won by Soviet young people is one result of this system of institutions and of the caliber of the teachers they provide.

Music is the only art for which there is an organized system of

Children of extraordinary musical promise at eleven-year
boarding school of Leningrad Conservatory

schools for children *not* planning to make it a career. There is a
small number of ballet schools comparable to those for children
of musical genius. There are two 11-year schools below the college
level for painting and sculpture, aside from classes in drawing in
the compulsory general curriculum. Extracurricular school-spon-
sored drama clubs, and clubs and courses at the Pioneer Palaces
and Houses are available in these arts.

Children between ten and seventeen who show an aptitude for
sports are admitted to one of the thousand after-school-hours athletic schools for training in one or a number of sports. These schools
explain in part the Soviet victories in the 1956 and 1960 Olympics.
That they are not connected with the regular schools these children
attend may help explain the absence of athletic hero-worship in
the Soviet school system.

Blind children go to special boarding schools for the compulsory

Blind girl learns to draw from embossed pictures and
with special drawing instruments

eight years of schooling. For deaf-mutes the regular school system
includes special kindergartens; they are trained to work on a par
with normal individuals. However, a system of sheltered workshops
exists for the blind who are unable or unwilling to work out in the
world. Some five hundred occupations are taught to the blind.
Blind children are taught to appreciate art through embossed reproductions similar to the Braille system.

Extraordinary efforts are made for mentally retarded children.
They, too, are educated in boarding schools. Class size is held
down to ten or twelve. The goal is to give them, in eight years of
schooling, at least the education others absorb in half that time,
plus useful skills. Girls, for example, are taught sewing, dress-
making, and the household skills. Each child is under constant
supervision of a psychologist trained in organic disorders of the
nervous system, and consulting physicians are on call. For children

who cannot tolerate memory drill—in arithmetic, for example—
the teacher, having explained the concept of length and volume,
will illustrate this in needlework, modeling, and drawing classes.

Good education depends, of course, upon the teacher. When
Sputnik I caused a sudden interest in the United States in the
educational system that provides the foundation on which Soviet
scientific achievement is built, the American government sent a
delegation of educators to Russia. President Eisenhower's Commissioner of Education, Dr. Lawrence Derthick, reported on his
return:

We saw no evidence of any teacher shortage. Teacher work loads
and other working conditions are advantageous. Teacher prestige is
high; salaries are at the levels of those of doctors and engineers (in
fact, a fully trained doctor and nurse are regular members of each
school staff); only the best are chosen to teach—one out of six who
apply.

Since 1963, principals have been elected by the teachers and
staffs of each school.

UNIVERSITIES, COLLEGES, PROFESSIONAL
AND TECHNICAL EDUCATION

The magnificent new buildings of Moscow University stand at
the highest point in the capital. Built under Stalin, it is named for
its founder, Mikhail Lomonosov, son of an Arctic coastal fisher-
man, contemporary of and comparable to Benjamin Franklin in
the range of his interests and knowledge.

The United States and the Soviet Union are the only two countries that have developed college-level education on a mass scale.
The United States has 3.5 million (not counting two-year junior
colleges), and the Soviet Union 3 million college and university
students. The population of the U.S.S.R. equals that of England,
France, West Germany, and Italy put together, but it has *four
times* as many college students as all of them combined.

The U.S.S.R. gives the name "university" to only forty of its
766 higher educational institutions. The universities have the specific purpose of training researchers and teachers, largely for the
college level, while the colleges (the Soviet term is *institut*) produce
practicing professionals. Since 1963, all university students have
been placed in either a research-oriented or teaching-oriented
"track" from the day of admission. This is not a closed issue: one

university president ("rector") objected in the press at once. Another contended that the departments are too specialized, and do not provide sufficiently for the great number of overlapping fields (biophysics, for example) that exist today.

A university graduate is free to enter a profession, and a college graduate may choose to teach or do research, but the effort is made to direct the most promising individuals interested in science to the forty universities. Universities vary, but virtually all have departments of history and languages (studied in relation to each other), economics, law, physics and mathematics, chemistry, biology, and geography. While there are *instituts* of economics, law, medicine, and the arts, as well as polytechnical colleges—all similar to comparable colleges in the United States—most of them specialize in very narrow single fields: motion-picture engineering, for example, or fisheries technology, or naval engineering.

Like elementary and high-school education, Soviet higher education is now in a period of adjustment from an essentially academic system to one combining work with study. The stated purpose is both to close the psychological gap that had reopened between the thinking man and the working man, and to graduate people able to step into professional jobs with the least problem of adjustment. College applicants with two years of experience in any kind of work are given preference, but a minimum of 20 per cent of freshman admissions is reserved for students who have not worked, so as to save room for particularly promising high-school students. In actuality, 40 per cent of the students entering college day sessions in 1963 had never worked. Evening-session and correspondence-division students are, naturally, people with jobs. Fifty-six per cent of college and university students in 1963 had full-time jobs as well.

It is felt that people entering those fields in the humanities that shape the course of conduct of their fellow men—law, journalism, philosophy, and economics—must have a minimal knowledge of the practical problems of daily life and work. In these majors, therefore, every entering student without exception is required to have held a job for at least two years.

After admission, this pattern continues. Freshmen courses for persons who plan careers in history, language, literature, and economics are given only in the evenings or by correspondence, and the students are required to hold some kind of job. Full-time study begins in the second year, and even then a history student does practical work in archaeology, ethnography, or in museums, and a language student goes out to study dialects in the field. Law students spend three months of their third year at a job in court, a district attorney's office, or local government.

Only in special fields of engineering and science based on complex theoretical knowledge are the first two or three years devoted to full-time study and laboratory work of the classical academic type. But this is then followed by a year of practical work in the chosen field, and then return to school.

In most nonhumanities fields—and this covers nearly 90 per cent of all students—the student, during the first two years of college, holds a production job in the very industry for which he is training, and takes evening or correspondence courses, which are followed by full-time study thereafter. This is entirely aside from, and not to be confused with, the requirement of two years of work experience before entering college. On the other hand, in the universities, with only one-tenth of the Soviet student body, education largely follows the traditional full-time pattern, the requirement being merely that students acquire "work skills in their specialty in the process of study."

At present, nearly half of all students study full-time, the rest in evening and correspondence divisions after work. The part-time students enjoy extraordinary privileges to make up for the educational and financial handicaps. In addition to regular vacations, evening students get twenty days' leave at full pay for laboratory work and examinations in the first and second year, and thirty days' in each subsequent year. Correspondence students get thirty and forty days', respectively. Another thirty days', paid, is granted for the nationally uniform government examinations. During the final year, four months' additional paid leave is granted to complete the Soviet equivalent of the thesis. In addition, students have a day off a week at half pay for the last ten months before graduation, and may take another day or two each week without pay, with no danger to their jobs. An additional month's unpaid leave may be taken during the final year. For this month the student draws a standard scholarship grant from his school.

As in every other aspect of Soviet life, tangible incentives are provided for maximum effort and ability. Virtually all full-time students receive scholarships of approximately the amount earned by the unskilled to semiskilled worker. However, there are 2,200 Lenin scholarships for the very best undergraduates, which provide the pay level of a skilled worker, and one hundred for graduate students at the salary level of an engineer. There are also, as in the United States, scholarships for excellence in specific fields. All Soviet students are now required to perform duties as laboratory assistants, look after residential quarters and recreational facilities, and contribute time in cafeteria service and in study-room and dormitory monitoring. Students are also urged to help young working people to advance in culture, skill, and education through spare-time activities in single workers' dormitories, and in recreation centers and libraries. Many students do engage in this type of civic activity.

College courses run from four to six years, most being of five or five-and-one-half years' duration. For example, engineering, law, and economics courses are five years, medicine six, including the period called pre-med in the U.S. Evening and correspondence college courses are one year longer than the equivalent courses in day session.

Classes meet six days per week. Thirty-six hours per week are carried in the earlier years and, with study, it is estimated that the full-time student puts in fifty-five or sixty hours per week. Yet nearly all belong to the national student athletic association, and many Soviet Olympic athletes are students. The youngest Ph.D. in the Soviet Union until 1963 had also been Moscow University high-diving champion and wears a gold emblem awarded for several summers in Siberia as a volunteer farm pioneer under Khrushchev's virgin-lands project.

American experts in various professions have made on-the-spot studies of Soviet schooling. The magazine *Electrical Engineering* reports that the diploma received by any Soviet engineer on graduation represents education equal to that required for the Master of Science degree for American engineers, because the Soviet student has had 5,100 hours of instruction plus twenty weeks of industrial practice in a 5½-year course, while the American has had three thousand hours or less and no industrial practice. Yet the Soviet Union graduates three times as many engineers per year as the United States. Except for medicine, in which the American graduate's stiff course gains him the title M.D. while the Russian is designated "physician," and for teacher training, in which the Soviet college course is only four years, it is generally true that the Soviet professional has been educated to the equivalent of an American master's degree.

The education in literature and history given in Soviet high schools compares favorably with the equivalent courses at the *college* level in the United States. Therefore, the humanities have been omitted from Soviet higher education and it has been exceedingly technical and specialized, as is American college study starting in the junior year, which is generally at the level of Russia's freshman year. Less than 10 per cent of the Soviet student's time, before the recent reform, was given to foreign language, economic theory, and political philosophy combined. That represented the total offering of the humanities to engineering students, except for an additional elective year of language and a semester of philosophy. No music, art, anthropology or psychology is offered, although again it must be said that the high school offers some grounding here. Additional language work has now been added, and a required course in "esthetics": appreciation and theory of the arts. Another reform, in 1963, reduced required courses to thirty hours weekly in the first four years, and twenty-four in the fifth and sixth, with six hours of electives.

The U.S.S.R. offers two advanced degrees: "Candidate," which corresponds to the American Ph.D., and "Doctor," which demands study and research well beyond anything required in the U.S. The "Candidate" degree requires three years of postgraduate study and a thesis, and five or more years of undergraduate work.

In addition to the sociological objective of producing professionals and intellectuals with a feeling of identity with working people, the current Soviet reform has two other goals. One is to train students to do more independent work, rather than merely to memorize and acquire a skill to enable them to do a job. The other is to provide a rounded education.

Instruction traditionally rests very heavily upon lectures, which now absorb more than half the student's time. A lecture usually runs uninterrupted for two hours, with all questions reserved for the end. This practice was very sharply criticized by the group of Academy of Science members, top science administrators, and college heads, whose proposals for improving high-school education we cited earlier. They believe that the student's time should mostly be given to seminars and independent study and laboratory work. They requested a complete overhaul of all curricula and that the study of cybernetics and computers be instituted at all technical colleges. They want the student to be given a monthly over-all examination, and that if he fails to keep up over a three-month period he be dropped from the department. They proposed that experimental university departments organized on this basis be established in the autumn of 1963 in Moscow, Leningrad, and Novosibirsk.

Students at Lumumba University, Moscow

The organization of higher educational institutions differs from the American. All posts, from full professor down, are thrown open in competitive examinations every five years. Faculties seem to be reasonably stable, however. As in Soviet high schools, college and university examinations are oral, and the student is subjected to peppering by a board of examiners.

There is little doubt that American and Soviet higher education have both benefited from the exchange of visits of top figures during recent years. American college presidents have come back with a determination to strengthen their institutions in the sciences and to increase educational opportunities for talented students from poor families. Their Soviet counterparts have been impressed with the training for independent work, the use of discussion, and the liberal-arts breadth of our system, as well as the use of our colleges and universities for research. Eight per cent of Soviet students are now engaged in research projects.

Today the foreign contacts of Soviet education are increasing at the student level. Thirty-eight Americans entered Soviet institutions in the fall of 1961, and forty-eight Russians came to the United States. In 1963, foreigners resident in the U.S.S.R. were granted the same rights of enrollment as Soviet citizens. There is a very heavy program for students from the Communist-led countries, and an entire university, Lumumba University, has been built for people from the underdeveloped and primarily neutral countries. There are fifteen thousand foreign students in the U.S.S.R. from eighty countries, of whom 2,700 are in Lumumba University.

Prorector Pavel Erzin stated that there were African, Asian, and Latin American students at Moscow State University, the Medical Institute, and other Moscow colleges. He explained that people could graduate from Lumumba University a year early, because it omitted social and political subjects compulsory in other Soviet institutions. The point is that many governments would object to their students receiving indoctrination in communist political theory. Lumumba also has a preparatory period of one to three years, depending upon the level of education with which students arrive, because high schools in the underdeveloped countries vary greatly in quality and curriculum. The preparatory course also teaches Russian, which is essential, of course. A number of Soviet students also study at Lumumba. The faculty-to-student ratio is extraordinarily high: one to four.

I shared a cabin for several days on a Baltic steamer in 1962 with three Nepalese students vacationing from their studies in Moscow. They were neither enthusiasts for nor hostile to the U.S.S.R., but they had experienced no segregation or discrimination.

The higher educational system we have described is expanding rapidly. Forty per cent more graduations in the seven years 1959–1965 are planned than in the preceding seven years, and facilities and funds are being provided accordingly. The goal for 1980 is eight million students.

6: Earning a Living: The Professions

GETTING THE JOB

One night I was being peppered with questions on a Leningrad street corner, and this one came out of the crowd: "Why don't the unemployed in America go on strike against it?"

Ridiculous? Of course: a man who doesn't have a job can't quit it. But to my Soviet questioner the idea of not having a job was so abstract that he obviously could not deal with it realistically. Very possibly the concept of a strike was equally meaningless to him.

This does not mean that a Soviet citizen gets a job in some automatic fashion, or that he is not allowed to quit. Automatic employment would mean assignment to a job—and Russians don't like that any more than Americans. Those who leave school with any salable skill—and we have seen that the school system is now designed to provide this to every graduate—have no problem at all. Bulletin boards advertise jobs on almost every street corner. The afternoon papers are full of "help wanted" ads.

As in the United States, the children of workers in particular industries or trades have the inside track to work in those fields. However, children tend to leave the parent's occupation if it is particularly difficult. This is true of coal mining, for example, although there are plenty of jobs in the mines, and wages and con-

ditions are tops for the U.S.S.R. Miners work a six-hour day, and
earnings are so high that half of all miners own cars. Automobile
ownership is very rare in all other occupational groups.

Under the recent educational reform, all Soviet children now
in school will have a specific trade and some work experience in
it when they get out of eight-year school at the age of fifteen. Industry is under government orders to reserve specific numbers of
jobs for practical work-training of school children in the upper
grades. A 4-hour workday is enforced for fifteen-year-olds, for
which they get a full day's pay. Where piecework is done, their
rate is almost twice that of the adult worker. Between the ages of
sixteen and eighteen the workday is six hours, also at a full day's
pay. Workers under eighteen get a full month's annual vacation,
and it must be given them in the summer. They must not be assigned to night, overtime, or underground work. No wage or
salaried work can be exempted from any of these laws.

Management is delighted to train people who will stay to work
in the particular enterprise, but there is no requirement that the
student do so. And he is in a seller's market. Among other things,
young people like to travel, and until they start families it is quite
common for them to take a job somewhere and move on after a
while to see some other place. The only people who have to take
the particular jobs offered them are newly graduated day-session
college and technical high-school students, who are required to
work where assigned for three years. The latter group don't seem
to object: they go to school to learn a particular skill and they are
quite happy—and take it for granted—that a job in that skill is
waiting for them upon graduation.

There is a small minority of college graduates who leave no
stone unturned to stay where they can enjoy the comforts of the
big city, and preferably the biggest cities—Moscow, Leningrad, or
the capital of their native republic. Very often they are children
of professional people or intellectuals and have led lives as soft as
the U.S.S.R. can offer. Some parents use connections and pull to
keep their children near home. Admonishing such people, the press
notes that the public at large has paid for the education of the
minority that receives a college education, and has also met their
living costs, and that the least they can do is to work where their
services are needed. The great majority take the jobs offered.
Graduates usually have a choice of three positions, but all three
are apt to be in relatively underdeveloped—and understaffed—
parts of the country. But some take jobs out of the fields in which
they are trained so as to remain in their home cities, a few simply

loaf at their parents' expense, and a tiny handful turn to crime. In 1963 the law was changed so that diplomas are issued only a year after graduation, on recommendation of the place of employment to which the student was assigned.

There is no unemployment insurance, because joblessness of any duration does not exist, and there is no evidence of serious hardship as a consequence of the brief interruptions when people change jobs. There are almost always two breadwinners in a family. Two weeks' pay is provided upon dismissal, call-up into the armed forces, refusal by the worker to accept transfer to another enterprise, or if a temporary layoff exceeds one month. The management of the enterprise, or the government body supervising it, is required to retrain workers displaced by automation. If the new job requires relocation, the worker gets a month's pay, allowances for his family, and travel costs. Two million workers displaced by automation were reabsorbed into the economy in 1958–1960, while hours were cut from forty-six to forty in the same period. The total number of jobs in 1962 was higher by 2.6 million in 1962 than a year earlier. Job opportunities increase by about that many every year.

ON THE JOB

The Soviet working day is seven hours (six in mining or work under unhealthy conditions and for teachers, physicians, and others whose work involves great nervous strain). The workweek may not be over forty hours in any employment, and averages a bit less. Saturday is a five-hour day. In industries whose employees are chiefly women, they have requested and gained a 5-day week of 8-hour days, so that Sunday does not have to be used for shopping and housework.

As the pledge to reduce the workweek from forty-eight hours to forty without loss in pay was kept on schedule, the Soviet worker believes that reduction to thirty-five hours (thirty in underground work) will occur as promised, starting in 1964. This is to be accompanied by institution of the 2-day week end for all. There is no evidence that the Soviet worker seeks overtime work. When the job demands overtime, the law says that it must not exceed four hours in two consecutive days or ten hours per month, and it must have the approval of the local union.

This is one of the two provisions of Soviet labor legislation that is most frequently violated. With a planned quota to be met each month, managers work lagging departments overtime during the last third of the month. Consequently, wage bills run higher than planned, because overtime earns time-and-a-half for the first two hours in all work without exception, manual, office, or professional, big city or small town. Double time must be paid for subsequent hours. Holiday work gets double time, but the worker may accept another day off instead. Management often pressures workers to take this alternative. This pressure and the actual working of overtime are among the most common labor-union grievances.

The night shift is generally an hour shorter than the day shift, except where the day is less than seven hours, or when a continuous production process (blast furnaces, chemicals) requires three 8-hour or four 6-hour shifts. Night shift bonuses range from 14 to 20 per cent.

There are six paid holidays per year: the Revolution, November 7–8; May Day, also with two days off; New Year's; and Constitution Day, December 5. None is religious, although Christmas, Easter, and many other religious holidays are celebrated in the countryside even by those who never go to church. All wage and salary earners get a minimum of two weeks' paid vacation. A very large percentage gets three weeks, a month, or even more as special inducement for work in the Far North, eastern Siberia, desert or high mountain areas. There is a very pronounced labor shortage in summer, when most women with young children simply take an extra month off without pay to go to a summer place or their parents' farm.

The minimum wage is about one-half a good factory wage. In the Soviet Union, however, no industry or occupation is exempted from the minimum. Wages may be garnished only as provided by law, and not more than 20 per cent of any pay check may be deducted except for family maintenance or to repay thefts or embezzlements. Vacation pay or compensation money (sick pay, etc.) cannot be touched.

Management's attitude toward the provisions giving special protection to working women seems to be strongly affected by considerations of efficiency and economy. There is never any trouble about confinement leave, because this comes out of social insurance and not the factory pay roll. Women can and do hold all kinds of jobs, including top management positions, particularly in technical capacities. Women construction superintendents are not at all uncommon, particularly if they are engineers or otherwise specially educated. But there seem to be a good many violations of the rules regarding the hiring of pregnant women (who are not supposed to be refused employment despite the fact that they go on leave nine weeks before confinement), and regarding their transfer

and that of mothers of infants to day work and light jobs. Nor
are there enough plant day nurseries to satisfy the law that says
every working woman's child must be provided for. A plant that
obeys the law in these respects gets less output per ruble, as it does
with juvenile workers enjoying a full day's pay for a shortened
workday. The same factory manager who is required to obey the
labor laws is also judged—and his bonus is paid—on the economics of his operation, and so a conflict of obligations arises. This
is another field in which much depends on the strength and per-
suasiveness of the union—whether it will yield to the pleadings or
threats of management.

Working conditions, such as illumination, ventilation, and protection against exposed machinery, are poorer than in the United
States except in specially dangerous trades (high construction;
mining), but are excellent by world standards.

LABOR UNIONS

Union membership is not compulsory. Dues are not deducted
before the worker gets his pay check. The idea is that the personal contact between the employee and the volunteer who collects
the dues allows people's complaints and suggestions to be heard.
All fields of employment, including farm labor and the professions,
are organized. Almost everyone belongs to the unions: membership averages 96 per cent, but it is much lower in seasonal trades,
such as lumbering engaged in by farmers who want to earn extra
money.

Union organization is industrial. Everyone employed in a particular enterprise belongs to the same union, from the sweeper to
the factory doctor. Unions are very active in civic affairs outside
the place of employment: inspection of stores and public services,
and so forth. Inside the plant, the union's word is law on matters
of safety and health: it has the legal right to close down an operation if its inspectors find that the laws are not being respected.
The unions are also legal agencies for distribution of government
appropriations for social insurance of all kinds. Of course, the individual's benefits are spelled out precisely in law, and the union
must carry it out exactly. The advantage of having the unions do
this work is that they have real knowledge of the individual's
circumstances through volunteer committees, and can assist people
in learning their rights, which, as in the United States, are quite
detailed and specific. Thanks to this variety of functions, one-third
of the 66 million union members are active in their unions on a
regular basis. (The total number of wage and salary earners is

She's a foreman at Moscow's major power plant

68.4 million.) Sixty per cent attendance at union meetings is
normal. In the United States it averages less than one per cent.

There are elaborate protections against managements that may
wish to intimidate active union members. The law guarantees that
anyone elected to a paid union post (or to public office or other
paid office) must be given his job back, or another at the same
level, upon completion of his term in office. A man elected to a
nonsalaried union post (shop steward, deputized labor inspector,
social insurance representative) cannot even be shifted to another
job without the union's approval. The local union enjoys the right
—and in recent years this right has been exercised on numerous
occasions—to demand the firing or disciplining of management
when it violates labor law or fails to live up to the union contract.

—but she still makes dresses for her daughter

This is one of the means most effective in preventing strikes. When top management posts are open, the union has the right to voice its views on the candidates.

In general, union rights and privileges are extraordinary. Union approval is required when management wishes to change a worker's job assignment for more than one month. No one may be fired without union approval, except for specified posts in top management. Piecework output quotas must satisfy the union, as must office or plant work rules. Safety engineering regulations are established jointly by top government bodies and the national union bodies. Industrial sanitation regulations, drafted by the Ministry of Public Health, must have the agreement of the central body of organized labor in the Soviet Union. A few years ago

Steel union housing committee checks construction
of workers' homes with builders

there was a long and heated argument over whether the system of
factory physicians should be retained or whether they should be
reassigned on a geographic basis. The unions insisted that no one
could understand the prevention and treatment of industrial disease
and accident like a doctor in the plant. They won.

No plant may open, start work, or move without union approval
of physical conditions.

The unions must be involved at the drafting stage when laws on
labor and the living conditions of working people are drawn up.
They participate in drafting production and capital-investment
plans. Soviet labor unions are unique in that they are the final
authority in grievance procedures when grievance committees com-
posed of equal representation from labor and management have
been unable to agree. Management may appeal to the courts only
on the ground that the union decision is in violation of the law. If
the union's decision is merely a matter of discretion within the
law, management has no recourse. On the other hand, if a worker
is dissatisfied, and his union has decided in favor of management,
he does have the right to go to court. The purpose is to protect
the working man if management has a stranglehold on local union
officials, which has happened sometimes, as one may read in the

Soviet press. Thus, *Izvestia* reported, April 24, 1963, that the manager of a government farm and the local union head had made a worker lose several months' wages by trying to harass him into leaving that farm, where they regarded him as a troublemaker. In an editorial note, the newspaper demanded that the culprits be compelled to reimburse him out of their own pockets.

Despite the elaborate provisions for handling conflicting interests, I have not noticed any conflict when I have visited factories in each of my three trips to the Soviet Union. Factory managers are usually former workers. They have often risen from the ranks in the very same plant. Many of them got their first experience in administration in union posts, which, as we have seen, deal with matters that we usually think of as management's field. While some clashes arise out of hatred, jealousy, conniving for favored treatment, they are more apt to be the result of conflicting responsibilities: labor law on the one hand, and the executive's duty to get production out as quickly and at the lowest cost possible.

Workers are encouraged to take a great variety of courses, including formal education. Technical and managerial posts in their own constantly expanding enterprise are often the reward. Engineering colleges that may award degrees were recently established at five of the country's largest and most progressive industrial plants. In the rest of industry, workers are nominated for admission to colleges and universities by the unions and management. They are paid their full salaries, well above scholarship-grant level, on condition that they return to the same place of employment upon graduation.

Workers think: "How can we strike when the plants belong to us?" But the personnel employed in the plant are not the owners. It is the public which owns the plant, and the ownership is exercised by some level of government, depending on whether the enterprise serves national, regional, or local needs.

THE PROFESSIONAL PERSON

In 1961, a Moscow borough with over a quarter-million population had seven private physicians, one self-employed dancing master, and one photographer in business for himself, among forty-eight people registered as working for themselves. The rest were mainly craftsmen. But the same district had at least five hundred salaried physicians, in addition to salaried music teachers and the like.

The Soviet professional person is free to practice privately upon payment of an annual license fee approximating a month's income.

However, even fewer do so than is the case with doctors in England, where socialized medicine also exists. Most professions are salaried. Lawyers, for instance, are either salaried employees of particular industries, labor unions, or government; or they receive wages from co-operatives after the fashion of an oversized multi-partner office in our country. Each attorney in a co-operative is paid the fees he himself earns. Free legal advice is available to all labor union members and their families, who constitute virtually the entire nonfarm population. Labor-union lawyers are particularly respected by working people because, in a virtually no-strike situation, proof that the law is on your side is especially important. Additional free legal advice is available to women through the mother-and-child consultation centers throughout the country.

The co-operative law offices are patronized largely by persons engaged in civil suits, and by defendants in criminal cases. There are only 152 lawyers in the suburban portion of Leningrad Province, which has 1.2 million population. The maximum fee permitted in a civil case is equivalent to a month's pay for a semi-skilled worker. Such a fee is very rare, and would be charged only where property of much value (a house, for example) or a very considerable sum of money, is at issue. In criminal cases, the maximum fee in "simple" cases is 15 per cent less than in civil trials. In "complex" cases, there is no ceiling, but there is a maximum fee per day in court. It is equal to the day's pay level of an experienced engineer.

The relative prestige of the professions is different from that in the United States. In the U.S.S.R., the greatest respect is accorded to people engaged in increasing the country's production or ability to produce, so engineering ranks first among the professions, both in public standing and in income. One reason for the high salaries is to attract students to engineering. Three times as many are graduated per year as in the United States, and the total number in the U.S.S.R. is far greater.

Education and medicine rank next in public esteem, but salaries are substantially lower. I met an electronics engineering graduate who was expecting to earn, on his first job, as much as his father, a physician of many years' standing. Physicians and educators in top administrative posts are very well paid by Soviet standards. If the quality of a person's work is recognized as constituting scientific achievement of a high order, he enters the country's top earning bracket. Science and the creative arts are the highest paid fields of all.

7:   Agriculture

Only since 1962 has the urban population of the Soviet Union been larger than the rural. Therefore, the government has always had to consider the peasants, and the rural population serving them and dependent upon agriculture. In turn, the needs and state of agriculture have governed many acts in other fields; thus, we have been compelled to consider the history of agriculture in our general chapter on history. But let us review it briefly here.

The first Soviet action with respect to farming, taken the very night of the Revolution, November 6–7, 1917, was to nationalize the land and divide it among the peasants, without charge. For the next twelve years they worked it privately but primitively, for there was no farm machinery and the horse-drawn implements were poor. The traditional village system of dividing the land so each peasant would get a piece of the good, the average, and the poor soil left him with widely-separated strips. Each strip was usually so narrow that a tractor-drawn implement could not turn in it even if there had been one.

All countries that had modernized farming were capitalist. The economic principles under which modernization had taken place were capitalistic and included: private ownership of land and of machinery, the right to buy and sell land and to hire farm laborers, and to sell products at prices determined on the open market, subject to some government regulation. The Communists would not permit this road to be followed, on the ground that a new division of the country folk into the very rich and the very poor would result. They also feared that private enterprise in the countryside, in a very largely rural country, would swamp socialism in the cities. But to industrialize the country, they needed both a source of labor and farm products to feed, clothe, and shoe the city workers. Modernization of agriculture was essential.

The approach the Communists chose was new: "collectivization." This meant organizing the peasants into co-operatives in which land holdings, tractive power (horses at that time), and implements would be merged. Income would depend not upon one's contribution in property, but solely upon one's work. The richer peasants naturally objected. So did a great many of those in the middle ranks, who feared—rightly, it proved—that the collective would not take as good care of horses and cows as each man on his own. The government rallied to its side the poorest peasants and those in the middle who would support it, exiled the wealthy, popularly called *kulaks* (fists), to Siberia and the north, and brought cruel pressure to bear to compel the sale of produce to it at prices it established. When peasants concealed the grain, they were tortured, as we have reported in quoting the Communist writer Sholokhov in a letter to Stalin. When, in some areas, the peasants refused to plant more than enough for their own needs, punitive battalions took even this from them, and there was little left to eat. Peasants slaughtered and ate their cattle rather than surrender them to collective ownership.

There is great controversy over whether famine conditions existed in some areas after the harvests of 1931 and 1932 as a consequence of collectivization. An experienced and respected American traveler in Russia of that day, Sherwood Eddy, reported as follows:

Our party, consisting of about twenty persons, while passing through the villages, heard rumors of the village of Gavrilovka, where all the men but one were said to have died of starvation. We went at once to investigate and track down this rumor. We divided into four parties, with four interpreters of our own choosing, and visited simultaneously the registry office of births and deaths, the village priest, the local soviet, the judge, the schoolmaster and every individual peasant we met. We found that of 1100 families three individuals had died of typhus. They had immediately closed the school and the church, inoculated the entire population and stamped out the epidemic without developing another case. We could not discover a single death from hunger or starvation, though many had felt the bitter pinch of want.*

A broader survey by a particularly competent observer is reported thus:

On the other hand, a retired high official of the Government of India, speaking Russian, and well acquainted with tsarist Russia, who had himself administered famine districts in India, and who visited in 1932 some of the localities in the U.S.S.R. in which conditions were reported to be among the worst, informed the present writers at the time that he had found no evidence of there being or having been anything like what Indian officials would describe as famine.†

The Webbs, the most distinguished contemporary British sociologists, devote fourteen pages in the book quoted to the question of famine. They had traveled widely in the U.S.S.R. in 1932 and 1934 and found that by contrast to the famines of 1891 and 1921, when "literally several millions of people died of starvation," in the collectivization crisis "any increase in the death-rate due to accompanying defective nutrition occurred only in a relatively small number of villages." ‡

Yet there are equally respected observers who say that famine did occur, among them Walter Duranty of *The New York Times* and Maurice Hindus. Just one thing is certain. If there was a famine, it was the last in Russian history. Thirty-four years of the eighteenth century were years of famine, according to agricultural records; in the nineteenth century, there were over forty. In the present century, 1901, 1905, 1906, 1907, 1908, 1911–12, and 1921 were years of famine. Some day we will know the truth about 1931–33 in the countryside, but no one claims that there has been famine in the thirty years since then, although they included years of invasion by the Germans, devastation, and postwar reconstruction. Rations were very short in World War II, 1941–45, but gross farm output rose 63 per cent from 1945 to 1949. Isolated peasant deaths from hunger did occur in 1947.

The fact is that collectivization worked. Urban food rationing was ended step by step in 1934 and 1935. The 1937 crop was the

* Sherwood Eddy, *Russia Today,* New York: Farrar and Rinehart, 1934, p. xiv.

† Beatrice and Sidney Webb, *Soviet Communism,* New York: Scribner, 1936, Vol. I, p. 259.

‡ *Ibid.,* p. 260.

Gradenitsy is a typical collective farm village in the Ukraine.
The local smith's daughter is a Moscow opera star

biggest in Russia's history till then. In 1928, there were 27,000
tractors in the entire immense Soviet Union, but by 1940 there
were 531,000. In the latter year, 62 per cent of spring plowing,
56 per cent of spring grain sowing, and 46 per cent of harvesting
was done by tractor power. There were 135,400 tons of mineral
fertilizers manufactured in 1928 and 3,237,700 in 1940, the last
year before Hitler's invasion; fertilizer output multiplied *twenty-
five* times in a dozen years.

THE COLLECTIVE FARM

When the smoke of collectivization cleared in 1934, there was
a system in which groups averaging several dozen families had
merged their land and work cattle. After they had delivered to
the government a fixed quota of farm produce at low prices, they
could sell the surplus to the government at more realistic prices,
or to individual customers in farmers' markets at prices set by the
free play of supply and demand. No middlemen were allowed.

The net income, in cash and produce, was then divided among the members in proportion to the work each one did. This was measured on a complicated scale based both on time put in and type of work done. The decision about this division was made by vote at an annual general meeting of the members.

The meeting also elected a board of directors and a chairman, who had great powers of management. Although the voting for the income-sharing system and for the board of directors was conducted on democratic principles, that for the chairman was not. Except in the very few cases where the farmers' own manager proved highly efficient, the Communist Party county organization "recommended" someone it thought would be a good manager, often a complete stranger. The peasants quickly learned that it was best to accept him unanimously. This system still exists, but a whole generation of farmers has grown up under it, and their attitude toward it has changed. They find that the "recommended" people today are increasingly well-trained, and the Party wants the farms to be as productive as possible. The farmers retain, and make use of, the right to vote these chairmen out if they prove incompetent, but they now go to the Party as a matter of course and ask for a better man.

In organizing the collectives, the government eventually came to realize that it was dealing with people whose feeling for property could not be entirely ignored. As a result, in addition to the earnings from work on the collective, each family is now allowed a plot with which it does exactly as it pleases. The plot is large enough to produce a small market surplus of vegetables, eggs, milk, and occasionally meat, when an animal is slaughtered. The owner sells this produce in farmers' markets for whatever he can get. As a result, nearly ten million people, chiefly women in farm families, spend all their time in this private enterprise and in housework. Nearly half the milk cows in the country are privately owned, but the law permits only one per family.

Until Stalin's death in 1953, farming was managed as a source of food, raw materials, and labor for the cities. The rise in farm output just about kept pace with the increase in population. Prices for farm produce were held low and taxes were high in order to squeeze out every possible ruble to finance the growth of industry. Farmers even cut down their fruit trees so as not to lose by the taxes on them, and in Stalin's last year there was a drop in livestock head count because the cost of production was higher than the prices the farmers had to accept for cattle.

This was a danger signal, for livestock had risen in numbers steadily since the war. One of the first acts under Khrushchev (who has headed the Communist Party since Stalin's death, although others held the premiership for a while) was to increase sharply the prices paid to farmers for meat and dairy products. Later, all compulsory deliveries of farm produce to the government were abolished, even though the government is naturally the largest buyer under the Soviet system. Small collective farms were merged and merged again under the prodding of the Communist Party and the government, so as to find a unit that would have the maximum advantages of large-scale operation and the availability of trained experts. The huge bureaucracy of the Department (Ministry) of Agriculture was dissolved and its trained people were told to go out and get jobs in the countryside. The thousands of government-owned machine-and-tractor depots were dissolved, and their equipment sold to the collective farms themselves. Previously these depots had done the actual farm work requiring machinery, and had been paid in produce. The farms had often complained that the depot would not follow their instructions, and losses or inefficiency resulted. Later still, the government set up a chain of machinery sales-and-service outlets.

Under Stalin, a central planning office far away set up an output plan and quota for each farm, and said, deliver or else. The Khrushchev administration gave the farms the right to do their own planning instead of having to carry out government plans to the letter. However, the Khrushchev policies were not based only on the existing collective farms. The enthusiasm of the country's young people was called upon to open vast unused lands in the east. One hundred million acres were put to the plow, most of it in three years. This is equal to the cropland of the entire American West, Southwest, and some of the prairie states. Most of it was organized not as collective farms but as "state" (government-operated) farms. It earned $3 billion clear profit in nine years.

THE STATE FARM

State farms are completely owned and operated by the government on a wage-and-salary basis. They are becoming increasingly important. There are eight thousand of these immense operations. They average eight hundred employees each, on a year-round basis, which makes it possible for them to have families. The families have homes, truck gardens, chickens and a cow, and are quite well off by comparison to farm laborers anywhere. While (until 1964) the collective farmer had to save for illness and old age, the state-farm worker belonged to a union, and was covered in sickness and retirement by the government plan covering all wage-and-salary earners. Apparently, state-farm workers came to put in more time tending to their private cows and small animals than was good for their efficiency at their salaried jobs, for in 1963 Mr. Khrushchev called for private livestock ownership on state farms to be abolished, but that provision be made to the farmers for ample supplies of the butter and meat these animals had provided. This is the sort of thing that is decided from the top in the U.S.S.R., with no vote by the people involved.

The state farms concentrate on producing the key crops and what is needed to provide variety in the city diet. Throughout the country, wherever a collective farm proves incapable of making a go of things for many years, the government offers to take it over as a state farm and put the members on regular salary.

It is hoped some day to have a single type of farm, rather than the collective and state farms of today. One purpose is to reach a uniform type of public ownership in city and country. This result is not to be arrived at by taking over the collective farms, as happens to inefficient ones today. The expectation is that they themselves will gradually go over to the payment of regular monthly wages, build up their treasuries so they can pay pensions and sick leave (some already do), and make capital investments for improvement and expansion in partnership with the government.

The collectives will ultimately become indistinguishable from the state farms. The Soviet leadership also hopes that the collective farms will eventually become satisfactorily efficient in livestock farming, poultry raising, and vegetable growing, in addition to crop farming. It is expected that the members will then voluntarily give up their small private plots as inefficient, and will sell their cows, chickens, and pigs to the collectives, thus eliminating the last field in which a kind of private enterprise still exists. But no date has been set for this.

The result of the two major farm policies of the Khrushchev administration—cash incentives for the collective farmers and opening vast new tracts of virgin soil—is that the percentage increase in farm output in the eight years after Stalin's death in 1953 was greater than in the forty years before that.

My third visit to Russia, in the summer of 1962, came only a few weeks after a sharp rise in retail prices for livestock products: meat and dairy goods. I asked people about it everywhere: Soviet

New homes of state-farm families in virgin-soil territory,
Kazakhstan. Whitewashed exteriors indicate that
these pioneers are chiefly Ukrainian

tourists from all over the country wandering around the Kremlin,
townspeople in Zagorsk outside the "Vatican" of the Russian
Orthodox Church, fellow passengers on a railroad train and in the
Moscow and Leningrad subways, people relaxing in the park near
my hotel, workers at a factory, students at Leningrad University,
crew members on a Soviet ship. I walked into butcher and dairy
shops, looked at and priced the foods, watched the customers,
talked to them and the salespeople.

I asked whether the price rise had affected their diet. They
laughed. In a typical Russian gesture people would level their
hands at their chins and say: "We eat up to here." "We still turn
down the fat meat." A girl clerk behind a dairy counter even said
to me: "Stay in this country. Life is good here." Everyone I spoke
to accepted without question the government's explanation that the
price-rise money was needed for defense.

The United States Department of Agriculture statistics say the

Russian averages 2,985 calories a day, which is a shade more than the West or East German, the Swede, the Italian, and the Bulgarian, and a shade less than the American, the Canadian, the Frenchman, the Czechoslovak. The Russian is right up there with the best-fed peoples on earth. The amount of meat produced in the U.S.S.R. per head of population is 2½ times the world average. Annual Soviet meat production rose from 5.8 million tons in 1953 to 9.4 million in 1962. This figure will have to be more than doubled to provide as much meat per person as in the United States. On the other hand, the U.S.S.R. passed America in butter output per person in 1959. Soviet milk production is also greater than that of the United States, but because the population is larger, it is slightly (5 per cent) less per person. Vegetable and, particularly, fruit production, are very far behind America, although rapid progress is now being made. Government fruit purchases from agriculture for sale in the cities were 20 per cent higher in 1962 than in 1961. Until science frees agriculture from dependence on climate, and makes it possible to equalize the fertility of all soils at negligible cost, farm produce in the U.S.S.R. will have to be more expensive than in the U.S. This is chiefly because the climate is so much colder, but also because of water and wind conditions. It is quite conceivable that when Soviet industrial products become attractive to American buyers for quality and price, probably about 1970, United States farm produce will find a permanent and large market in the U.S.S.R. This was foreshadowed by large purchases in the U.S., Canada, and Australia in 1963, when the Russian crop fell back to the 1959 level because of a very bad winter and spring.

The job of agriculture is to feed the people and provide the raw materials to clothe and shoe them. The Soviet farmer gets that done. In 1959 and 1962 I never saw anyone, city or country, wearing rags or patched clothes, anyone barefoot. Yet the percentage of the population engaged in agriculture had dropped from 80 per cent to 40 per cent since I was there in 1931. Today, farms are feeding *seventy million more townspeople* than then, but at that earlier time there were rags to be seen, there were birch-bark sandals and even bare feet, and there were very short rations.

Nevertheless, the Soviet leaders and their press are constantly complaining that things aren't going as they should on the farms. One of the steps taken in recent years to improve the situation has been reduction by merger of the original number of collective farms to about one-sixth. Early in 1962 there were 41,300 collective farms, embracing 16.4 million farm families, averaging exactly two members per family working in the collective. Among these forty thousand farms, one can find examples of almost anything, from the very worst to the very best. One advantage of the merger is that it has been possible to provide 60 per cent of the collective farms with chairmen who have a specialized high school or a college education. But what of the other 40 per cent, in which these large enterprises, averaging four hundred families each, are managed by people with less than high-school education? It was to meet this situation that the Party and government instituted a new measure in 1962. Essentially, this is a system which for the first time provides management of farms from above similar to that which exists in industry. Each "state," approximately equal in size and population range to states in the United States, now has a Regional Board of Farm Production and Procurement. Beneath the Regional Board are "county" Production Boards. They consist of experienced and highly trained agricultural experts, with a variety of backgrounds: farm machinery, crop raising, collective-farm chairmanship, state-farm management, livestock, etc. The county boards have staffs of traveling "inspector–organizers," each of whom is responsible, on the average, for six collective farms, about ninety thousand acres, including forty thousand under crops.

The inspector–organizer visits a farm, finds out what's wrong, and if necessary returns with some of the specialist experts from the county staff. They work out a plan to improve the situation and have funds on which to draw for promising undertakings where capital is needed. Beyond that, the inspector–organizer's job is to pick up good ideas and working methods from the better farms and pass them on to the weaker ones. The county board also holds conferences on special problems—animal husbandry, for example. One purpose is to free the harassed farm chairman from daily detail and give him a chance to think out his problems in perspective, and in the company of experts.

A sharp upswing in production may be ahead for another and much simpler reason: hard cash. Until 1963 agriculture was deliberately treated as the stepchild of Soviet government investment. Moscow's economic policy has been, and still is, to give major stress to industry until it has reached the level of that in the United States and then to surpass America if possible. Therefore, the government has put vastly more money into industry than into farming. The value of all installations and equipment in all manufacturing and the construction industry was *thirty-seven* times greater in 1960 than in 1928, when industrialization began. But the value of farm buildings, equipment, and livestock had multiplied less than *three* times. As a result, while the output of industry rose thirty times during that period, the output of agriculture rose 80 per cent, or less than twice. Thus, industry progressed almost as rapidly as the amount of money put into it. Agriculture showed a much lower rise in output per ruble invested. Experts say that you can't expect as much return on investment in agriculture because harvesters, for example, can only be used during the few weeks when the crop is ripe, and must stand idle the rest of the year. The same is true of plows, seeders, and so forth. Factory equipment, on the other hand, can be used the year round.

In November, 1962, the Communist Party Central Committee, which makes policy in the Soviet Union, decided that the country could now afford both industrial progress and to put a ballroom gown on the agricultural Cinderella. In 1963 alone, the money ordered invested in agriculture was as great as in the whole seven-year period, 1946–1952. That, of course, had been the Stalin period, when farming was at the bottom of the priorities list and the country was much poorer. But the 1963 investment represented an 83 per cent jump over the amount originally scheduled for that year when the present Seven-Year Plan was drafted in 1959. Tractor production in 1963 was scheduled at 325,000, equal to the combined production of the three highest prewar years. Tractors would have plenty of work to do: 28 million acres had been added to the crop area in 1962 alone. In 1962, 39 per cent more fertilizer-manufacturing capacity was put into operation than the previous year. The poor crop in 1963 resulted in a decision to put even more money into fertilizer and irrigation because four-fifths of all cropland suffers periodically from drought. Fertilizer output trebled from the last year under Stalin to 1963. In 1965, it is to be up to the U.S. level of 1962. By 1970 it is to reach three times that American figure. This is to make possible a further 80-million ton rise in grain crops, on top of the 60-million ton increase from 1953 to 1962. The bad crop of 1963 caused the U.S.S.R. to buy 11 million tons of grain abroad. The increase sought for the future will go chiefly to feed cattle and put more meat on the table.

Clearly, Mr. Khrushchev and his associates are looking forward. What interests them is not so much that the Soviet farmer already produces *four times* as much per man-hour as before the Revolution, but that it still takes three or four Soviet people on the land

Home of farm truck driver: three rooms plus kitchen

to get the results produced today by one American. What concerns them is not that meat production per head of population has increased over one-third since 1953, even though this is why the man in the street says he eats "up to here." The Soviet leaders know that today the American still gets five pounds of meat for every two pounds available to a Russian, and the difference in the production of eggs, another protein food, is the same.

While the Russian gets all the calories he needs, and is growing healthier all the time (the average fifteen-year-old Moscow schoolboy weighs 22 pounds more than one that age in 1925), his diet is much less varied and not as well balanced as the American's. This is why Russians follow grain harvest reports in September the way Americans follow the baseball pennant races.

The Soviet citizen develops new tastes and demands as his income rises. The leaders want their people to live as well as and better than Americans, and believe that their system will enable them to accomplish this. Part of this has to be done by industry, and for this they need more workers and technicians. The one

Harvester-combine assembly line

way to recruit them in a country that is steadily reducing the length of the working day is to increase the efficiency of agriculture so more people can come to town or do nonfarm jobs in the countryside.

The countryside is changing. Many collective farms have pooled resources with neighboring collectives to set up small joint hydroelectric plants, creameries, feed mills, brickyards, construction enterprises, and other improvements. Therefore, the village, which used to consist of peasant huts, a church, and a primitive flour mill, without so much as a store, is beginning to display the diverse activities of an American small town in farm country. But the process is only beginning.

A leading American farmer, Roswell Garst of Iowa, was given four full columns in *Pravda,* February 13, 1964, for his opinions and advice on Soviet agriculture. He wrote that in 1955, when he first observed it, the Soviet Union was thirty years behind the United States, but in 1963, the gap was only eight years. He said that the U.S.S.R. was now very close to America in the use of hybrid seeds, making rapid progress in mechanization, and in fertilizer would do in the 1960's what America had done in the 1950's. He recommended a higher production of insecticides and herbicides, and vitamins, antibiotics, and protein feed additives, which the Soviet Union has barely begun to manufacture. He urged that paved rural roads be built to assure an all-weather supply of fuel and fertilizer to farms, and of produce to town. (Russia is fifty years behind us in this, which explains the frequent temporary food shortages in cities.) He recommended that the U.S.S.R. order fertilizer factories from the U.S., and samples of the latest American farm and road-building machinery, which are the world's best. He said that the U.S.S.R. leads the world in some fields, such as the artificial insemination of sheep on a mass scale.

8: Medicine, Mental Health, Social Security, Insurance

When a person gets sick, even for a few days, everything in his life—job, study, recreation—is upset. What happens then?

The Soviet citizen goes to see a doctor without hesitation. There are two reasons: it costs him nothing and it assures continuation of income. He does not have to budget for health insurance, doctor bills, hospital bills, fees for surgery, tests, or X-rays. If he wants to pay for what he can get free, there is a handful of doctors who practice privately—quite legally—after their salaried hours, and a few clinics in the largest cities which charge a fee. These doctors give their paying patients more time, and some people feel that if they pay for something, the quality must be better than what they get free. Also, there is less waiting at the pay clinics. But paid medicine—individual and clinic—is a very small part of the whole.

The Soviet citizen regards medical care in exactly the same way as he regards education. It is something that he does not have to think of in terms of his budget. It is there when he needs it. New York City's Commissioner of Health, Dr. Leona Baumgartner, reporting on a visit to a Soviet polyclinic, wrote:* "There he [the patient] sees his own physician. . . . Some families I talked with . . . had obviously had the same physician for years."

* *The New York Times Sunday Magazine Section,* May 17, 1959.

129

A doctor's certificate of illness is needed to draw sick leave pay. That is a further incentive to seeing the doctor as quickly as possible. There is no waiting period: sick time is paid from the first day one can't work. This covers every wage and salary earner in the country. It is a matter of law, and does not depend upon a labor union and the nature of its contract, or upon management practices.

Sick leave pay ranges from 50 per cent to 90 per cent of normal income, varying with seniority and other factors. The purpose of the seniority advantage is to induce people to remain at a particular place of employment, in a country where jobs are always available. The law protects one's job until recovery or until doctors have ruled that the disease (or incapacity due to injury) is chronic, and the particular duties can no longer be performed. In that case, if he can work at all, the individual must be found work at the same place, if work within his more limited capacities is available. Otherwise he seeks it elsewhere. In both cases he gets, in addition to salary (unless he can still earn as much as before), one of three rates of disability pension, depending upon whether disability is total or partial and, if partial, how extensive. Rehabilitation training is also provided. If a limb has been lost, the artificial replacement is free. In 1959 I was still aware of war invalids, but in 1962 wooden peg-legs were no longer in evidence, so I imagine that all who needed artificial limbs had received them, at least in the largest cities.

What kind of medical care does this system provide? American physicians, both members of numerous government and medical-society delegations and private visitors, agree that: (1) splendid human warmth and attention is shown to Soviet patients; (2) there are ample facilities and an extraordinarily high number of doctors, nurses, and attendants in proportion to patients; (3) buildings and generally available equipment and instruments are poor or backward or both, by American standards; and (4) the training of the average physician and nurse is less complete and less satisfactory than in the United States.

This system has helped to bring about: (1) the lowest ratio of deaths to total population in the world; (2) a doubling of the life span since the Revolution, so that today it is almost equal to that in America; (3) the most rapid population increase (births minus deaths, as per cent of population) in any major country, not counting immigration. Weaknesses include an infant mortality rate (from birth to first birthday) still higher than the American,

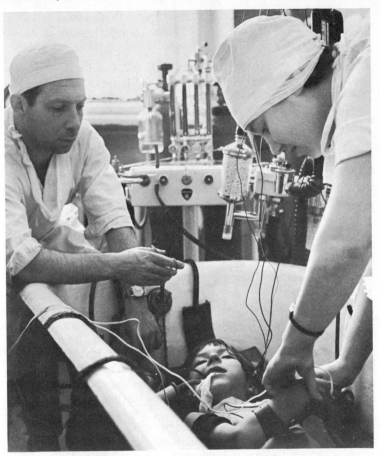

Chilling patient in water at 50°F. permits heart operation
without excessive anesthesia

and substantial tubercular and intestinal disease rates, reflecting
crowded housing and a background of poverty. But there are seventy centers equipped to revive people "dead" an hour or more
from heart stoppage; 3,500 had been saved through mid-1963.

Bubonic plague, cholera, and such are long gone. New cases of
syphilis are fantastically few. This is a measure of the almost complete disappearance of prostitution, the nonexistence of male prostitution (in a population of 223,000,000 one can find individual
cases of anything, but that becomes an unpleasant curiosity, not a

matter of statistics), and the extraordinarily high public morality, on which all visitors are agreed. John Gunther writes, in *Inside Russia Today*:*

Prostitution has virtually disappeared in the U.S.S.R. . . . Homosexuality is . . . practically unknown. . . . There is no homosexual problem on a national basis even remotely comparable to that in several Western societies.

Malaria has been eliminated to the extent that, in 1961, an institute in the Uzbek Republic specializing in this disease had nothing further to do, and was converted to another purpose.

If the average Soviet doctor has poorer training than his American counterpart, and hospital and examining facilities are generally less satisfactory, how has a lower death rate and a nearly equal longevity been achieved? The answer lies in the Soviet approach, which is preventive. Vaccination law is uniform throughout the U.S.S.R., so it is impossible for a controllable disease to hang on somewhere because of unsatisfactory local legislation.

Next to sanitation, vaccination, and unhesitating application for treatment because it is free of cost, the most important factor is preventive examination. Because of frequent and inclusive examination of the adult population, Soviet medical statistics report cancer death rates to be several percentage points—several thousand human lives—lower among women than in the U.S., probably because of earlier discovery and treatment. They make no claim to any more effective treatment. A Soviet cancer specialist, Dr. Nikolai Blokhin, was elected president of the international medical organization in that field in 1962.

A very weak spot in the Soviet system is the rural situation, where only 11 per cent of the physicians serve half the population of the country. Despite the government inducement of *higher* pay for rural service, a vacation twice as long, and preference in postgraduate training, plus attractions often offered by village authorities such as free rent, a cow and chickens to provide milk and meat for their families, Soviet doctors tend to stay in the cities, where cultural and professional facilities and opportunities for their children are greater. Yet the 44,000 country doctors, and twice that number of trained midwives and "doctor's assistants" (practitioners with diagnostic training above that of a trained nurse), are able to keep rural health at a level not significantly

* John Gunther, *Inside Russia Today,* New York: Harper and Row, rev. ed. 1962, pp. 361, 362–63.

different from the urban. This is largely because of the system of preventive medicine we have described, plus free aerial ambulance service for emergency and serious cases.

MENTAL HEALTH

Aside from the emphasis on prevention, the other great difference between Soviet and American medicine lies in psychiatry. The Russians do not accept Freudian theories, and many base their work on Pavlov. A. R. Luria, a Soviet figure world-famous for his work with mentally defective, retarded, and ill children, put it rather colorfully: "Psychoanalysis interests itself in the depths. . . . *We* are interested in the *heights,*" and he points his finger heavenward. His point is that Freud, by basing human behavior on sexuality, omits the rational factor that distinguishes human beings from the animal world.

The Russians have been quite willing to adopt Western discoveries that have demonstrated not only calming but possibly curative effects in mental illness, such as tranquilizers. On the other hand, it is against established policy to use physical restraint, such as straitjackets. Soviet psychiatrists say that it is bad both for the patient—by justifying and increasing his hostility—and for the personnel, in that it gives them a lazy way out. They have not used brain operations such as lobotomy. They say that improperly functioning or nonfunctioning brain cells may perhaps be restored to normal activity, while destruction of cells merely damages the brain and produces a more docile patient by reducing him to a subnormal level. They use insulin shock, but employ electric shock only as a last resort because autopsies on dogs have shown that electric shock always leaves severe brain damage.

How is it possible to manage highly disturbed patients without physical restraint? Besides suggestion, hypnosis, re-education through reasoned discussion, sleep induced by electricity (a Russian development) or drugs, and the tranquilizers, there is another factor. Dr. A. D. Gurewitsch of Columbia-Presbyterian Medical Center in New York wrote, after two visits to Russia:

There is one nurse for four patients in the Soviet Union, as against one nurse for about eighty patients in our psychiatric hospitals. . . . One physician for sixteen patients in Russia, with more than 150 patients for one psychiatrist in this country.

In other words, there are enough trained people to make it possible to take the time to calm a disturbed patient.

Woman doctor, Glafira Medvedieva, heads
medical school in Vitebsk

The standing, salary, and working hours of the Soviet medical profession give it the same status as the teaching profession has in the American social scale. Physicians' working hours are thirty-five per week. A doctor who is a mother (most physicians are women) will frequently arrange with others for her schedule to be three eleven-hour days, leaving four days for her family. The research scientist in medicine is paid at least twice the salary of an experienced practitioner. The top men in the profession—very few women have reached the very top as yet—earn ten times as much as practitioners, when they attain election to the Academy of Medicine.

Hospital workers receive privileges related to the dangers to health which they face. Attendants in psychiatric hospitals and active tuberculosis wards, and hospital cleaners, laundry workers, and dishwashers work a 6-hour day. Likewise, the basic vacation of two weeks for nurses is increased, for hospital personnel in difficult services, by from one to six extra weeks: some enjoy an eight-week vacation.

THE SENIOR CITIZEN

Most people rely on pensions when their working life is over. The pension rate is very high, averaging 60 per cent of maximum annual earnings. People who had been earning the minimum wage permitted by law receive a 100 per cent pension. Pension rates scale down to 50 per cent for high-income people. There is a maximum pension, which is equal to the level of a skilled worker's normal wage. High-income people are usually in nonphysical occupations and are best able to continue working, full or part time, after retirement. The retirement age is sixty for men and fifty-five for women, and is reduced to fifty and forty-five for the most unhealthy occupations.

To qualify for a pension upon reaching retirement age, a man must have put in twenty-five years of wage or salaried employment, and a woman twenty. To induce people not to change jobs, a 10 per cent higher pension is paid to people who have worked at the same place fifteen years or more. Recognizing that any pension of less than 100 per cent of former earnings may work some hardship, a bonus of 10 per cent is paid to pensioners who are supporting an infirm member of the family, and 15 per cent if there are two or more such.

The bulk of the urban population is covered by pensions as described above, and seven million people were drawing old-age benefits before social security was extended to include collective farmers, in 1964, increasing by 50 per cent the number thus protected. The regulations were also improved that year to allow pension-age miners, and farmers, to draw full pension in addition to full earnings if they go on working. Other working pensioners will draw 50 per cent of pension plus earnings except in Siberia, where it will be 75 per cent because life is harder. Twenty-six million people draw pensions of all sorts, including veterans'.

One reason for the limited popularity of life-insurance policies in the U.S.S.R. is that the chief reason for buying them—assurance of income to one's family should one die or be incapacitated—is not applicable because of the social security system. Survivors' insurance, which protects the wife whose husband has died, may equal the total earnings of the deceased. Permanent disability insurance ranges from little less than former earnings to more than 100 per cent, if money for special care is needed. But personal insurance in the U.S.S.R. exists alongside of social insurance.

The types of insurance one may buy include: life insurance under several plans; insurance against loss of physical earning ability; accident insurance; and an annuity paid for in a single premium (presumably by withdrawal of savings from a bank). The type of insurance regarded officially as giving fullest protection pays either upon attainment of a given age, upon death prior to that age, or upon accidental total or partial incapacitation. This "term" insurance may be bought by persons sixteen to sixty years of age for terms of five, ten, fifteen, or twenty years. Medical examination is required, except when insurance is for a lump sum not greater than about six months' income of the average earner. Premiums are payable monthly, quarterly, or at other agreed intervals. The only compulsory personal insurance is for travelers: the premium is part of the price of the ticket. Personal property of all sorts may be insured against theft, fire, and natural calamity.

Teachers, librarians, doctors and other medical personnel, and some other categories, receive length-of-service pensions after twenty or twenty-five years, as do the military. This may be one reason that the medical and teaching professions accept lower salaries than do others. Another explanation for these service pensions may be that these professions are staffed largely by women. They are usually married, and might otherwise be inclined to quit working before having put in that many years in their profession. In any case, they are an extraordinarily privileged group as a consequence of this provision. They may continue working without loss of this length-of-service pension.

Despite the inducements to stay on the job, most people do actually retire before they are wholly incapacitated for work. An unusual effort is made to involve them in public affairs. Usually they are encouraged to act as volunteer inspectors—of housing conditions in their apartment blocks, or of service, prices, and honesty of weights and measures in the stores of their neighborhoods.

Geriatrics as a medical specialty was started somewhat later in the Soviet Union than in the United States, except for an interest in what makes some people live to advanced ages. A medical society in this specialty was organized in 1961. Centenarians are surprisingly numerous throughout the country. Increasing longevity is indicated by the fact that there are eight million people over seventy, while twenty years ago there were little more than half as many. Of twenty million people past the maximum retirement age of sixty, only 120,000 live in homes for the aged. A

Old-age pensioner gets free legal advice

Retirement home for actors

pensioner who stops working is exempt from further taxation of his home (private homes are normally taxed at 1 per cent of their value, annually). Persons who believe themselves eligible for pensions or social insurance of any kind also enjoy the privilege, written into law, of being able to have legal papers drawn up for them free of charge by any law office.

One's home, furniture, piano, paintings, the fruit trees in one's garden plot, the cow, pig, goats, fowl one may keep there, the buildings erected to house them: all of these are private property in the most complete sense. This property may be bought and sold, except for the land, which is public property allocated by local government for individual use, and has no price. However, its use may be transferred to the purchaser of property or an orchard thereon. (Purchase and sale as a way of life is illegal; the transaction must be from user to user.)

At the owner's death, personal property goes to his heirs, and to them alone, either as provided in a will, or by law if no will is left. The property of husband and wife is treated as belonging equally to both, even though only one may have been the bread-winner. Property may be willed for special purposes: a general has left his home to house a kindergarten; war veterans have left theirs to the Soviet Peace Committee. However, the law provides that a surviving wife (or husband) as well as minors and incapacitated dependents must inherit set minimum shares in the estate. Savings accounts, on the other hand, may be willed outside the legacy. Disputes over wills and inheritance are settled in court, and re-ports of cases sound very similar to those encountered in Ameri-can practice.

9: Party, Government, and People

As I walked down Leningrad's main avenue on a recent visit, I noticed two buildings, on opposite sides of the street, each flying the national flag: red with gold hammer and sickle. The smaller of the two buildings housed the offices of government for that section of the city. The building across the street was Communist Party headquarters for the same district. I turned to my Russian companion and said:

"How come the Party has a larger building?"

"In our country," came the reply, "the Party leads."

He couldn't have put it more precisely. People in non-Communist countries think of government as having only one head and body. In the U.S.S.R. it has two, although the same man usually occupies the top positions in both: First Secretary of the Communist Party and Prime Minister of the government. Whenever different men have held these jobs, the Party leader was clearly the more important. When Molotov headed the government for many years, Stalin was head of the Party. When Malenkov and later Bulganin headed the government in the first years after Stalin's death, Khrushchev headed the Party and soon came to be premier as well.

Important new measures are published as joint resolutions of the Central Committee of the Communist Party and the U.S.S.R.

Cabinet. Less significant ones are issued by the Cabinet alone. The most vital ones are decided by the Party's Central Committee alone. If the new measures do not agree with the Constitution, it is the Constitution that is changed at the next meeting of the Supreme Soviet (congress), which is the body that has the power to do this in the U.S.S.R.

In November, 1962, for example, the Party Central Committee decided on a complete reform of the government (and of the Party) of a type never previously undertaken. To resolve the conflict of industrial and agricultural problems, which claimed the time and attention of government and Party bodies, the Party simply ordered the entire governmental organization of the country divided in two. Since that time, there have been *two governments* in each of the "states" comprising the U.S.S.R. One is elected by the cities and towns, even when these are islands in farm country, and governs them. The other is elected by the countryside, and governs it. There is no such provision in the Constitution; there was no prior discussion in the legislatures or in the press—not even in the specialized publications for the Communist Party. The Central Committee decided it, and that was that.

The American press maintains some very able correspondents in the Soviet Union. There has been no censorship on outgoing dispatches since 1961. These men frequently send news or opinion that the Soviet leaders would rather not have appear. Actually, such material does appear almost daily in *The New York Times*. But no foreign newspaperman, including those who have excellent and long-standing personal contacts among Russians, has suggested that anybody complained about this act of the Central Committee or even thought that it was in any way improper.

It is important to realize that Soviet people simply do not think about government in the same manner that Americans or Englishmen or, say, Italians, do. Every Soviet citizen is raised from childhood to regard the Party leadership as deserving the credit for his country's progress. Usually the people he respects most are among the *ten million* Party members. One does not enroll in the Party. The Party recruits by inviting the most respected individuals, be they scientists, factory workers, or housewives, to join.

THE COMMUNIST PARTY

Partiinaya Zhizn'—*Party Life*—the Party's house organ with half a million circulation, is available on newsstands and by subscription abroad. Read it and it becomes clear that the Party is

Steel worker at extreme left, second from bottom, is member of the
Communist Party Central Committee, which runs the Soviet Union

anything but a secret society. Within five years after Stalin's death
in 1953, some of its clubs had gone so far as to abolish private
meetings altogether, even for business purposes, although the editors of *Partiinaya Zhizn'* believed that to be wrong. The Party
rules do not provide rigid regulations governing club meetings.
Ordinary members and lower-level officers do not hesitate to write
this national magazine with complaints about their superiors, and
sign their names and addresses to them.

In 1958 a woman wrote the editors: "May Communists speak
out with criticism of shortcomings at Party meetings open to the
public?" The Party organization of the housing-and-services department of her factory had held an open membership meeting.
Current maintenance and major repairs to "company"-administered
housing was discussed. A Party member rose and criticized short-

comings in the department. Others, including the writer of the letter, backed him up. Subsequently they were called to a Party executive board meeting. The Secretary (president) said they had behaved improperly because their remarks had undermined the authority of the department head and given non-Communists reasons to draw conclusions he thought undesirable.

The issue of *Partiinaya Zhizn'* that published her query carried the editors' reply:

If an open meeting is called, this is not for purposes of parade, not just for the record, but so as to permit a free discussion of a problem, to hear different points of view, to reveal shortcomings and indicate measures to eliminate them. . . . If Communists do not set the example of criticism at meetings open to the public, but keep silent because of the false conception that criticism of shortcomings in his work may diminish someone's authority, such meetings won't be worth very much.

The Party maintains its standing with the people by keeping its ear to the ground and by trying to satisfy their needs and complaints. In the same magazine (No. 5, 1960, p. 52), we read of a Communist welder who went to the Party Secretary at his chemical plant.

We're not being treated right. The water supply to our houses goes on and off. And while I'm at it, I may as well get all our beefs off my chest. There's no place to go at night. If you want to see a picture or get a book out of the library you have to go downtown. Things are tough for our wives. To put the kids in nursery school they have to go into town in the morning before they can go to work. This kills two hours every day. You ought to hear what people are saying.

This was summer, and a few days later there was a meeting under the shade trees in the courtyard of this man's apartment block. The Party Secretary was there, the acting mayor of the city, the factory manager, the union local chairman, and other influential citizens. They listened as the people made complaints and suggestions. Shortly afterward a general conference was called of all the Party members in that borough. Within a few months the results were totaled up. The water supply had improved. A day nursery had been opened right in the neighborhood. The factory library opened a neighborhood branch, with evening programs of movies and talks. Stores were opened. A hospital and a clinic were under construction. Now new problems were being tackled: home delivery of milk (it is only a few years since the U.S.S.R.

Volunteers planting trees near new apartment houses

has had enough milk for this to be considered), smog control, and home heating by power-plant waters.

Even more important than the magazine we have been quoting is one called *Kommunist*. In its issue of September, 1961, there was a letter from a woman who was a mother of three children, a schoolteacher, and a Party member of nineteen years standing. It was typical of the new tendency to demand that women be equal not only on the job and in the eyes of the law but in personal life, and that this be a rule of Communist behavior:

It is not at all uncommon that some Communist is looked up to on the job and among his comrades as an ideal. And what kind of man is he at home? In the best cases he gives his wife his pay check and complete freedom of action, which means the right to hold a job and to come home and prepare the meals, do the laundry and the rest of the housekeeping, *and* take care of the upbringing of the children. Mama has to be able to do everything. Papa hasn't got the time: either he's at work, or he is out on Party assignments, or at meetings, and when there's nothing else, he's got to "raise his level" [Sovietese for pursuing your education by reading]. The mother doesn't succeed in doing everything; gradually something loses out.

The ten million rank-and-file Party members have a chance to speak out on major problems of their organization during the period of general discussion before its Congresses, which are held every four years. The new long-term platform (program) submitted to the membership for its consideration before the 1961 Congress proposed to limit the number of terms *elected* officers could serve. The woman who heads the Party in a factory in the oil city of Baku offered an amendment that *appointive* officials, too, should have to be replaced at stated intervals, in Party, government, labor union, and business posts.

A delegate to a local Party conference in Tashkent said the proposed program was "not sharp enough with respect to bureaucracy, red tape, and a mechanical style of work." A letter in the national political-leadership magazine, *Kommunist,* objected to the provision that particularly outstanding leaders could be exempted from the limitation on number of terms served if they got three-quarters of the vote. This member wanted even top people to have to be rotated to other posts. A newspaperman wrote that in elections to local soviets "people are nominated whom the voters have not only never seen, but sometimes had never even heard of." He wanted the program to contain a specific commitment "decisively to uproot bureaucratic distortions of the Soviet electoral system."

Other members were concerned with the idealism of the organization. One wanted the Party rules to state that members are required to give their children a proper upbringing as a condition of retaining their membership. Another wanted the rules to spell out that promotion obtained through personal loyalty and friendship is not allowed. A third wanted heavy drinkers to be subject to expulsion under the rules. A fourth wanted Party members to be forbidden to make "unearned income" by renting out their homes or summer cottages. These suggestions were all given publicity by publication in national papers, and will therefore affect decisions as individual cases arise, although the rules as adopted were less specific:

Every Communist should observe in his own life and cultivate among working people the moral principles set forth in the program of the Party . . . mutual respect in the family circle and concern for the upbringing of children; intolerance of injustice, parasitism, dishonesty, careerism, and money-grubbing. . . .*

* *Rules of the Communist Party of the Soviet Union,* London: 1961, U.S.S.R. Embassy, p. 20.

PARTY STRUCTURE, POLICY-MAKING, LEADERSHIP

The basic direction of Party policy is set by its conventions ("Congresses") held every four years. The delegates are elected. The democracy of the elections depends upon the initiative of the members. In some places individuals acquire the powers Americans associate with political bosses, and put up slates of candidates, but the general trend in recent years is toward increasingly open elections.

The Party Congress elects a Central Committee, which must meet at least twice a year. The Committee has 173 voting members plus 155 alternates with consultative vote and the right to speak. Since 1957, this committee has been the real seat of power in the U.S.S.R., rather than the sixteen-man Presidium it elects, or the first Secretary (Khrushchev) the Presidium has chosen. But the Presidium and the Secretariat do the day-to-day work of running the Party and the country.

The Central Committee elected in 1961 is quite different from earlier ones. In the past the Committee had consisted exclusively of politicians. Although they were nearly all workingmen and peasants by background, in recent years almost all of them have been college graduates, usually in engineering, but their work has been politics.

The present Central Committee (term: 1961–1965) includes people of authority who are not politicians. There are a number of distinguished scientists, headed by the President of the Academy, Keldysh. There are also several writers, including Sholokhov, the giant of Russian letters, and the immensely popular older poet, Tvardovsky. As editor of the literary magazine, *Novy Mir* (*New World*), he has published the most rebellious and critical writers of the post-Stalin era. But the most striking single addition to the Central Committee is Valentina Gaganova. She is a textile-mill forelady who gave up a well-paying job heading a smooth-running team to take over, instead, the worst crew in her mill. This meant a considerable cut in pay because the pay was based on group output. She upgraded four consecutive poor groups this way, with a loss of income each time she started anew.

She represents, on the Central Committee, the public morality that, it is hoped, will be typical of the Communist society of the future.

It is the Presidium of the Communist Party that most nearly corresponds in power and authority to the Cabinet in the United

Mikoyan votes as former British Prime Minister Macmillan looks on

States. Although the Presidium is not chosen on a nationality basis, this factor clearly plays a role, just as regional and religious representation do in making up the American Cabinet or selecting a new member for the Supreme Court. Nine of the sixteen Presidium members are Russian, which is exactly in proportion to the ratio of Russians in the population. There are two Ukrainians (the next largest nationality), one Belorussian, one Uzbek (a novelist as well as a professional politician), one Georgian, one Armenian, and one Finn, Otto Kuusinen, who was an elected member of Finland's parliament for ten years when that country was part of the Russian Empire before World War I.

The best-known member after Khrushchev is the international trouble-shooter for the Soviet government, the Armenian Anastas Mikoyan, whose parents were both illiterate. His father was a carpenter. One brother is a factory worker, now retired. Another is a distinguished engineer, one of the Soviet Union's leading plane designers. One sister is on a collective farm; another manages a small handicrafts co-operative. The other Soviet leaders are of similar humble origins. Khrushchev, Mikoyan, and Kuusinen are the most liberal of the present membership, perhaps because they are the oldest, and have the clearest first-hand picture of how Stalin's personal dictatorship developed.

While the Presidium makes day-to-day policy, a body of nine men called the Secretariat carries it out. Nikita Khrushchev's actual title in the Party is First Secretary. Below its Congress, Central Committee, and Presidium-and-Secretariat, the Party is organized, as one would expect, on a territorial ladder corresponding to the regional structure of the country. But since November, 1962, the Party, like the government, has had two separate "state" organizations. One is for agricultural areas, county seats, colleges, and farm research institutions on the one hand; the other is for industrial cities and everything associated with industry. Governing bodies at each level are elected at periodic conventions. However, the Central Committee shifts executive officers around the country in accordance with the importance of jobs to be done and the qualifications of the individual. Members and officers at each level are required to adhere to instructions from above, subject to their power to replace their superiors at the next Party election.

COMMUNIST YOUTH AND CHILDREN'S ORGANIZATIONS

The Party draws new members largely from the Komsomol, the Communist League of Youth, which has twenty million members. This is about one-third of the age group of fifteen-to-twenty-eight that is eligible to belong. Half the members are high school and college students; the rest have jobs. Admission is supposed to be on merit, but the rules are loosely enforced. The Komsomol is really more a service organization than either a political or a social one. Until recently, social and recreational activities were provided for young people not by this organization but through their schools, places of work, neighborhoods, or athletic clubs. Now the Komsomol also does this. The Komsomol rallies young people to take part in the kind of civic volunteer activities we describe in detail below in discussing government. But it serves particularly as the means of getting people to develop pioneer areas, because young people are naturally less bound by family responsibilities than older ones. In 1962 alone Komsomols numbering 130,000 took construction jobs in Siberia and elsewhere.

The opening of the virgin-soil country so as to stabilize the Soviet food supply has been done chiefly by youth volunteers recruited through the Komsomol. But the Komsomol will take responsibility for staffing a particular part of some major construction projects in the better developed parts of the country as well. This organization channels the enthusiasm and competitive spirit of youth for this purpose. In 1963 its pet project was fertilizer

Young people pioneering Siberian industry live in tents such as these

plants, to help increase the country's food supply. The Komsomol puts out the country's liveliest daily national newspaper, which often has exciting discussions on morality and the other things that young people particularly talk about. On such occasions, it receives tens of thousands of letters.

In our chapter on education we referred to the Young Pioneers, the co-ed Soviet equivalent of the Boy and Girl Scouts. Officially, this is also an organization of a Communist nature. Actually, it deals very little with politics and a great deal with plain good citizenship and good deeds of kinds that are familiar to us. However, the "graduation" of Pioneers into the Komsomol at age sixteen serves to bring them that much closer to eventual membership in the Party.

THE STRUCTURE OF GOVERNMENT

Although the Party leads, the government governs. The nationality structure of government was discussed in Chapter 3 (the fifteen constituent republics, plus autonomous republics, territories and regions). To this there is no parallel in the U.S. In addition to the divisions mentioned earlier, the republics contain regional structures. The areas that correspond to American states are called *oblasts;* larger, usually partially underdeveloped, territories are called *krais;* those similar to American counties are termed *raions.* The very largest cities have a special standing, something like Washington, D.C. However, both the *krais* and the great cities and their citizens have the same rights as the "states" and the people in them. Recall once again the very unusual system of separate "state" governments for farm areas and industrial areas. The latter administer cities, islands of industry in rural areas, and even fairly large isolated industrial plants and the "company" towns of their personnel.

The system of government is called *soviet,* which is the Russian word for "council." It originated in spontaneous councils of representatives of workingmen, peasants, and soldiers during the Revolution of 1917. During the revolutionary period, the soviets were legislature, executive, and judiciary all rolled into one. In principle, they still exercise all power. In actuality, there is a considerable division of powers.

The lawmaking body of the U.S.S.R. is the Supreme Soviet, which resembles the American Congress in having two houses. One, the Council of the Union, is elected strictly in proportion to population. In the other, the Council of Nationalities, representation is by nationality, not numbers. Each full republic has twenty-five seats, and lesser nationality units have fewer seats.

Under the 1936 Constitution, which established this structure, the Supreme Soviet is elected every four years by secret ballot. Everyone over eighteen has the right to vote. There are no property, residence, or literacy qualifications. Nearly everybody does vote. Speaking to a Leningrad housewife, I said I had always been puzzled by the Soviet system of nominations, because there is only one party and no public primaries. I asked her who did the nominating. She said: "The people active in politics. Isn't that the way it is in your country, too?" Because of the way she said that, and the bitter complaints she had been making about housing and about the attitude of her neighbors toward herself as a Jew, I was very surprised at her answer to my next question: "Do you vote?"

She looked amazed. "Of course we vote! We dress up in our best clothes as for a most solemn occasion, and we congratulate each other on the elections."

"But why do you vote?"

"Because the best people are nominated, and they do the best they can for us."

I would imagine that the idea of having more than a single

candidate on the ballot had never entered her mind. To her the system that operates in her country works, and by and large she thinks it works for her benefit. She can vote "no," and if "no" votes are a majority, Soviet law provides for a new election, usually with a more popular nominee. Very few candidates are rejected by "no" votes because it is true that the Party does go to great pains to nominate those whom the voters will regard as "the best people."

For example, when a new city council was elected in Moscow in 1963, the selection of the final candidate proceeded as follows. At the immense Ball-Bearing Works, a proposed candidate was nominated by meetings of workers in each of two departments. A third department named two people, each of whom would represent the constituency well, in its opinion. Then the factory-wide union executive board met with the factory Communist Party board, with a number of other people invited who were active and respected by the personnel. They went over the four names in this meeting, decided on one, and submitted it to a general nominating meeting of the plant personnel. It was at this stage that approval became cut-and-dried, with the nominee receiving a unanimous vote, essentially guaranteeing endorsement of his name at the next stage. The meeting also elected two people to represent the factory at a constituency meeting of Party, union, and other organization leaders. This gathering heard the nominations advanced in this fashion by the personnel of every place of employment (schools, hospitals, scientific institutions, offices, department stores), and chose a final nominee to offer the voters on election day.

The city council of 1,084 members (one per six thousand in the city's population) reflects this system, for it consists of 476 workingmen and women, 131 union, government, and Party officials, eighty-five scientists and college faculty members, 238 industrial executives, engineers, and technicians, forty-four school principals and teachers, fourteen writers and artists, twenty-five military men, and forty-six in other occupations, or housewives. The council is clearly too large for the week-to-week work of decision-making. For this purpose it elects an executive committee that is more nearly the size of city councils in Western countries. The full council membership functions in committees and individually to look after the voters' needs and complaints. In closely built-up large cities, one can hardly walk a block without seeing a sign on an entrance saying: "City Soviet Member . . . lives in Apartment . . . and receives visitors from . . . to . . . o'clock on . . . days of the week."

The fact that elections are regarded as meaningful, despite the absence of opposition on the ballot, was indicated by a controversy that raged in the public press in 1963. It was over whether or not school principals should be elected by their teachers and other staff members. Some educators and school administrators felt that election would reduce the principals' authority, continuity of policy, and so forth. Teachers replied that they would have more confidence in elected principals, who would have to be on their toes, because their continuance in these posts of responsibility—and better salary —would depend upon the satisfaction of people with whom they work every day. The decision went in favor of election as the method of choice, and that is now the rule. The system of nomination is exactly the same as in the factory described, with a secret ballot for or against the final nominee.

One doesn't have to be a Party member to be elected to public office. A majority of the people elected to village councils are not in the Party. Even at the very top level, the Supreme Soviet of the U.S.S.R., about a quarter don't belong to the Party. However, the top government officers are always Party members. Like the soviet of Moscow or any other city, the U.S.S.R. Supreme Soviet consists of people who are not professional politicians for the most part: Ulanova the ballet dancer, Ehrenburg the outspoken novelist who has been publicly attacked by Khrushchev, major scientists, leading executives, the country's most respected shopworkers and farmers, the best schoolteachers. A disadvantage of this system is that the country would suffer a great loss if these people left their professions to spend most of their time in committee or otherwise engaging in politics. This is one reason the Supreme Soviet does not exercise the full power it constitutionally enjoys. It usually meets twice a year for a period of a week or less to vote on bills suggested by various branches of government. It appoints standing committees to meet well in advance of its sessions to give these bills thorough consideration, and always accepts their recommendations.

The Supreme Soviet sounds most like the American Congress during budget discussions, when members will stand up and argue that an appropriation be included for a bridge across a river in their district, or for more housing there than the bill called for. The committees meet to consider the proposed changes, the Finance Minister (Secretary of the Treasury) states why the administration feels some should be accepted and some should not, and the budget is passed, amended somewhat, but not a great deal.

Nina Morozova, twenty-five, graduate of evening college,
is member of Supreme Soviet. Here
she meets with constituents

Most of the year, Congresswoman Morozova works
as a team chief in an
electrical plant,
where her civic activity won
her the nomination

Here the Congresswoman encourages schoolgirls
to keep the neighborhood green

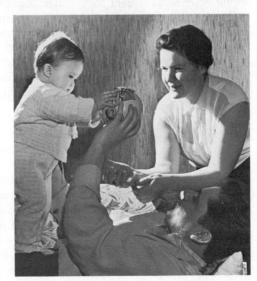

And here she is
at home with
baby and husband

For example, at the December, 1960, session, the Minister was faced with requests for more money for apartment-house repairs. Since the low rents paid for apartments do not even cover the costs of major repairs, government has to meet the bills. Constituents exert great pressure to get better maintenance than is actually given. The budget committees of the Supreme Soviet amended the administration's budget upward for this purpose, and showed how income could be increased to meet the cost. The government accepted this as well as a proposal to increase capital investments in the republics within the limits of the increased income.

Individual deputies (congressmen) were still not satisfied. Said Finance Minister Garbuzov: "Congressmen Malinin, Bayramov, Mohammed Ali, Kiselev, Gegeshidze, Congresswomen Konduchalova and Vakhabova, and Congressman Panov have, in their addresses, proposed that additional funds be assigned for major repairs. . . ." He then noted that the administration's draft had provided a 17 per cent increase in this over the previous year, and said: "In the light of the size of the increase in appropriations for these purposes, it is not possible to raise them further at the present time." * But then he accepted a proposal to loosen government control over the purse strings of local industries by allowing them to have their own working capital. Passage of that kind of bill would be an achievement for a congressman in any country.

Another representative requested the government to meet 50 per cent of the costs of drainage for land improvement in his district. The answer was yes. Another complained that the legal limits on funds for village governments were outdated, preventing them from doing their job, and was told that the Finance Ministry would give this its consideration. Two years later a reform was adopted to meet this problem.

The chairman of the country-wide Planning Commission is a member of the Cabinet, and he took the floor to present the administration's reactions to proposals in his field. The budget committees of the two houses had proposed to raise still higher the planned increase in output of leather footwear, confectionery products, and fruit-and-berry wines, by over a hundred million dollars, and the government accepted. A committee and several individual representatives proposed a further increase in the manufacture of certain industrial products. The planning chief noted that they were already scheduled to rise between 18 and 32 per cent in one

* *Izvestia,* December 24, 1960.

year's time, and that a further increase would be uneconomical in the over-all picture. He promised that his commission would take another look at problems of equipment supply, so that perhaps these congressmen's republics could expand manufacture on their own.

One reason the budget goes through with little change is that the bill presented has already been gone over carefully by sub-committees of the Supreme Soviet budget committees. In a typical year, one subcommittee examined proposed expenditures for medical services, cultural activities, education, and administration; another looked at the figures on farming and domestic commerce; a third dealt with the machinery industry; a fourth with consumer-goods industries. Government officials from these ministries appeared before the subcommittees to justify their own estimates.

As in other countries, Cabinet officers have the most difficult time when faced with charges of extravagance and inefficiency in their departments. In 1959 the Minister of Culture was attacked from the floor for hoarding expensive furniture and equipment, and even clocks, in his offices. He was replaced not long afterward. A unique Soviet procedure is that the government's daily newspaper, *Izvestia,* which has a national circulation of six million and is printed simultaneously in twenty cities, follows up on congressmen's complaints, interviewing Cabinet ministers to find out what has been done about them.

Since the Supreme Soviet meets for such brief periods, it delegates its lawmaking powers between sessions to a smaller body, its Presidium (not to be confused with the ruling Presidium of the Communist Party). This body passes interim legislation, which has always obtained the approval of the next meeting of the Supreme Soviet.

The Supreme Soviet also chooses a prime minister (called, in the U.S.S.R., Chairman of the Council of Ministers). He nominates his Cabinet (Council of Ministers), which the Supreme Soviet then approves. The Cabinet actually does the day-to-day work of governing the country, with the sixteen-man Presidium of the Communist Party creating basic policy. The most important figures in the country belong to both.

The lack of an opposition party (whether capitalist, or "revisionist" or "dogmatist" communist or socialist) is most clearly seen in the lack of open opposition on matters of basic policy. Nor is there discussion in the mass media of subjects the Communist Party doesn't want discussed. No public disagreement on any foreign-policy matter has been expressed in government or in the press for a quarter-century, until after the event. No representative has ever raised a question in the Supreme Soviet on, for example, why German-language schools are allowed for the German minority, but no Yiddish-language schools for the 400,000 persons (20 per cent) of the Jewish group who regard that as their native tongue. When the Communist Party attacked certain trends in the arts, no cultural figure on the Supreme Soviet expressed disagreement with Premier Khrushchev, although some—Ehrenburg, Tvardovsky—did so through other channels. Today, such silence is no longer because of fear of execution or imprisonment, or even of loss of income. For politicians it would mean the end of their careers. For others it would mean a loss of popularity that would destroy their standing, because the very same Soviet citizen who might agree with the critic believes that it is wrong to "break ranks" against the Party's will. But, as we have seen, in those fields in which the Party sees no objection to disagreement, it is vigorous, open, and functions in a manner very similar to that in countries with multiparty systems. And the number and importance of these fields is increasing.

JUSTICE AND POLICE

Justice in the U.S.S.R. is administered by legally trained judges elected for 5-year terms, each assisted by two lay judges elected for very short terms. The former are salaried; the latter are not, but their wages or salaries from their regular occupations continue while they serve. All problems—law, fact, guilt or innocence, and the sentence—are decided upon by majority vote of these three. Actually, the two citizen associates (who are like jurors but have broader powers) usually go along with the judge on law, because they can't possibly know it as well as he. On other matters they show more independence, depending upon their education, personality, or strength of character.

I once wandered into a civil court in Leningrad and heard the two citizen judges hear and rule on a noncontroversial but technical matter in the absence of a professional judge. They had a far better knowledge of the law than one would expect of non-lawyers. They were careful to frame their judgment in a manner that would stand up to examination by other legal bodies if this were necessary. The chief judge of the district was kind enough to make time to talk to me, although I had no appointment and offered no references. When I asked him to explain the good legal knowledge of the juror-judges, he said that he and the other professional judges conducted evening seminars for citizens who had been elected to these posts.

There are appeals courts and a supreme court, which is strict about insisting that lower courts adhere to the legal rules of evidence and procedure. Soviet law differs from American law in that both parties can appeal in a criminal case: if the local prosecution feels that a person acquitted is really guilty, it can appeal to a higher court. The prosecutor is part of a single national system of attorneys-general, called the Procurator's Office, which has the duty under the Constitution of seeing that justice is done and the law upheld in all respects. Under Stalin, each such state's attorney ran a one-man show, and was responsible only to the man above him. Today, he works with a board of citizens deliberately drawn from different walks of life, who are to assist him and to restrain prosecutions they may regard as unjustified.

It was not the ordinary police, uniformed or plainclothes, but the former political police (called successively "Cheka," "GPU," "MVD") who knocked on the door at 3 A.M. in Stalin's day, and who tortured confessions out of innocent people. When I first visited the Soviet Union in 1932, I remember two regular policemen taking over the wagon of a milk black-marketeer about whom they had been tipped off. One policeman told the suspect to drive to the police station. He replied with a string of curses. The policeman flushed red, but merely picked up the reins and drove off, with the man seated alongside him.

On a more recent visit, in 1959, a crowd engaged me in conversation on Leningrad's main avenue late at night. At about 1 A.M., a policeman came up, asked us to consider that people were trying to sleep in the apartment buildings above us, and wouldn't we call it a night. One man actually said: "He's only a peasant," and the crowd simply closed in tighter around me. I tried to move toward my hotel, but it took an hour to progress a block, with questions and discussion going all the time. At 2 A.M. a paddy wagon came up, and a policeman started asking the members of the crowd for identification. No one was threatened or arrested or lined up against the wall, and no one fled. But this time the crowd drifted away.

Today the police are being replaced and supplemented by citizen volunteers, unarmed and of both sexes and all ages. Outside my hotel near the Leningrad city limits I was chatting with two teenage youths, tall and husky, one evening in 1962. Two short, slight

Volunteer patrol officer reprimands fellow student

women came up, wearing the red armbands that are the sole badge of authority of the volunteer auxiliaries, and asked the boys for identification. One claimed he had left his at home, and the other admitted he was under sixteen. One woman said to them: "You know it's past curfew for you. Go home!" They started to go, but I turned to the women, told them I was a foreigner trying to learn about things, and asked if they would let the boys remain so we could all talk. They agreed. I said:

"You are women, you do happen to be small, and you don't carry weapons. How does this work?"

One replied: "Force is not the point. One must teach with the word."

I said: "But what if someone took a swing at you?"

One of the boys answered: "It would go very ill with him indeed." It was clear he approved.

A few days later I learned that the need for force must be negligible. After watching the system of volunteers in the streets and parks and dance halls for several evenings, I arranged an appointment with the chiefs of the citizen volunteers for that industrial borough. Both were engineers, one a research man in the mechanical field, and the other chief of quality inspection in a furniture factory. Their district, with 175,000 people, has only *three* regular armed policemen on day duty, and *four* on night duty! But it has seven thousand citizen volunteers, each of whom gives one evening per month. This means that there are 230 people patrolling in pairs or groups each evening in an area with the population of a fair-sized city. We asked what kind of disorder they usually had to deal with, and they said rowdy drunks. I personally had not seen one during my week in that area, except for a man who thought young people talking with me outside my hotel were trying to buy things for resale at a profit, and who stormed at them: "Aren't you ashamed of yourselves?"

Asked about sex cases, the two chiefs looked at each other in puzzlement. There had been no rape case in the three years they had served. Narcotics cases were unknown. Both such types are reported from time to time in the Soviet press, but every indication is that they are extraordinarily rare.

Asked about juvenile delinquency, they said it was not a great problem. Their schools were of the "lengthened-day" type, providing supervised recreation and homework-rooms after class until time to go home for supper. Factories provided shop activities for those who liked this. There were plenty of summer replacement jobs for youths, particularly because women with young children take unpaid leave in addition to their vacations. The borough also had four elaborate community centers, two parks with amusement and sports facilities, four movies, and various club houses, not counting Leningrad's downtown and city-wide facilities. Even the smallest places of employment had recreation "corners," with books and papers, television, and games. In small towns, where such facilities have not been provided, juvenile delinquency is a problem, and there have been some violent attacks on police and citizen volunteers.

We asked what happened when someone was picked up for disorderly conduct? In every case without exception, the offense would be discussed at the offender's place of employment, with his fellows

Order is kept by students

present. There were courts of public opinion, and in cases serious
enough to require judicial action, some citizen, usually from the
offender's place of work or apartment house, served as friend-of-
the-court prosecutor, and someone else as defender. The idea was
to involve every possible person in a feeling of responsibility for
maintaining a decent atmosphere in the neighborhood.

I once asked Professor Kerimov, head of Leningrad University's
law school, what he thought of these extralegal bodies. He is
particularly devoted, as an individual, to the concept of government
under law, but he thought these citizens' bodies were a fine idea.
He said people would much rather face a formal court of justice
than the men and women with whom they have to live and work
from day to day: "A man is picked up drunk, this is reported to
his buddies on the job, they call him on the carpet and say: 'What
kind of reputation are you trying to give us?' He feels this, and

their attitude toward him until he straightens out, much more strongly than he feels a fine levied by a judge."

The regular courts may even entrust serious cases to the courts of public opinion if the individual is believed susceptible to rehabilitation by the pressure of public opinion and by friendly assistance. Only one such person in two hundred has been found to commit another crime within a year. The vast majority never do. In extreme cases the informal courts have the power to order people to leave the city for two to five years, if it is felt that they would be kept on the wrong track by their associations there or they would be troublesome or potentially dangerous to decent citizens.

How much crime is there in the U.S.S.R.? While in the Soviet Union, I encountered a woman officer of the court of nationally known Judge Leibowitz of New York. He had written eyewitness descriptions of Soviet courts and penal systems for *Life*. She said to me: "There just isn't any crime in this country." What she meant, of course, is that there is very little.

Most of Moscow's passenger transport is run on an honor system, with the passenger putting the fare in a box at the other end of the vehicle from the driver, and taking a receipt himself. In Moscow, there are hundreds of snack bars, factory cafeterias, and bookstalls without sales people or cashiers. People pay and make their own change on an open-till basis.

Wages are paid in cash, not checks. There are now thousands of places of employment where the paymaster brings in a box with the total amount of cash to be paid a crew or entire shop, and individual wage slips for signature. People come up at their convenience and take the amount of money specified on their slips. The system works. It is by no means universal. Even more interesting, because it involves not only financial honesty but honesty of judgment, is a system in which workers on piece-and-quality payment systems individually calculate what is due them. This was first tried in a factory department with a thousand workers. The total wage bill was found to be exactly equal to that calculated by management's experts, although there were doubtless individual errors in both directions. Today some hundreds of thousands work on this basis, but that is only a small fraction of the total number of wage earners. In the U.S.S.R. this honor system is described as an "early sprout" of communism, the system they hope to have developed in its essentials by 1980.

What happens when a court does issue a finding against someone? In the house organ of the Justice Department of the Russian

Republic, *Sovetskaya Iustitsiya* (*Soviet Justice*), for March, 1961, we find a court officer, rather like a probation officer and clerk of court combined, describing her work. When people are fined, some pay at first notice.

The second category consists of those who fail to appear at court despite having received a summons. They assert that the fine to which they were sentenced is unjust and flatly refuse to pay it. One has to visit these people, try to awaken their sense of responsibility, *convince them that the decision of the judge was right*—and very often this gets results.

A third type just won't pay, and have their possessions taken away to compel payment. She writes that, by organizing her time properly, she finds it possible to make several visits to a person who has failed to make payment. Apparently, exceptional efforts to convince people are made before fines are collected by possession.

Some people are sentenced to imprisonment, of course. Of the prisons, Judge Leibowitz wrote in *Life,* June, 1959: "The Soviet advancement in this field is so remarkable as to make our American methods seem positively archaic." Krukovd Penal Colony, which he visited, is in "bleak, unprepossessing buildings," but has

intelligent, humane, farsighted administration from top to bottom. . . . Prisoners . . . did not have the beaten, shamed look of the American convict. . . . You have to know intimately the sickly, sullen atmosphere of the average American prison exercise yard to appreciate what I saw and what I *felt* as I watched these Russian convicts this brilliant, sunny day. . . . They ate in comfort: four men to a table and plenty of food for all. . . . They are actually paid just as much for the work they do in prison as they would receive for corresponding work on the outside. It is hard to realize how important that single fact is. . . . They earn and pay for their own keep. . . . The remainder goes to the support of their families so that the families are not a burden to the government either, as they are in our country.

According to U.S. Assistant Secretary of State W. Averell Harriman, prisoners' wives are allowed to visit with them privately once a month. Wife and family may spend a week with the prisoner three or four times a year in rooms provided for this purpose.* Mr. Harriman's prison observations agree with those of Judge Leibowitz, and what he saw of the volunteer law-and-order squads and their attitudes corresponds exactly to my own experiences described earlier in this chapter.

* *The New York Times,* June 3, 1959.

In 1959 the maximum prison sentence was cut from twenty-five years to ten, with fifteen for a few very grave crimes. Life imprisonment is unknown. The minimum age of criminal responsibility was raised from fourteen to sixteen in general, with some specific exceptions. The death penalty may be applied for treason, espionage, premeditated murders of particular cruelty, large-scale embezzlement of public property, and to prisoners who commit violence in jail. Death sentences handed down in recent years include sentences for bank robbers who committed murder in the course of the robbery, ringleaders of gang attacks upon police stations in frontier-type towns where the authorities were campaigning to restore order, drunken drivers who killed persons with their vehicles, professional counterfeiters and currency black-marketeers, and officials found guilty of repeatedly accepting large bribes. Individuals who helped the Nazis run concentration camps, and who killed and tortured prisoners, are found now and then, tried in public, and the major offenders are usually sentenced to death.

The chief district judge who received me in Leningrad in 1962 told me that a murder trial was in progress in that court building. I walked in and sat down among the spectators. Attendance was small, consisting largely of relatives and neighbors of the deceased woman. The murder was a typical crime of passion, with some of the trappings of a mystery. The prosecutor asked for the maximum sentence for premeditated murder without aggravating circumstances. She pointed out that the prisoner knew that the woman killed would leave a young child with no one to care for it. The court agreed, and condemned the prisoner to the longest term the law allowed: ten years.

My own impression was that the defense attorney had made an excellent case for the plea of not guilty by reason of insanity by showing that his client had a record of hospitalization for mental illness, although the prosecutor had brought medical witnesses who testified that the defendant was sane at the time of the crime. I left with the feeling that the chances were good of reversal on appeal, with commitment to a hospital instead of imprisonment. In 1962, 8 per cent of verdicts, and 35 per cent of sentences, were appealed; 20 per cent of appeals were successful.

The openness of the Leningrad judge with me was not unusual. I had had the same experience three years earlier in Sochi on the Black Sea, where I wandered into a police station and told the man at the desk that I'd like to talk to a judge. He phoned several, found one who was in his chambers and who was willing to see me right away. Court was not in session but he was trying to clear cases from his calendar by agreement, and was receiving visitors requesting action or official documents. A woman had been in a fight with another on her job and demanded court action, claiming she had been the victim. The judge turned the case over to her union. He remarked to me that they were now having organizations of the citizenry settle matters that required education in public behavior rather than punishment. A Ukrainian judge on vacation was seated behind him to observe procedure in the Russian Republic, and nodded agreement.

The next petitioner had spent his enterprise's money, had been fired and ordered by the court to make good the loss. Apparently there had been no move to jail him. He explained to the judge that he hadn't yet found another job—his record didn't help, I'm sure —and this was why he had not yet made any move to repay. The judge set a firm date for repayment.

Another man had gone to his former wife's house late at night and gone to sleep in an empty bed. His ex-mother-in-law pulled him out of bed, he said. The judge's records showed she had testified that he had struck her. He denied this. The judge pointed out that he clearly had no right to be in the place, and said he'd strike the complaint from the calendar if the man would apologize. The man refused point-blank. The judge said: "You don't want a court record," but when the man refused to yield, the judge set date for trial eleven days later. Asked by the judge where he lived, the man answered: "Nowhere." To me the case looked like a reflection of the housing crisis. Having been divorced, the man no longer had the right to share the room of which his former wife was the official tenant, and he hadn't been able to get another in this crowded resort city.

A lawyer came in for a client who apparently had had quite a criminal career. A government bank representative came in to ask for a lien on a house, because a borrower was a month overdue with a quarterly payment on a loan. The judge said: "She's *promised* to pay, hasn't she?" "Yes, but she committed herself to pay a month ago." "No lien, but I'll issue an order that she must pay within two weeks."

GOVERNMENT OF THE REPUBLICS AND OTHER LOWER LEVELS

The governments of the fifteen constituent republics and of the autonomous republics within them are like that of the U.S.S.R., except that the legislatures (Supreme Soviets) have only one chamber. The relationship between the Communist Party and the government is also similar at each level. Since Stalin's death, these legislatures have been acting more and more like true governing bodies than rubber stamps. For example, legislation of the Supreme Soviet of the Ukraine in recent years includes, in addition to the budget, the economic plan for that republic, bills for improvement of government administration, measures for education, the procedure for recall elections, public health, culture, the judiciary, and criminal law. In 1962 it adopted a divorce law far more liberal than that of the U.S.S.R. as a whole. No republic during the period of Stalin would have dared to exercise "state's rights" to this degree. It also passed a distinctive law governing the provision of arms and munitions to civilian enterprises, their storage, and conditions of use. The purpose of this is to have arms available to the population for guerrilla warfare, which the Ukrainians had to wage in 1918–1920 and 1941–1944, when 175 city and county committees of the Communist Party led underground resistance behind the German lines.

The relationship between the republics and Moscow at present has some of the flavor of the United Nations. Each maintains a Permanent Delegate and staff in the Soviet capital. In Stalin's day this structure was a hollow shell. For example, the number of matters handled by the Belorussian Republic's delegation rose from a scant twenty or twenty-five per year until 1953 to seven hundred per year since 1959. They now include matters of vital interest such as measures to speed the development of particular industries, financing of the economy, and farm improvements. The republics draft their own economic plans and budgets and see them through nine federal executive and legislative bodies (Cabinet departments, banks, committees of both houses of the Supreme Soviet) to final passage. The permanent delegates expedite delivery of their republics' manufactures to other Soviet republics through federal co-ordinating agencies. They also maintain contact with foreign companies through the federal Ministry of Foreign Trade.

The most important thing that has been done to make the republic governments truly significant has been turning over to them almost all industry and business. Local government has a very high degree of citizen participation. Many new departures in all aspects of Soviet life start at the local level. They find approval in government and Party, which then use their authority, prestige, and publicity facilities to spread them throughout the country. For example, here is an editorial in *Izvestia,* the government's official national newspaper, October 23, 1960:

Currently, the gradual process of transfer of certain functions of government into the hands of the organized public is proceeding on an ever-widening scale. This is a complex process whose directions are as yet unexplored, and wherein established practices do not exist, and practical experience is either lacking or very limited. All the more aid and support must therefore be given to the pioneers in this work. There are a number of cities in the Ukraine where the [paid] departments under the borough councils were eliminated more than a year ago, and their functions have been taken over by standing committees of the citizenry. . . . It is the duty of the local government and of business management to give day-to-day support and assistance to all positive initiatives by the people.

In *Pravda,* September 3, 1961, the mayor of a Siberian coal-mining town of 300,000 described how citizens help out. His is a raw town, for it had only ten thousand people in 1926, but it now has a repertory theatre with a permanent company of professional actors, *120 libraries,* a score of community centers, and about seventy-five schools. There is a school of mines, a mining research institute, and a school of nursing. In addition to mining, industries include food processing; manufacturing clothing and lighting equipment; and repairing mining, electrical, and grain-handling equipment on an industrial scale.

He writes that thirty thousand people in this one town—about one adult in six—belong to some volunteer committee assisting in one or another aspect of public affairs. Sanitary committees of 5,800 members make sure that streets and houses are kept clean; 4,800 parents participate in school activities; 280 people look after the problems of the retired and aged; 530 women belong to councils concerned primarily with the problems of the housewife; and more than 1,800 participants in 360 courts of public opinion set up in housing projects and private residential blocks, settle quarrels among neighbors, quiet noisy people, and handle similar problems. Volunteer store inspectors number 140 citizens. They found violations of official retail prices by storekeepers and cheating on weight and price by customers. Thousands give one evening a month to the unarmed auxiliary police.

This Siberian city also has 712 street committees with about four members each. Another item from a city in Central Asia tells us more about these citizens' organizations. A committee consisting of a dozen people was chosen by a community of a few square blocks for neighborhood improvement. Building bees were arranged by this committee to fix the streets, repair the irrigation ditches and bridges, build a recreation hall, a tearoom, a store, a branch post office, and a phone booth. The people provided the labor and the borough government provided materials and equipment. A medical office, a library, and an appliance rental store are maintained by persons of the appropriate skills who contribute their time. The people have torn down the walls that traditionally isolated Uzbek family compounds from one another. The committee is called upon to assist in personal problems, such as protecting a girl whose parents seek to marry her off against her will in Eastern tradition, or a woman whose husband won't let her work out of the house at a job she wants.

A shade under half the population of the U.S.S.R. still lives in villages. Yekaterinovka is an overgrown village on the Volga four hundred miles southeast of Moscow. Of its four thousand inhabitants, five hundred attended a town meeting there, reported in the press because it adopted resolutions sent on to national and state authorities. The Finance Minister was petitioned to change the system of taxation. The idea was to penalize self-employed skilled craftsmen who have been growing rich (by Soviet standards of wealth) by repairing homes and appliance and charging whatever the traffic will bear. Said the collective farm chairman:

Semyon Gorbunov, truck driver by trade, age thirty, doesn't take any kind of work except the kind you hide from the internal revenue people. Let him tell us where he got the nerve to take $132 for roofing from old Gorelov, who has to make do on a pension, when he only worked a day and a half at it!

Another resolution went to the state government:

The town meeting of Yekaterinovka village feels it is essential for a construction agency to be set up here. The prospects for the improvement of our village guarantee that it will be kept busy. The more than twenty enterprises and offices, the collective farm, and the inhabitants themselves are greatly in need of such a building organization. . . . This agency would be a profitable operation. However, in order to launch its activities, financial support—a line of credit—is needed. The "firm" also will need an allocation of building materials. The town meeting requests the state government to reply with a statement as to the aid the village can expect to receive for establishment of this construction team.

Discussion of this problem, then of expanding the line of products of the village factory (remember that all business is publicly owned), and then of reviving forgotten folk crafts grew into a general conversation on the future of the village. The mayor spoke and was then besieged with questions: "What about central heating for the whole town?" "Why does a broken TV have to be hauled all the way to Bezenchuk for repairs?" "When are the police going to put up road signs in the village?" "What's being done to keep tractors off the streets?" "Isn't it time we set up an inquiry bureau?" (As there are few private phones, the phone book cannot serve as general directory, and a public information booth serves this purpose.)

Yekaterinovka has no public bathhouse (recall that inside plumbing is almost unknown outside the cities). When a schoolteacher brought this up, the meeting really exploded. The teacher waited till the noise died down, then said that the authorities couldn't do everything, and it was about time the village took a leaf from common practice in Soviet cities, and built the bathhouse by volunteer donated labor. The town accepted the proposal.

"REFERENDUM BY DISCUSSION"

The public is periodically asked to speak out in a distinctive Soviet institution that might be called referendum by discussion, although this applies only to internal affairs, and even then excludes what we would call political, rather than economic issues. But when the Party and government are considering a bill deeply affecting the public welfare, there is truly an extraordinary amount of discussion in print and at meetings by the citizens at large.

In 1956, there was a complete overhaul of the pension and old-age security legislation. Twelve thousand letters were published in the press and studied by the committees putting the bill into final form. In 1957, there was a major revolution in management. Industry was freed from federal management and placed in the hands of "state"-level governments. This was of tremendous public interest. Sixty-eight thousand letters were published, and 2.3 million people put forward ideas and suggestions at half a million meetings across the country.

The next year the planned targets of the current Seven-Year Plan were printed. They affected every aspect of people's lives: housing, jobs, education, health provisions, cultural facilities, wages, prices, and much else. On this occasion 300,000 letters were published in the country's papers and magazines. It goes without saying that people wouldn't bother to write if they didn't know, from previous experience, that their ideas would be taken into consideration.

Similar discussions have taken place during the Khrushchev administration on (1) the new code of labor legislation, (2) the thoroughgoing education reform, (3) the breakup of government farm-machinery depots and the sale of this equipment to collective farms, (4) the regulations governing the treatment of juvenile delinquency, (5) the rules of the courts of public opinion to which we have previously referred, and (6) the involvement of the public in the unarmed auxiliary police. The amount of freedom allowed by the press in publishing opinions varies. In the case of the farm-machinery issue, the papers did not publish a single item objecting to the whole proposal, but carried a great deal of sincere and practical discussion of how the farms were to pay for the machinery they acquired. On the other hand, discussion of the education reform pro and con was absolutely wide open, and no personalities or organizations were spared.

THE PRESS

In addition to these frequent special discussions on particular matters of national interest, the press is for both Party and government the preferred means of daily presentation of information and propaganda. It also serves as a channel through which citizens can voice their objections and propose alternate solutions when they believe decisions of an agency of the federal or lower government may hurt the public interest or their own. For example, the location of a major public improvement is often controversial.

In October, 1961, the Cabinet member in charge of power-dam construction announced that a plant to make three times as much electricity as Grand Coulee would be built at a point on the Ob River in Siberia where the land was so flat that the resulting reservoir would be as big as all of Czechoslovakia. Geographers published their opposition to this, stating that if the dam were built higher on the river, a deeper, smaller reservoir could be used, and much land now marshy could be saved, drained, and put to practical uses. Another scientist supported this in print, saying that there was oil in the territory to be flooded, and that recovering it from beneath the waters would be much more expensive. A writer then wrote a hard-hitting article in a national newspaper, the *Literary Gazette,* saying that a country that expected a population of 300 million in twenty years could not afford to flood so vast a body of land. A railway construction executive said that felling the forests on the flooded areas would open southern Siberia, which is already cold enough, to arctic winds from the north now slowed and modified by the trees. A scientific body then sent out exploring parties which found that the marshlands to be flooded had enough peat to fuel three power plants as large as the projected hydroelectric plant. But the dam builders went right ahead with their initial intention. At this point the *Literary Gazette* hit at them again, saying that their approach was narrow-minded and departmental. Finally, the extremely powerful magazine *Kommunist* published the opinion of a top scientist saying that the land in question should be drained, not flooded. The controversy ended in a very interesting way. In May, 1963—nineteen months after the initial announcement—the State Planning Commission of the U.S.S.R., one of the highest bodies of government, decided that the project had given insufficient consideration to the question of deforestation and oil and gas fields in the zone to be flooded. It ordered a complete new survey. Most important, this top body made this decision public *in a letter to the newspaper that had campaigned against the initial decision,* the *Literary Gazette,* which has a circulation of a million.

Other papers include *Pravda,* the most influential of all, which is the official organ of the Communist Party and has 6.7 million daily readers. This alone is twice the total circulation of the entire newspaper industry of Russia under the last tsar. Next in rank is the government's paper, *Izvestia,* which sells six million. Among other national dailies with circulations over one million are *Komsomol'skaia Pravda,* unique in that it is aimed at the sixteen-to-twenty-five age bracket; and *Trud,* which is published by the labor unions. All cities have local papers. Magazines do not circulate as widely as in the West, although one called *Krestianka* (*The Peasant Woman*), sells over 3.5 million copies.

The press is the most important means of national communication. Kurgan is a state capital in Siberia. Six members of a do-it-yourself housing co-operative there sent a letter to *Pravda.* Fifty families had already moved into homes they had built with their own hands. They wrote:

Just one thing is bothering the residents. This is the indifferent attitude of the plant management [at their place of work] and of the local organs of government to their needs. The tract of do-it-yourself homes has no electricity, piped water, bathhouse, restaurant or pharmacy. . . . We have to go to work on foot . . . about two and a half miles to the plant. . . . Many of these questions can and must be solved by plant management. This is provided in this year's union contract. But the management is in no rush to do this, and it has the silent agreement of the local union leadership.

Neither the city officials, the plant management, nor the union officers could have been happy to see itself laid out before a nationwide audience. Letters of this kind do not die with their publication. The papers follow up. For example, *Pravda* published a story that an important state-level business official had used his position to have a great deal of money spent to improve the apartment house in which he lived. Six weeks later it carried a follow-up that this man's Party superiors had found the story to be true, and had asked the appropriate government authorities to fire him from his job. They did so, and he was also dropped from all Party posts.

Each department of a Soviet newspaper has its own phone number. *Pravda* has three numbers just for calls to the letters-to-the-editor department. No other department has more than one. Annually, one reader in fourteen writes a letter to *Izvestia*. It publishes fifteen items a day, written by readers, many as articles.

Non-Soviet points of view are presented regularly in the press through its foreign news coverage. The Soviet viewpoint is strongly favored in treatment, of course. Sometimes hostile views are presented directly, as in 1956, when the press presented queries by British members of Parliament to the Soviet government about the Hungarian insurrection. Speeches by former United States Secretaries of State Acheson and Herter were published in full, and *Izvestia* presented to its national audience the full text of the interview former President Kennedy granted its editor. In the summer of 1962, television, radio, and the papers carried speeches by Americans, Englishmen, and Frenchmen at the World Congress for Disarmament and Peace held in the Kremlin under the sponsorship of Albert Schweitzer, Pastor Niemoeller, Bertrand Russell, and others, opposing Soviet armament and bomb-testing policy. In 1963, Kennedy's end-the-Cold-War speech of June 10 was carried in full in *Pravda* and *Izvestia*.

A commission to draft a new constitution for the U.S.S.R., to replace that of 1936, was established by the Supreme Soviet in 1962. Khrushchev said the new constitution must "raise socialist democracy to a still higher level . . . provide even more solid guarantees for the democratic rights and freedoms of the people, guarantees of strict observance of socialist legality" and "define the

principles of the foreign policy of the Soviet Union." He promised
that the constitution would be discussed "together with the whole
people" before adoption. In 1962 and 1963 discussions were held
on the new codes of criminal and civil law and the new marriage
and divorce laws, which were to be incorporated, in their basic
principles, into the new constitution. Since the press is the major
channel for such discussion, as it is for discussion of practical,
everyday affairs, there are now five million "worker and rural correspondents": citizen volunteers who write regularly for the papers.

10: The Status of Soviet Women

"Don't turn to grandma for advice!" warns a headline in a Soviet magazine for farm women. Her good will is far outweighed by ignorance. She was probably illiterate until after the Revolution. When grandma was a girl, many peasant mothers gave birth in the fields. Factory girls often had their babies alongside the loom in a textile mill or in the mill-yard. Infants died like flies, and mortality among mothers was shocking. Only one child in twenty was delivered with qualified assistance. Birth control was unknown; illegal, unsanitary abortions took a tremendous toll.

Today, prenatal and maternity medical care is universal. The country has 14,000 women's and infants' medical consultation centers which keep expectant mothers under observation to the time of confinement, teach them proper care of the child, and treat the sick. These centers supposedly offer birth-control clinics and instruct in physical and psychological painless childbirth techniques. As of 1958, half of all Soviet women had in this way been freed of the physical agony of childbearing. The figure today is doubtless higher.

Few contraceptives are produced. Unwanted pregnancies occur. In the postwar years this led to a rise in illegal abortions. In 1955 the Soviet government gave up trying to fight abortion practices by a combination of education and aid to mothers married or not,

Rosalia Prusova, metallurgist, and child. The decoration is
highest Soviet honor: Hero of Socialist Labor

and reinstituted legal, hospital abortion. It is free when medically
justified, and costs $5.50 otherwise. But traditional concepts of
shame remain. *Izvestia* admits that illegal abortions are still common in the case of unmarried girls and even married women who
don't want pregnancies to become known.

In publicly owned establishments, all women—industrial workers, office employees, professionals (all professional occupations

are salaried positions in the U.S.S.R.), state-farm workers—are allowed eight weeks' prenatal and eight weeks' postnatal leave at full pay. This can be followed immediately by the annual paid vacation if the individual wants it then, and then by three months' unpaid leave if she desires. Only if she remains away from work after this does management have the right to change her job status in any manner. The paid postnatal leave is increased, on doctor's affidavit, in case of a multiple birth or abnormal delivery. Pregnant women and nursing mothers cannot be assigned to night work or overtime. Nor may they be sent on business trips after the fourth month of pregnancy. (Women number 53 per cent of all employed college-trained people, including three out of four physicians, two out of three teachers, more than half the economists and statisticians, two out of five agricultural experts and veterinarians, one-third of the lawyers and judges, and three out of ten engineers, so this is a realistic provision.)

Co-operative enterprises meet costs such as maternity leave out of their own funds. Therefore, the law does not set standards for them as high as in publicly owned establishments, for this might be too heavy a burden for weak co-ops.

There is a continuing effort to convince women to have babies, once conceived, as a matter of health. This is aided by such institutions as the round-the-clock nursery, in which mothers can place their infants for the whole week, taking them home only on week-ends and holidays. These are an inestimable boon to unmarried and widowed mothers, and those whose housing conditions are worse than the generally unsatisfactory average. Among women between twenty-five and twenty-nine, the birth rate is four times as high among those having adequate housing as among those who do not live in separate apartments, private homes, or rooms of ample size. The over-all birth rate is among the highest on earth but is dropping steadily. A Soviet study showed that the only possible practical measure to reverse that downward trend would be an even more rapid rise in housing construction than is now the case.

Infant mortality is among the lowest in the world: one in thirty-one, in 1961, and is only one-eighth of what it was in 1913. One reason for this is that the number of doctors in obstetrics and gynecology alone is larger than the entire Russian medical profession before the Revolution.

Each newborn child is registered automatically at the local consultation center, and the first visit by a nurse is the day after the mother has returned from the hospital with her baby. The center follows the child to the age of fourteen. One of its functions is to provide baby formulas and foods, and special diets for older children when needed. These consultation centers all have legal departments that provide free advice (their other services are also free). Thus, the unwed mother, the abandoned wife, the divorced woman whose husband is not paying alimony, can obtain both physical and the legal aid at a single place. In the countryside, the same services are offered at the county health centers. The latest medical advances are available to country people: 60 per cent of confinements in the cities are by painless childbirth, and 44 per cent in rural areas.

In 1963, year-round day nurseries and kindergartens could accommodate a total of 6.2 million children in the age groups from two months to six years. This represents a doubling of these facilities in five years, and provides by far the highest level of preschool care in the world. Nevertheless, these institutions can care for only one-fifth the number of children in this age group. Therefore the great majority of children continue to be looked after by their own families all day.

Admittance to day nurseries is not controlled by one's income. The fee is only 15 per cent of the cost of maintenance, including meals. It is cheaper for a child to be in a nursery than at home. But there are just not nearly enough, although rapid expansion continues. On the other hand, opposition to letting one's child out of the home during these years is still very strong.

The fullest provision of children's facilities is in the summer. Camps, children's health resorts, trail camps, and summer day-camp sites for the permanent kindergartens and nurseries care for seven million children; three million children attend seasonal rural nurseries when the demand for farm labor is at its height. For these children it is, as I have had a chance to see, a lovely life.

Camps and kindergartens—I have observed both—provide love and warmth and successfully teach co-operativeness and respect for what belongs to all, and yet leave room for robust individuality.

I remember the amazement of everyone in my party at the splendid condition of the elaborate dolls in a kindergarten we visited. It was hard to believe that they were in constant use. But there was no doubting the sincerity of the motherly staff. They told us that the children kept them that way just because they were for everyone to use: to spoil your own toy is stupid, but to spoil that which others will use is bad. And what, we asked, when a

Railroad yard traffic conductor

child does something that is bad—as surely must happen? Of course it happens, they said, but then the earliest opportunity is taken to tell a story or play a game that will illustrate the good way to do the particular thing that had been done wrong. The child is not scolded. Whether the little child ever does it again, or how many times, I do not know.

Officials and educators in the Soviet Union say that expressions of selfishness, superstition, backward traditions in family life, and a lack of interest in or contempt for manual occupations may be traced to the fact that children are still largely raised by doting parents—and particularly grandmothers.

Whether because the war-torn lives of parents and grandparents were so difficult, or for whatever other reason, there is a distinct tendency to coddle children in the family, and to protect them against physical effort. This is something the authorities try to undo in the school system, where a determined effort is made to give a type of training that will break down the widespread feeling that manual labor is beneath the dignity of a person with a high-school education. However, I spent a good deal of time talking to teenagers in Leningrad in 1962, and got no feeling that they looked down upon physical effort or manual labor, although they naturally hoped to go on to work that would use their brains.

Soviet women certainly do not think of themselves solely as

mothers. Like American women, they are "joiners," perhaps to an even greater degree. Also like women in other countries, they feel that there is a place for organizations of women alone, although they participate to a high degree in organizations open to both sexes.

As in the United States, women are particularly active in parent associations. But the last several years have seen the emergence of groups called women's councils. They are at present local bodies, although there is some demand for a national organization. These councils may come into being merely to organize a party for children, but in the course of this simple activity someone will bring up the need for a new kindergarten, and the council continues in existence to see this through with the local authorities. Meanwhile the matter of unsatisfactory service in local stores may have come up, and the council will crusade on this, since the stores are all run either by municipal authorities or co-ops. In one Ural Mountain city the size of San Francisco, there are 160 neighborhood women's councils headed by a city-wide representative body. In addition to engaging in the activities mentioned above, they act as public monitors of the health services and of hostels for young working people. They work with the local school system to organize leisure-time activity and recreation for children and adolescents, and press for the introduction of home economics courses. They give much attention to adult education. They are also active in promoting the planting of flowers and greenery throughout the city.

Three hundred women belong to a council in a huge shipyard on the Black Sea. The council keeps after both union leadership and management to make sure that women with young children and women who are studying on the side, work only on the day shift. It encourages women to improve themselves through organized study, and prides itself on the fact that 80 per cent of the women in the plant attend school at one level or another. It has also set up sewing, embroidery, and cooking classes, medical examinations, and lectures on sanitation and hygiene. It has been particularly insistent on adequate and proper shower and bathing facilities. Finally, with the characteristic interest of Soviet labor in matters of production, it sent a delegation to a similar shipyard in Leningrad, hundreds of miles away, to determine why their output per person was lower than that in shops with identical equipment. The delegation became convinced that this was because the Black Sea yard had an inefficient organization of work teams. The women's council then persuaded management to place people of

At the hairdresser's

different skills in a single team, so that a complete job could be done by that team without loss of time. In a Soviet shipyard women are not found only in office and clean-up jobs. At this particular place they do most of the painting and installation of insulation, as well as carpentry. They operate the huge cranes, and the head of the women's council is the chief of the foundry's testing laboratory and also a member of the Supreme Soviet—the parliament of the U.S.S.R.

This is not at all unusual. Fatyana Fyodorova, another member of the Supreme Soviet, is now assistant manager of the Moscow subway, which she helped to build with her own hands. The present Minister of Culture, Yekaterina Furtseva, began work at the age of fourteen in a textile factory. That a woman, Valentina Tereshkova, was one of the first half-dozen Soviet cosmonauts, should have been no surprise, for the U.S.S.R. also had the only woman regular-airline jet pilot, and the only women sea captains.

Valentina Tereshkova, Cosmonette No. 1, in training

But women still rejoice at each new "first" for their sex. Mrs. Audrey Topping, wife of *The New York Times* bureau chief in Moscow, reported in that paper, June 30, 1963:

While the world's first space woman, Valentina Tereshkova, was whirling through space, a 10-year-old Russian girl rushed over . . . with news of a new baby sister named Valentina. "All the girl babies born in the hospital except one are being called Valentina," she explained.

But while sharing the most extreme rigors of the masculine world, women have abandoned the early post-revolutionary trend to look and act masculine. Mrs. Topping adds:

Junior Lieutenant Tereshkova . . . wears her hair in the latest, most popular, short, fluffy "kitten cut." . . .
There are more than fifteen hundred small hairdressing shops in Moscow, and one large beauty parlor that can handle 350 women a day. Women are beginning to be diet-conscious. It is no longer popular to be plump, although Russians definitely prefer a sturdier build than is fashionable in the West.

11: Science

Science enjoys an extraordinary status in the Soviet Union. Nobel Prize winning physicist Glenn Seaborg, chairman of the U.S. Atomic Energy Commission, reported on returning from a visit to Russia in 1963 that he was

struck by the number of people with backgrounds in engineering or in one of the sciences who are in responsible positions *not* directly involved in the administration of scientific or technical functions. . . . Mr. L. I. Brezhnev, Chairman of the Presidium of the U.S.S.R. Supreme Soviet [i.e., chief of state] is himself a metallurgist.

Dr. Seaborg was also impressed by the fact that the very act of having earned a Ph.D. automatically entitles one to eight weeks' paid vacation per year for life.

The underlying reason for this attitude toward the sciences is that Lenin believed, with Marx, that human progress is in all respects closely related to man's conquest over the forces of nature. It was a natural consequence that government should assist science in every way possible.

In 1918, when the Germans were as deep into Russia as they were again under Hitler in 1942, Lenin had the confidence and vision to lay down a "Draft of a Plan for Scientific and Technical Work." One hundred and seventeen new scientific institutions were founded in 1918–1920, while the Civil War and foreign invasions were being fought. These were years when water had to be carried into laboratories by hand because piping in the unheated rooms had cracked. Solutions froze and crystallized. Members of the Academy of Sciences shared their short rations with the animals they used in experiments. Even under these conditions, the government provided money not only for work of immediate practical value, but grants to publish complete editions of classic writings.

As soon as the fighting ended, top scientists were sent abroad to purchase equipment which Russia was then unable to produce. Young researchers were sent to study in Europe as early as 1923. There was great boldness in advancing young men. Nikolai Semyonoff, who later became the first Soviet winner of a Nobel Prize, was put in charge of a laboratory at twenty-four. Boys of nineteen and twenty were given the chance to do original research from their sophomore years in college. When Semyonoff was told to set up a laboratory in 1920, *he* comprised its entire scientific staff. But only eleven years later, when he established the Institute of Physical Chemistry, he had a staff of *fifty* well-trained men. He writes:*

The twenties, the formative years of Soviet science, were wonderful and truly romantic. They saw young people from all segments of society streaming into science with an enthusiasm that baffles description and with comparable mental and physical endurance, which made for rapid progress in their creative endeavors. Pouring into colleges and universities were young people who until then could not have dreamed of getting an education. They were young factory workers, peasants, apprentices, shepherds, and young soldiers.

This was exactly the make-up of my own class at Moscow University in 1932, when I spent a year in the U.S.S.R.

The outside world was not unaware of Soviet science even in those days. The Arctic then was almost as mysterious and forbidding to most men as outer space is today. The Russians were the first to invest heavily in mastering the Arctic, convinced that it could meet their need for a navigable northern seaway, and for minerals and fish.

In 1928, front pages throughout the world carried the story that a Soviet icebreaker, the *Krassin,* found members of an Italian dirigible expedition that had crashed on the return trip of a flight from Spitsbergen to the North Pole and back. More amazing for its day was the depositing of four researchers at the North Pole by

* *Soviet Weekly,* April 21, 1960.

Woman physicist at control panel of proton synchrotron

four 4-engined aircraft in 1937, with supplies and equipment for a year on the ice, and their rescue as the floe was about to break up many months later, far to the south.

It was in 1934 that Professor Semyonoff published his first volume of research into chain reactions that later won him the Nobel Prize. Also in 1934, the Academy of Sciences was given the job of co-ordinating the development of Soviet science. Thus, the U.S.S.R. pioneered by perhaps a decade in introducing the principle of unified planning into science.

Before the Revolution, Russian science had produced men of genius: the chemist Mendeleyev, the physiologist Pavlov, Tsiolkovsky of rocket fame, but these were isolated giants. By 1940, there were ten times as many scientists as in 1914.

World War II compelled the evacuation of many institutions from the main centers of science, besieged Leningrad and frontline Moscow. It stalled progress in many fields, while attention was centered on those of immediate importance to the war effort.

Science was not exempt from the dead hand of Stalinist conformity during and after the war. Einstein's relativity theory, Linus Pauling's resonance theory of chemical structure, the classical biology of Virchow, the genetics of Mendel, and, later, Norbert Wiener's cybernetics (the basis of modern computer-controlled processes) were all officially described as philosophical heresies. Dissent in science and scholarship actually cost the lives of numerous Soviet historians, educators, plant geneticists, and even Orientalogists. Physicists and chemists, however, simply went on applying and developing modern science by avoiding the forbidden labels for the theories by which they really operated.

Yet Stalin was fundamentally convinced that science is the foundation of modern progress and continued to provide funds lavishly for education, equipment, and research. Moscow University's magnificent new science buildings were erected in his lifetime. At his death, there were thousands of people trained and working in physics in the one city of Leningrad alone; in 1917 there had been only twenty. The education, funds, facilities, and encouragement created an atmosphere in which fundamental discoveries were made. In 1950, for example, Tamm and Sakharov put forward the idea that thermonuclear reactions, which produce heat no material can withstand, can be controlled by confining them within magnetic fields. All thermonuclear research throughout the world is conducted on that principle at present.

Every known field of science, theoretical and applied, is pursued in the Soviet Union. In 1962, the Academy of Sciences had 4,300 projects under way. The invention of surgical staplers to suture blood vessels instantaneously makes it possible to remove an entire lung in twelve minutes under local anesthesia, with the patient awake and breathing. It formerly took two hours and deep anesthesia. More experimental, but already in use in a New York hospital, is a Soviet sleep machine that crowds a full night's sleep into two hours, and is used to help treat emotional disturbances. At the other extreme from these practical developments is the research of a geographer who believes that Nicholas of Lynne, an English Carmelite friar, sighted the New World 130 years before Columbus. There is a linguist whose painstaking and brilliant work led him to decipher the ancient writing of the Mayas. An anthropologist has devoted his lifetime to doing two hundred portrait sculptures of ancient man from skulls, based on the difference in the degree of development of soft facial tissue depending on bone structure.

Vladimir Wechsler, head of Institute of Nuclear Problems,
sees first photos of new nuclear particle

The first Soviet scientist to do research at an American university was Dr. George Debetz, who arrived in 1957 to study a
collection of Eskimo skeletons. The next man came to the United
States under the exchange agreement to pursue his study of fungi.
Soviet graduate students at the University of California have included people writing theses on Jack London and Mark Twain as
well as men interested in gas pipeline engineering.

Today, most of the world's scientific achievements are recognized and their creators credited and honored in Soviet writings
(Mendel in genetics and Freud in psychology are exceptions). The
"philosophers" who denounced Einstein, Pauling, and Wiener are
told that they'd better learn something about science and examine
the reasons for the failure of their own philosophizing to leave
room for such discoveries. Scientific controversies rage, and in
most cases the politicians keep hands off. In 1962, some prominent
people asked the Central Committee of the Communist Party to

intervene on behalf of a man who claimed he had a cure for cancer, whom the recognized leaders of medicine regarded as a quack. The Committee issued a public reply saying that it was not competent to resolve such a question, that attempts to do so in the past had had harmful results, and that any action was up to the people who did know what it was all about.

But this approach is not applied to Mendel and Freud. Biology editors are still removed when they open the doors to Mendelian ideas, and in 1959 I was unable to find Freud in the card catalogue of the Soviet Union's largest library! The reasons are basically two: (1) no way has yet been found to explain their theories in terms of the dialectical materialist philosophy of Marx and Engels, and (2) the practical results of their work are regarded as being not adequate to prove their theories beyond question. A third reason is political: many of Stalin's followers are in the sciences and some of his ideas hang on. The process of overcoming them is still under way.

But rulings have been adopted that have made it possible to cleanse science of some of those who got ahead at a time when political connections, fraud, and the willingness to use rumor against a competitor were important in scholarly advancement. It is now possible to strip a man of his master's or doctor's degree if he is found to have achieved it by "borrowing" little-known work done by others.

On the other hand, favorable publicity is heaped upon individuals like the young geologist in Siberia who, with the aid of the newspaper *Izvestia,* bucked his superiors and twice fought his case clear up to Moscow to prove that territory scheduled to be flooded by a dam contained immense deposits of rare ores.

Some Soviet meteorologists believe that the Arctic can be "unfrozen" by damming Bering Strait between Alaska and Siberia. Others think the effect would be the very opposite. Both sets of views are published, and the issue will doubtless be resolved by a combination of improved knowledge, small-scale experimentation, and joint work with American scientists.

The most far-out ideas are published and discussed if there is competent training and evidence of any kind to support them. There are Soviet scientists who think that mental telepathy exists, others who believe that there *is* an Abominable Snowman; still others are convinced that the enormous explosion in Siberia early in this century was caused by the destruction of a nuclear-propelled space ship from a more advanced civilization. One man believes that the Biblical story of the destruction of Sodom and Gomorrah describes a nuclear attack by intelligent beings from outer space, so closely does it correspond to known information on atomic explosions. He thinks enormous parallel-inclined hewn rocks still in place not far away, so heavy that there is no explanation for how they were transported, were a launching track for the ship's take-off from this planet. On the other hand, in 1959 Nobel Prize-winner Igor Tamm, and nuclear physicists Kapitza and Artsimovich, verbally flayed an astronomer who claimed that time was a source of energy. His knowledge of physics, they said, did not extend beyond what was known at the end of the last century.

Freedom for the imagination to range where it will has not hampered disciplined accomplishment. This is demonstrated above all by Soviet pioneering in space flight. The space age was opened in 1957 by Sputnik I, orbiting the earth. The next step was to put life into orbit. This was done a month later in the second sputnik, which carried a dog that survived a week, a trip made possible only through studies in many fields of biology and the solution of technical problems with no precedent: atmosphere maintenance, feeding, damping of take-off shock, and the like.

The moon-hit by Lunik II in 1959 represented progress in entirely different fields. It required calculation of the trajectory to another heavenly body moving in space at a different speed and in a different direction than the earth, which rotates meanwhile on its own axis. Also necessary was the highly accurate aiming of a vehicle along that path, and its propulsion with precisely the force and accuracy needed to put it onto that course without overshooting or undershooting.

A new chapter in the practical application of electronics and remote control was opened later in 1959 when Lunik III circled the moon, aimed a camera at its unseen side, and televised the pictures back to earth on order.

In 1961 Yuri Gagarin became the first human being to orbit the earth, and Gherman Titov stayed up for a day. The next year Nikolayev and Popovich made the four-day flight on which they maneuvered to within four miles of each other. An American scientist calculated that this paired flight required the control force on the ground to measure immediately the unavoidable slight difference between the planned and actual orbit time of the first capsule. They then had to recompute completely all the fantastic calculations for the second capsule, and have the count-down for the second cosmonaut under such flawless control that his vehicle would take the air exactly 23 hours 32 minutes after the first. At eighteen thousand miles per hour, an error of one minute would have put the men three hundred miles apart, not four.

The second two-capsule flight, involving a record eighty-two orbits by Valery Bykovsky and a three-day flight by the first woman in space, Valentina Tereshkova, took place in June, 1963. They maneuvered to within three miles of each other.

Kenneth Gatland, Vice-President of the British Interplanetary Society, commented:

In many ways a woman may be more suited to isolation and to the meticulous scientific tasks which will be required in the future scientific outposts in space for orbital laboratories and exploratory posts which certainly will be established on the moon during the seventies.*

That women cosmonauts are part of the long-range Soviet plan became clear when, in answer to a foreign newspaperman's question as to whether she would continue to take part in space exploration if she had a family and children, Miss Tereshkova replied that "many of the women cosmonauts were married." Her back-up pilot was also a woman.

The fact that Miss Tereshkova had been a sport parachutist only, and not a flier, drew attention to the fact that the Soviet male cosmonauts, although pilots, were far less experienced than their American counterparts, all of whom were required to be test pilots. An analysis in *The New York Times* offered the following explanations:†

One is that the Russians have more confidence in their automatic equipment than United States space experts have in theirs. . . . The Soviet Vostoks are so large that it is possible to put in all kinds of back-up equipment that can be turned on if any part of the main system breaks down. . . . Two or three of the four Mercury orbital missions would have had to be terminated prematurely had there not been really skilled pilots on board.

The Soviet flights were all in cabins large enough to permit free movement, and Bykovsky floated free for one and a half hours in each twenty-four. Air-tightness, air purification, and temperature control were such that the spacemen were able to orbit with their visors open, the space suits being merely an emergency precaution. Their five-ton ships were capable of coming to earth undamaged on dry land, and they themselves were able to leave them without

* *The New York Times,* June 6, 1963.
† *Ibid.,* June 19, 1963.

Spacemen 1 and 2: Gagarin (one orbit) on right;
Titov (twenty-four hours) on left

assistance. This was a further step toward landing on the moon, where neither water to cushion the shock nor human assistance in emerging would be available.

Human space flight is clearly something that cannot be achieved by countries in which science has achieved nothing more than, say, the development of powerful rockets. Engineering and technology must be highly sophisticated. Industry must be able to produce the fuels safely, in quantity, and to unvarying standards. It must be able to manufacture the extraordinary metal alloys and the heat-resistant ceramics to withstand fantastic frictional temperatures.

Workmanship must be flawless, or the rocket won't take off, its timing will be off, its course won't be accurate, it will leak air, its life-support systems will fail, its radio and television contact will be lost, it will burn on reentry, it will land in the wrong place, or it will crash on landing. Astronomy, mathematics, geodesy, the force of terrestrial magnetism, computer design, physiology—the list could be extended to eighty sciences in which there must be no serious weak spots if men are to leave the atmosphere and come back alive and in good health. The United States and the Soviet Union are thus far the only two countries in which these conditions, plus economies powerful enough to meet the financial burden, exist.

However, there are certain fundamental differences between science in the U.S.S.R. and in the West. One difference was illustrated by a special conference of the Soviet Academy of Sciences in 1959 on the value of science in the practical experience of factory workers. A machinist was given the floor. He had increased the rate of revolution of his machine to increase its output. When he could no longer safely raise the r.p.m., he increased the distance the cutting tool travels along the work per revolution. Metals theory said this was virtually impossible, because the surface produced would be uneven. He tried hundreds of tool-edge shapes, and found one that permitted a tenfold increase in "feed," with smooth finish. The scientists had to revise their theory.

The U.S.S.R. provides a partnership between practical work and science. The machinist couldn't explain why his cutter worked: it was up to the scientists to discover the principle involved, which could then be applied generally. They, in turn, would not have believed that theory required improvement if not for the doggedness of the machinist. The Academy brought them together.

The importance of science in the Soviet scheme of things is indicated by the fact that the head of the Government Committee for the Co-ordination of Scientific Research is automatically a Vice-Premier, making him a member of the inner Cabinet. The head of the Academy of Sciences has been elected to the Central Committee of the Communist Party. As a result, when general changes in government organization occur, the organizational structure of science must necessarily be modified accordingly.

In 1963, the U.S.S.R. Academy of Sciences was given the right to co-ordinate the activities of the academies of the fifteen republics, and to assign specialization to particular research institutes and agencies throughout the Soviet Union. In addition, a central management body now exists for the research needed for each branch of industry, to avoid overlapping in the research and development efforts in applied science. The Academy is responsible for long-term research undertakings, the search for new principles, and for recommending practical applications of discoveries. It has its own immense network of institutes and facilities, with a virtually independent branch outside Novosibirsk, Siberia, built from the ground up since 1957, in virgin forest. In 1963 this branch had

1,627 scientists in twenty institutes erected in the six years. In addition, Novosibirsk University was founded, for training personnel for these institutes. The Novosibirsk "science city" experiment is regarded as so successful that two or three more centers of comparable size are to be built.

Everyone knows that recent discoveries of science may, if misused, destroy most of mankind. But few realize that the advance of science has also brought governments closer together. In 1959, the United States, the U.S.S.R., and ten other nations signed a Treaty on Antarctica that could well serve as a blueprint for world peace. They agreed that the continent shall be used for peaceful purposes only. No military measures may be taken and no weapons tested. Specifically, there must be no nuclear explosions of any nature and no dumping of radioactive wastes. Each nation has unlimited access to all ships, aircraft, stations, and equipment of all the others at any and all times.

This treaty has worked. American and Soviet scientists are permanently stationed at each other's camps and function as part of them. Aircraft land freely at each other's fields and are assisted on their way. Will the permanently inhabited continents someday live under a similar arrangement? Or, as a next step, could human exploration of the moon and the planets be such a joint effort of all mankind?

Scientists already do co-operate in fields outside the realm of the military to a remarkable degree. In 1962 the world's cancer experts, six thousand of them, met in the Kremlin; the world's sociologists met in Washington, D.C., and Soviet scholarly journals indicate that the Russians learned a great deal from practical American research techniques. Every year, major American and Soviet scientists meet at unofficial conferences, with the knowledge and encouragement of their governments, to discuss the broadest questions of human existence, including world peace. Perhaps it is significant that one such meeting took place in the United States during the very week of the Cuban crisis of October, 1962.

The United States and the Soviet Union today exchange scientific delegations in about half a dozen fields of atomic energy, according to Dr. Glenn Seaborg. Consequently, much that was formerly held secret is now being made mutually available. He said, after his official visit in May, 1963:

We were the first Western delegation since World War II to visit the Radium Institute in Leningrad, and the first to visit the Soviet reactor testing station near Ulyanovsk as well as the site of the seventy-billion-electron-volt accelerator at Serpukhov.

Since 1962, the two countries have co-operated in three peaceful uses of space: satellite weather observations, studies of the earth's magnetic field, and worldwide communications through the use of satellites. In 1962 and 1963 the U.S. Echo A-12 satellite was used in experiments on communications between the two countries. The two nations are agreed to conduct co-ordinated launchings of a system of operational weather satellites in 1964–1965. Schedules, numbers, orbits, and similarity of sensors and data to be obtained are discussed together, indicating how practical and advanced this co-operation has become. The information obtained will go to both World Weather centers, at Moscow and Washington. A similarly detailed program has been worked out for two additional satellites, one American and one Soviet, to gather information on the earth's magnetic field.

12:   Culture—Not by Bread Alone

Civilizations are remembered by their material achievements, their social organization, and the work of their uncommon men. But uncommon men have always been a source of irritation to the very civilizations they symbolized and stimulated. Socrates was made to drink the hemlock, Galileo to recant. In the United States, Thoreau and, more recently, the Hollywood Ten screenwriters went to jail; Arthur Miller and Pete Seeger went through indictment, trial, and appeals; Linus Pauling was hounded by the Senate Internal Security subcommittee; Paul Robeson was blacklisted.

It is the nature of uncommon men to gallop ahead, and it is the nature of governments to keep the whole nation pulling together as a team. The more reserve strength a government feels it possesses, the easier its hand on the reins in most cases, and the sooner it quits trying to harness the unbreakable horse.

So too in Russia. Every great writer of the nineteenth century —Pushkin, Dostoevski, Gogol, Lermontov, Turgenev, Tolstoi— was the victim of government repression at one time or another, of which censorship or suppression of their works was only the mildest form. The Soviet regime has traveled a path from great early freedom in the arts, through the murder of numerous writers and other creative artists under Stalin, to censorship and public criticism of Pasternak, Shostakovich, Ehrenburg, and Yevtushenko.

The founding leaders of the Soviet government were mostly intellectuals. Many were men of culture, and one of their purposes was to bring it to the people. In their view, all art represents ideas, even if only such broad concepts as optimism and pessimism, participation and escapism. As a consequence, they urged from the very outset that the arts be understandable to the people and that they help unite the people for the enormous undertaking of building an unprecedented way of life in an unbelievably backward land.

At the outset there was freedom in the arts except when direct political attacks were made upon the struggling new system. It was expected that the artists would themselves seek, and find, forms of expression that would communicate to the people at large in a people's revolution. The first art to do so was poetry. In a time of great emotion, when people were trying to speak with each other as never before, but were still largely illiterate, this was predictable. A vigorous young giant, Vladimir Mayakovsky, developed a new meter, new words, and shouted his challenging poems of patriotism, uprising, and satire of bureaucracy, to vast audiences. He was also a talented artist, and did strong posters in bold colors to go with his verses on the topics of the day. They were printed together and posted on street corners throughout the country. Mayakovsky was not the only significant poet. Alexander Blok, Demyan Byedny, and Sergei Yesenin, each with his own style, had a terrific impact.

For the first fifteen years there were painters and sculptors who did wholly abstract work, musicians who strove to imitate the noise of a foundry and who deliberately suppressed anything in their own work reminiscent of melody. But the people at large did not respond to this. Having been admitted to the ballet, the common people recognized the fairy tales, appreciated the fantasy, discovered and marveled at the grace and strength. They loved music with tunes they could remember. Modern architecture seemed cold to that generation: they craved structures with the opulence they envied in the landlord's house on the hill.

Other than poetry, posters, and cartoons, the first ten years after the Revolution produced little of lasting value. Later it appeared that this had been a period of gestation, for suddenly moviemakers, novelists, short-story writers, theatrical companies, and composers began to do work that has survived for thirty years. Some institutions, such as the Moscow Art Theatre, were not new to the scene, but had taken a decade to adapt to the new society.

The motion picture had been encouraged by Lenin from the outset, for he realized its tremendous potential in reaching the people. In 1925 Eisenstein produced *Potemkin,* and the motion picture became an art. For a dozen years afterward, an amazing series of films came from studios in several different cities, and won the Soviet Union a place of leadership in that art for that period. In a dozen different major story lines, they had a single theme—the people in motion.

Writers continued in the straightforward Russian realist tradition. Older men, even Maxim Gorky, who was an active revolutionist and aided greatly in the organization of publishing and assistance to new young writers, apparently did not find themselves capable of writing on postrevolutionary subject matter. They continued to work on themes from the period of their young manhood. But there are a number of fine novels and short stories translated into English that help us understand Russian history and the people of the generation from the Revolution to World War II. Among the best novels are Ostrovsky's *The Making of a Hero,* Sholokhov's *Silent Don,* and Alexei Tolstoi's *The Road to Calvary,* on the revolution and civil war; Gladkov's *Cement,* Katayev's *The Embezzlers* and Zoshchenko's uproarious short stories, set in the years of reconstruction and the New Economic Policy; the several novels of Leonov; Pilnyak's *The Volga Falls to the Caspian Sea;* Sholokhov's *Seeds of Tomorrow;* Ehrenburg's *Out of Chaos;* and Ilf and Petrov's *Twelve Chairs* and *Little Golden Calf* for the years of the first Five-Year Plans and collectivization. This last pair gives us a biting look at the United States in *Little Golden America,* which they visited in a cross-country tour. Other worthwhile authors to look for in English are Furmanov, Serafimovich, Fadeyev, Fedin, and Pavlenko.

But in the mid-thirties Stalin, who had been in power through all this renaissance, brought his fist down on political dissenters and free souls in the arts alike. His cultural spokesmen said: if a worker has to turn out a fixed quota per day, why should a writer escape the responsibility of contributing his skill? The result was a school of the arts that ultimately became an appalling deification of Stalin as an individual.

In Stalin's day, the penalty for dissent was a blackout of one's work, Siberia, or death. The greater the name, the more severe the penalty. As the young poet Yevtushenko puts it in *A Precocious Autobiography,* the best of all books on the U.S.S.R.:*

Remarkable Russian poets like Zabolotsky and Smeliakov vegetated in the Stalinist concentration camps. Young Mandel (who wrote under the name Korzhavin) was also exiled. I do not know whether his name will hold a position of greatness in Russian poetry, but I am certain that it will be written in letters of gold in the history of Soviet political thought. For he was the only poet who, in Stalin's lifetime, wrote and read poems against Stalin. His courage did actually serve, in a way, to save him, for he was regarded as insane. But he was exiled nonetheless.

But the fact that everything ultimately hinged on the decision of a single man, Stalin, meant that his taste could spare as it could condemn. So Sholokhov and Ehrenburg survived. For a period, the latter was carried on *Izvestia*'s payroll despite the fact that that paper would publish nothing he wrote.

The creative arts withered during the last decade of Stalin's life. The sole exception was music, which does not voice ideas directly except in vocal expressions and therefore cannot easily be held to account. Nevertheless, the politicians interfered here as well. As for literature, the situation is described as follows in Yevtushenko's autobiography, which has been published in English:

In the famous Stalin Constitution (adopted in 1935) we find these marvelous words: "In our country work is a matter of honor, of courage and of heroism." In practice, work was set up as something superior to man. It was deified, and every citizen had to make daily offerings to it. Artists were also obliged to make sacrifices to that abstract god, "work," and to reduce the spiritual life of the nation to the level of a description of the different aspects of "work."

Thus steel became the hero of many a novel. Others were devoted to building a house or planting wheat. Living beings played a secondary role in these works. They weren't alive, anyway: they were accessories serving to enhance the importance of work. The poets traveled from one end of the country to the other to see new construction projects or to admire the latest machines. The people who operated these machines hardly interested them. Ah! If machines could read! How they would appreciate the poems of that period! Unfortunately, to human beings they are of no interest.

But while the creative arts suffered, the splendid provisions made for bringing the arts to the people and for giving them the opportunity to develop their talents as performers bore rich fruit.

* *L'Exprès,* Paris, March 7, 1963.

The Red Army Chorus became world-famous before World War II. The violinist Oistrakh, the pianist Gilels, and a dozen other first-rate instrumentalists emerged in the 1930's, and were constantly pushed by an endless stream of brilliant newcomers. The most virile of ballet stars, Vakhtang Chabukiani, and the peerless Galina Ulanova, raised the Bolshoi Ballet to unprecedented heights. Moiseyev took seriously the injunction to refresh the arts at their roots among the people, left his position with the Bolshoi, and established his unsurpassed folk-dance troupe in Moscow in 1937. More Shakespeare was on the boards in Moscow than in London, more Lope de Vega than in Spain; Schiller was as well-known to the playgoing and reading Russian as to the German.

The war produced magnificent journalism, particularly Ehrenburg's. Among serious prose writers who continue to be significant today were Konstantin Simonov, Konstantin Paustovsky, and two who have emerged as leaders of the "second renaissance" which began in 1956, Nagibin and Nekrasov.

Within a year of Stalin's death in 1953, Ehrenburg wrote a novel, *The Thaw,* that revealed some of the truths of the dictator's rule two years before Khrushchev's revelations. In the novel he attacked "official" artists, mentioned anti-Semitism, and even allowed one of his heroes to have a love affair with a married woman. This would have been impossible under the moralizing role Stalin assigned to the arts.

As in every other field of Soviet life, the decade since 1953 was a battle between liberals and conservatives. In this struggle the weapons were words and, at times, censorship, but never jail or execution. Bold editors have lost jobs and regained them. Within the decade there were ups and downs. The first peak of freedom came in 1956. Because Budapest writers and their club played a major part that year in the bloody rebellion against a Stalinist government in Hungary, the Soviet leaders were fearful that Russian writers would demand political reforms more urgently than the politicians thought they could be granted. Therefore, the politicians silenced critics within the U.S.S.R. Pasternak was attacked bitterly for having his novel *Dr. Zhivago* published abroad because he could not have it published in the Soviet Union. In 1963, Yevtushenko had his autobiography published in France and was censured for it.

That these years showed a striking net gain for freedom emerges clearly from an interview given by Alexander Tvardovsky, poet and editor, to the United Press, two months *after* Mr. Khrushchev's "cultural crackdown" speech of March 8, 1963. Mr.

Ilya Ehrenburg, writer (cigar in hand), critic of Stalin
but himself attacked by Khrushchev, still speaks
out for "ideological coexistence"

Tvardovsky's magazine had published the "rebel" poets and authors when other editors would not. He is a member of the Central
Committee of the Communist Party, and this interview was published in full in its mass-circulation daily, *Pravda,* on May 12. In
it he dutifully supported the Khrushchev criticism of Mr. Ehrenburg's memoirs, and administered a slap on the wrist to that
writer and the young poets Yevtushenko and Voznesensky. But at
the same time he restated, from his position of literary and political authority, support for a list of writers whose attacks on aspects
of Soviet life have been searing and powerful and could not possibly have been published prior to the Khrushchev "de-Staliniza-
tion" speech of 1956.

In this interview, Tvardovsky praised such men as Vladimir
Tendryakov, whose stories have described inhuman rigidity in
regulations (a man dies because it is illegal for a farming executive
to assign a tractor to take him to the hospital). Another author

he mentioned with approval was Yuri Bondarev, whose novel *Silence* caused a furious debate when published in 1962. It exposed the atmosphere of terror, friendlessness, and helplessness of the purge year of 1937.

It was particularly encouraging to find Tvardovsky referring in positive terms to "Alexander Yashin, writer of many books of poems, and author of an excellent sketch, 'Wedding in Vologda.' " Yashin wrote that his very large native village "has no electricity, no radio, no club. In two years there has been no movie show." The village is cut off in the spring, the fall, and in heavy snows. The collective farm was doing so badly that its members were paid nothing the previous year. In an earlier story, he had contrasted the realistic concern of Communist Party members as individuals for the actual state of things, with Party meetings, where they sounded like puppets reciting a ritual.

Yashin was attacked on the grounds that he was negative and pessimistic. Tvardovsky supports him in the belief that if bad situations are to be improved, their existence must be recognized. Finally, Tvardovsky repeats his support for the book by Solzhenitsyn, *One Day in the Life of Ivan Denisovich,* with its crushing and unanswerable description of the complete rottenness and all-consuming injustice of the concentration camps. When that book was written, in 1959, the situation had improved to the point that the author could submit it for publication without fearing that he would be sent back to a concentration camp like that in which he himself had spent eight years. But it was in 1962 that the book was published, and then only because Khrushchev approved.

Because the critical speech by Khrushchev had led to fears that future publication by some of the individuals attacked would be barred, Tvardovsky closed by listing the names of persons his magazine would publish in 1963. These included, in addition to Tendryakov, whom we have mentioned, V. Nekrasov, who had been hauled over the coals for the evenhandedness with which he described the United States after a visit, and V. Aksenov, who had written a novel about the purposelessness and degeneracy of Moscow's "gilded youth": certain of the children of high-placed officials, scientists, and others. Aksenov and Yevtushenko continue to hold their posts as members of the editorial board of *Yunost* (Youth). This is the magazine which, with *Novy Mir,* has published most of the new literature of significance.

The best-known of the new writers is, of course, Yevgeni Yevtushenko, who has become internationally famous because he so often writes on touchy subjects. This doubtless is part of the explanation for his popularity in the U.S.S.R. as well, where he has had ten volumes of poems published, including two within a few weeks of each other early in 1963. They were printed in first editions of 100,000 each, which is fifty or a hundred times as large as the customary printings of books of poetry in English-speaking countries. Crowds of up to fourteen thousand have come to hear him at the statue of Mayakovsky in Moscow on the annual Poetry Day celebrated there. But other poets of his generation (he was thirty-one in 1964) are thought of more highly for their craft: Vladimir Berestov and Andrei Voznesensky, particularly. Several men five or ten years older, who experienced the war, are revered in Russia: Leonid Martynov, Viktor Nekrasov, and Boris Slutsky. They tend to write about "little" people and simple experience. In the winter of 1962–1963 the young poets filled Moscow's eleven-thousand-seat Sports Palace five times for readings of their recent works.

Volumes of translations of the poems of Yevtushenko and Voznesensky have been published in the United States. Recent prose writing may be found in *The Year of Protest, 1956,* an anthology assembled by McLean and Vickery; *Stories From Modern Russia,* edited by C. P. Snow and Pamela Johnson; the second volume of Sholokhov's "established" farm novel; the second volume of Ehrenburg's *The Thaw* (both appear together in English as *A Change of Season*); Simonov's novel of the first terrible months of Hitler's attack on Russia, *The Living and the Dead;* Ehrenburg's memoirs, *People and Life;* Fyodor Abramov's *A Day in the 'New Life';* Valery Tarsis, *The Bluebottle;* Alexander Yesenin-Volpin's poems and essays, *Leaf of Spring;* Dudintsev's *Not by Bread Alone;* Nekrasov's *Kyra Georgievna;* Boris Pasternak's *Dr. Zhivago,* some of his poetry, and an autobiography; and the Solzhenitsyn novel and Yevtushenko autobiography. Except for the Sholokhov novel and the Snow-Johnson anthology, these represent the Soviet writings most critical of things as they are in the U.S.S.R.

MOTION PICTURES

Motion pictures offer an art form in which we have been allowed a fuller glimpse of modern Soviet creativity, both in films with English subtitles, offered under the cultural exchange program between governments, and those that reach only art-film houses in the United States. *Ballad of a Soldier, A Summer to Remember, Peace to the Newcomer, The Cranes Are Flying, The House I*

Fourteen thousand people pack arena to hear readings by young poets

Gregory Chukhrai, director of *Ballad of a Soldier* and *Clear Skies*

Live in, Clear Skies, The Childhood of Ivan, Nine Days, Violin and Roller, and *Grown-up Children* have only one thing unmistakably in common: humanism. Five of these are set during the war, and not one suggests that Russians are better than anyone else, or that any particular nationality (German or American, for example) is worse than Russian.

Clear Skies was made by the same director, Gregory Chukhrai, who did *Ballad of a Soldier,* which was the best-liked of all recent Russian films in the United States. In *Clear Skies* we see the first attempt to deal in the motion-picture medium with what the atmosphere of the postwar years under Stalin, and then his death, meant to Russians. He shows some of the tragedy of that era through the lives of four or five characters. In its characterization of people the picture is convincing and winning. But it also attempts the exceedingly difficult job of trying to show the relationship between private lives and the formal organization of society. Here *Clear Skies* runs up against a Soviet reality that people with faith in democracy cannot accept: it presents membership in the Communist Party of the U.S.S.R. as a one-way street, a manifestation of devotion and support, but not a right of decision.

The Russians make wonderful films from classic literature, whether it be foreign (Cervantes' *Don Quixote*) or native (Dostoevski's *The Idiot*). They are equally good at putting ballet on the movie screen in a manner that takes full advantage of the film medium. The Prokofiev version of *Romeo and Juliet* is a rare combination of mime acting, dancing, music, and cinema art. They produce splendid documentaries—of science, war, or the daily activities of man—and singularly dull and pompous newsreels.

As in literature, the movie field reveals a widening of the area of freedom, but it is not unrestricted by any means. *Clear Skies,* which supports the dignity of the individual against an impersonal machine, was acceptable. But a film called *We Are Twenty Years Old,* which suggests that the youth of today have to find answers to a new set of problems to which their fathers and grandfathers can offer no set solutions, called down Mr. Khrushchev's wrathful criticism. Three months after his speech, however, a film studio in Kishinev which had produced two "new wave" films was still so determined to go ahead with its experiments in style that the leaders of the fifty-four Communist Party members in the studio refused to present the official position "in fear that they might be taken for dogmatists or be accused of backwardness and conservatism." *

On the international scene, the first joint American-Soviet movie production got under way in 1963 with preliminary work on the filming of *Meeting at a Far Meridian,* with actors, directors, and cameramen of both nationalities working together on location in both countries. "This is a real breakthrough in making motion pictures," was the view of the American producer, Lester Cowan. "We think 300 million will see the picture, and all will see Russians and Americans working together, not one making negative statements about the other." The story is of the professional and personal rivalries of an American and a Soviet scientist working on cosmic rays.

THEATRE

In *The Hospital Ward,* produced in the 1962–1963 season, playwright Samuel Alyoshin has a teacher say: "Now thank God I can think for myself. I understand now that a leader who wants me to obey without thinking is a tyrant."

But Anatoli Sofronov's drama, *Take Care of Your Living Sons,*

* *The New York Times,* June 6, 1963, quoting newspaper *Sovietskaya Moldavia.*

has the following as its very first lines: "Enough of speaking of tragedy. I am fed up with it. Cult of personality, cult of personality! Can't you find another subject?"

Clearly, the theatre does not dodge the most disturbing of issues for Soviet people. Theatre, like literature and the film, is an art of explicit meaning—or can be. In the theatre, Stalinism took the fantastic form of a theory of no conflicts. This reasoning ran: if everyone in Soviet society is good because there is no enemy class any longer, how can there be conflict? The result was preaching and, in the postwar years, empty houses. Even when greater freedom was permitted, the world-wide prestige of the Moscow Art Theatre tended for a while to overawe younger groups that were seeking new directions.

In the 1960's, Soviet directors and actors began to develop new styles of staging and presentation that had gained the support of their audiences. Even plays from ancient Greece, such as *Medea,* have been given an interpretation that, without changing a line, causes Russians to look into their own lives under Stalin. In general, new plays of merit are still few, and acting is still of a heavy style favored twenty years ago. However, the overrich naturalism of stage settings has been challenged by new directors and, with simpler backgrounds, less distracting to the audience, its attention has been returned to the human beings on the stage. As Brooks Atkinson writes: *

> By temperament Russians are superb actors. They have great physical and emotional power, and they dare to act on a big scale. They are also enormously cultivated. To them the theatre is not show business but an art, and they have the virtuosity to take it on that level.

Nikolai Pogodin, peasant-born playwright who died in 1962, was perhaps the best of the Stalin era. He had the ability to make plays on timely themes come alive. This was true of *Tempo* (1930) on the first Five-Year Plan; *The Aristocrats* (1935) on the rehabilitation of criminals on a canal-building project; a trilogy on Lenin; or on the virgin soil in a play dealing with young people who went out to pioneer (1956). The last of these was removed from the boards when a high official complained about it, but the playwright insisted that the producer could have refused to cancel it: he was no longer living under Stalin. Another older playwright is Ukrainian Alexander Korneichuk, best known for a wartime

* *The New York Times,* February 20, 1963.

play, *The Front,* assailing generals who sought to fight World War
II with the strategy and tactics of an earlier generation.

Live professional theatre exists everywhere in the U.S.S.R. (there
are 513 permanent repertory companies with an annual audience
of 80 million), and the writer is expected not only to entertain but
to have something of significance to say. He has the satisfaction of
knowing that his efforts, if they are meaningful, will be regarded
as more than merely an evening's entertainment. In a speech to
the Ukrainian Communist Party, Premier Khrushchev said:

Some collective-farm chairmen do not relish the image of Som, the
farm chairman portrayed in Korneichuk's *On the Banks of the
Dnieper.* Several have even written me to that effect. And there is no
denying that Som is a negative character. But tell me this, Comrade
Chairmen, do we or do we not have a few Soms among us? [*shouts
of "We have 'em" from the audience*]. . . . Therefore, Comrade
Chairmen, rather than bear a grudge against the author, get rid of
the Soms.

Not every playwright has the luck to have a good word said for
him by someone in that position. And so when satire is produced,
there are those who complain that the playwright had them in
mind as targets, and lower-rank officials bring pressure on local
theatres to take such plays off the boards. But nowadays the playwright fights back in the public press, and matters are eventually
settled on their merits. When Sergei Mikhalkov wrote a comedy,
A Monument to Myself, a local bureaucrat was sure that it was
aimed at him personally, and wrote the following complaint: "I
hereby inform you that I am not now and never have been a
parasite, a loafer, or a buffoon." The play had been produced
widely, and in some places such reactions caused it to be canceled.
But Mikhalkov wrote an article that was published in *Kommunist,*
the theoretical organ of the Party, a magazine with enormous
weight:*

Satire might be compared to drugs of such potency as the antibiotics. We all know, of course, that excessive use of antibiotics may
produce a reverse effect. Yet despite this they are generally more effective than a brew of dried raspberries, and what is more important
they help the human organism to combat infection. As for the danger
of carrying satire too far, this does not yet threaten either our theatre
or our motion-picture medium. . . . Paradoxical though it may seem,

* *Kommunist,* September, 1961.

works relating to the twenties and thirties are produced at the Moscow Theatre of Satire with greater daring, confidence, and resourcefulness than comedies dealing with current topics.

PLASTIC ARTS

Russia never attained the heights in painting and sculpture that it reached in the novel, the theatre, and music. Painters are exceedingly well trained. Institutional purchasing is still limited to meticulously realistic work, but individual buyers purchase what suits their fancy and pocketbook. Until the first showing of abstract and other nonfigurative work in Moscow in December, 1962, no artists' names had come to the world's attention as have those of Yevtushenko and some others in literature and the motion picture. One figurative painter and graphic artist, Prorokov, has much of the force of Germany's Käthe Kollwitz of thirty years ago in a somewhat similar style. A sculptor, Ikonnikov, has done powerfully realistic monuments to guerrillas and merchant seamen of World War II. His subjects are not heroes; they are a people stubborn and rugged to the point of heroism.

In 1962, there were some four hundred painters and sculptors in Moscow doing abstract and other nonobjective works. Khrushchev's tirades to the contrary notwithstanding, there is no evidence that these artists were politically disloyal or trying to "smuggle" foreign and hostile ideas into the country. They had had virtually no opportunity to see nonfigurative work. It remains to be seen whether their work represents valid creative effort. It certainly does constitute a legitimate protest against favoritism to paintings that are essentially colored photographs or topical political posters disguised as something else.

The leader in this effort is the critic and painter Eli Belyutin, whose Experimental Studio of Painting and Graphics attracted about one hundred and fifty members. The most publicized among the rebels is the surrealist sculptor Ernest Neizvestny, who is also the patron of young abstractionists. He also does realistic work that is exhibited without difficulty. The painter who has gotten most attention is Ilya Glazunov, whose "modernism" is of the pre-Impressionist period in Western Europe seventy-five years ago. One immense difference between the Stalin period and the present one is that Glazunov has been sent to Italy to study, where he will obviously be exposed to vastly more nonrealist painting than he could have possibly imagined. A more important difference is the way the Communist Party's Ideological Commission undertook to get creative artists in all fields to abandon "useless" or "harmful"

Soviet art is realistic in style. Tschaikowsky by Vilensky, 1947

experiments in styles hard to understand. It did not simply **hand** down an edict, instead, it invited 140 artists to a meeting and engaged them in discussion. At one such gathering, in December, 1962, all three of the artists we have mentioned spoke, plus Yevtushenko and two other controversial young poets. So did at least one of the young novelists regarded officially as having overstepped the line, and the protecting patron of all young experimenters in the U.S.S.R., Ilya Ehrenburg.

Nikita Khrushchev attended the meeting, listened, then spoke. He expressed his attitude very simply by saying that until the abstract artists could successfully explain to him the ideas expressed by their works, their mode of expression would not be acceptable in Soviet society. The essence of the position of the Communist leadership is that arts must communicate, and if they don't, they fail. They see no contradiction between their understanding that a very high level of education is needed to understand science, but that no effort or training should be demanded of the audience to understand art. The young experimenters have not gone unsupported by established realist painters, like Boris Ioganson, who wrote in December, 1962:

We have lived to see the happy day when bans and regulations telling the artist how he must and must not paint have ended. Art is art because it is discovery. And criticism is the study and generalization of these discoveries. No scholar, no theoretician, can foretell in which new form and on the basis of what tradition, really significant artistic works of genius will be created, and what truth about the world it will reveal to us.

In April, 1963, after Mr. Khrushchev had made his ultracritical speech on the arts, Mr. Ioganson rejoined as follows: "The struggle with alien ideology does not mean a drive to throw overboard as many of the achievements of modern Western art and the art of the past as possible."

While the controversy over what should and should not be produced and exhibited raged, the Soviet government pursued its long-term policy of enlarging the availability of art to the people at large. Two hundred and thirty-eight new museums and art galleries were established from 1957 to 1963; they displayed twelve thousand paintings and pieces of sculpture. Nine thousand art shows were held, and 45 million people went to see them in the six years. They included the work of some foreign abstractionists. Of the Fernand Léger exhibit in Moscow, Brooks Atkinson wrote: "I remember with respect the spectacle of a long line of Soviet citizens on a Sunday afternoon patiently standing in the snow and cold to see this series of paintings in an alien style." *

Seven hundred million art books, albums, and reproductions were printed in the six years and priced very low.

Until recently, opportunity to see Soviet art abroad was limited to the few world's fairs in which Russia participated and some special exhibitions organized on a governmental basis. However, in

* The New York Times, May 10, 1963.

Husband, machine-tool worker, and wife, power plant foreman,
at art museum. Visiting galleries is a very popular
recreation among city working people

1961, a London art dealer succeeded in buying some two thousand
examples of graphic art (the various black-gray-white or single-
color techniques). He exhibited them in London, where they drew
high praise. In 1963, he was able to buy oils, water colors, and
lacquer miniatures. His estimate of their merit was that they would
command prices of $400 to $2,000. He said of their style: "It is
all figurative art. There is no nonfigurative art to be bought. But
there is no stereotype that governs either the style or content of
the works."

MUSIC

Music is a field in flux. Prokofiev was prolific until his death
in 1953. Shostakovich and Khachaturian write interestingly and
skillfully, but their new works don't always excite. Men in the
nineteenth-century tradition—Kabalevsky, for instance—do work

Art class for workers of a farm equipment plant.
Union provides paints, easels, brushes

that is pleasing and attractive to listeners who don't object to melody and harmony in music. But these are all older men.

The official line is still against dissonance, the twelve-tone system, and other features characteristic of some contemporary composition in the West. Volkonsky, a young member of an ancient family of the nobility, moved from France to make his home in the Soviet Union a few years ago. His music is modern in the extreme. He is criticized in speeches by fellow composers, but that is all.

A major influence affecting Soviet musical tastes has been the interchange of performers and composers with those abroad. The leading Russian orchestras have played works by modern Americans when the latter have visited the U.S.S.R., and some of these have become part of the regular repertoire. A festival was held in the major city of Gorky to familiarize the public with modern music. Russian émigrés successful in the West, particularly Stravin-sky, have also greatly influenced new trends in the U.S.S.R. He received a tremendous reception when he conducted his own music in a series of concerts there in 1962 after an absence of forty-eight years.

Although political officials still rail against jazz—or some jazz —it is played all the time and everywhere, even in Soviet movies. Shostakovich urges that it be studied. Until recently it was played only for dancing (there are some three thousand bands), but now concerts are given. There are Dixieland combos and groups doing modern jazz. Benny Goodman was welcomed on his tour, but the hip fans had little patience with his old numbers, and sometimes chanted "Zoot!," wanting to hear Zoot Sims give out. Leonard Feather, author of the *Encyclopedia of Jazz,* who accompanied the Goodman band to Moscow, wrote in *Jet* of a Russian guitarist named Nikolai Gromin "who swings so hard and whose style is so brilliant it is almost impossible to realize it was formulated after a limited exposure to a few records."

It is not only in the removal, several years ago, of the ban against public performance of jazz that liberalization has shown itself in music. An opera by Dimitri Shostakovich that Stalin didn't like, *Lady Macbeth of Mtsensk,* was performed in 1963 after a ban that had lasted twenty-seven years. But Shostakovich was not satisfied with this. He wrote his Thirteenth Symphony, also pre-miered in 1963, entirely to poems by Yevtushenko, including the most controversial of all, "Babi Yar," which attacks anti-Semitism in the Soviet Union. After Khrushchev objected to the poem, Yevtushenko removed one line, added one other, and, according to *The New York Times* Moscow correspondent, the poem was essentially "unchanged and seemed to preserve the forcefulness of the original version." Yevtushenko himself insists that he made the change in response to a letter from a reader that made sense to him.

While Soviet music has gained fresh ideas from contact with the West, particularly the United States, since the cultural exchange program began, the West has also profited. The Oistrakhs on the violin, Gilels, Rikhter and Ashkenazy at the piano, Rostropovich on the cello, Galina Vishnevskaya and other vocalists, the Bolshoi Ballet and the Moiseyev Dancers have offered warmth, depth, integrity of performance, a moving involvement in their art, and a wonderful vigor in the folk dance. On the other hand, the Rus-sians have been surprisingly receptive to a number of Americans not very well known in their native land, the conductor Lorin Maazel, for example.

We think of the Soviet performers abroad as Russians, but cultural achievement among the smaller nationalities must not be underrated. The Kirghiz, who number only a million, inhabit a republic of mountains and plateau bordering China's Sinkiang Province in the very heart of Asia. A generation ago they were fairly primitive nomads, whose only arts were purely in the folk category. Yet here is how *The New York Times* reviewed the first Kirghiz ballet film to reach the United States, in September, 1962:

A big, lively stage work . . . vibrating with superb dancing. . . . Add to these a richly barbaric spangling of sets and costumes and the very faces of the dancers, members of the Kirghiz State Opera Company, with an arresting blend of Tartar, Mongolian, and Slavic features. . . . The picture certainly moves, as the dancers throng tented battlefields, ornate palaces, and, finally, an eerie underground kingdom, where two sweethearts overcome an evil witch. The dancers go to town, and for once a ballet heroine conveys real terror. But the incredibly mercurial Bibisara Beishanalieva [a typical Kirghiz name] as the sorcerer, goes the whole company one better by suggesting that she's about to take off into space.

In sum, the Soviet leaders still believe (and there is no reason to expect a change in this, given their basic philosophy of the common man) that art has to be intelligible to the people, and should inspire and encourage them, and give them rest. If art is a means of communicating thoughts and emotions, then forms that fail to communicate except to the creator and a small group who think they understand him, fail as art.

Though Khrushchev feels that art must be intelligible to him personally, the time is past when only a single opinion was permissible on such a subject. Therefore, one now reads articles in the Soviet press saying that if it is normal and proper to accustom to serious classical music those whose "natural" tastes are for folk songs, lyrical pop songs, and jazz, and if it is normal and proper to learn a foreign language for the sheer pleasure of appreciating its literature in the original, why isn't it natural to suppose that the languages of modern expression in the arts should also be taught and learned?

HOW THE ARTIST LIVES

Writers, composers, painters, and sculptors, by the nature of their work, are usually not salaried people. Writers receive royalties based on length of manuscript and copies sold. The royalty rate for poetry, science, scholarship, and other writings that cannot expect mass sale is over three times as high as for fiction, so that writers in those fields are able to earn as much as a novelist. Moreover, 10 per cent of the total retail intake from book sales is paid into the Literary Fund of the Writers Union, which collects close to $10 million per year. It uses this money to build rest homes, clubs, and special medical clinics for writers throughout the country, as well as nurseries, kindergartens, and summer camps for their children. It supports them while they are writing, gives them special grants to make trips to gather material, assists aged members in need, and pays all or part of the costs of their stays at rest homes or sanatoria. The Fund supports writers considered promising who have not yet established themselves as professionals and been voted into the Writers Union of 4,200 members. (There is a separate Journalists Union of 22,000.) The situation of composers and plastic artists is very similar. The Artists Union maintains studios for artists' use, galleries for exhibitions and sale, and art schools. In Leningrad, for example, a block of 25 × 25-foot studios, each two stories high, plus apartments for the artists and their families, was built in 1963.

The minimum price of an original by any of the 8,700 members of the Artists Union is about half a week's wage for a worker. The Ministry of Culture spends $4 million per year to commission works, as it does in other arts ($3,000–$4,000 per symphony, for example). Theatre people are salaried. Theatre companies are self-supporting except for troupes who perform in the languages of minor nationalities among whom, for whatever reason, a company may not yet be able to pay its way.

13: 1980

The new Program of the Soviet Communists, adopted at the Twenty-second Party Congress in October, 1961, says it will give the Soviet people, within twenty years, a living standard, working conditions, and leisure superior to that of Western Europe and even of the United States as it is expected to be in 1980. Space permits only a brief summary of the communist society the Program hopes for.

Whereas Soviet socialism permits two forms of joint ownership of productive property, co-operative and public, communism is to have public property only. Leaders believe that co-operative property gives the joint owners a narrow outlook, under which the interests of their own co-operative may be placed ahead of the public weal.

Under Soviet socialism today, the more skilled the operation or the higher the output, the better are the wages. Under communism, distribution is to be not in accordance with one's contribution to society but according to need. This is not understood as the needs of poverty—minimal survival needs—but the very opposite. It is promised that enough of anything that anyone can reasonably want will be produced so that one will obtain goods without exchange, that is, without payment.

It is understood that such a way of life can exist only if human beings develop the habit and the responsibility of working freely to the best of their abilities for whatever is the normal workday. Since everyone is expected to be able to get whatever he needs, no one, they imagine, will be jealous of anyone else getting more, since no one will be deprived. This is the most controversial of all communist ideas. It assumes that man is inherently good, and that selfishness and greed are consequences of the fact that the history of the race is a history of deprivation, under which some have been able to have everything only by taking from others all but a bare subsistence.

Communism is not a new idea. In the Bible we find, Acts 2 : 44–45: "And all that believed were together, and had all things in common; and sold their possession, and goods, and parted them to all men, as every man had need."

The Hutterite Anabaptists, who now have farming colonies in Canada, the Dakotas, and Montana, have lived in exact accord with this principle for four hundred years. But communists believe that for all people to want to live this way, there must be a level of abundance no country has yet achieved.

Government, or, as communists call it, the state, is to be re-placed, they say, by "public self-government." The Program pro-poses to start immediately by turning over certain government functions to voluntary membership societies (e.g. unions). Begin-nings in this direction have already been made in the past few years.

Communism also seeks to eliminate the traditional differences between town and country people by raising the farm worker and villager to the level of culture, living standard, and economic re-lationships of the city person. Another belief is that the difference between manual and mental labor will disappear. The work skills of the manual worker are to be raised to the level of a technician supervising automated equipment.

It is hoped that the many Soviet nationalities will, in the words of the Program,

draw closer and closer together in all spheres on the basis of a com-plete identity of economic, political, and spiritual interests, of fraternal friendship and cooperation. . . . Family relations will be completely freed from material considerations and will be based solely on mutual love and friendship. . . . Thus, communism puts an end to the di-vision of society into classes and social strata, whereas the whole history of mankind, with the exception of its primitive period, was one of class society in which division into opposing classes led to the exploitation of man by man, class struggle, and antagonisms between nations and states.

SPECIFIC GOALS

Having thus described the human society it believes will be possible after 1980 as a result of developments during the next two decades, the Communist Party then sets certain specific goals for the years before that. It pledges that by 1970 the Soviet Union will have the world's shortest working day, and a per capita production higher than that of the United States. The last goal will almost certainly not be attained by the target date, in the light of the Soviets' own estimate that their total industrial production was 65 per cent of the American in 1963. However, the established rates of growth in both countries indicate that total Soviet output may approximate that of America by 1970, although it will not yet be as high per person.

Between 1970 and 1980, says the Program, "abundance" is promised in material goods and cultural benefits. The country is to "come close" to distribution in accordance with need. There is to be "gradual transition" to public ownership only, as far as productive property is concerned. There will be no interference with private ownership of consumption property: one's house, piano, toothbrush, boat, or car. "The second decade" (1970–1980) is to provide solution of the housing problem. In fact, one-third of the entire population was rehoused in the six years ending in 1962. This is one of the Soviet accomplishments that is most impressive to the people of newly independent underdeveloped countries, and even to lands such as Italy and France, where the housing conditions of working people are very poor.

If the present rate of housing construction is maintained for the next dozen years, all people in cities would be housed, by 1974, with all the modern conveniences and no doubling up of families. But inadequate privacy within the family would still be the rule, for a family of three, including a teenager, is now entitled to only a one-bedroom apartment. The quality of the new housing is also quite poor, because of the tremendous speed of construction and the inexperience of the vast new labor force in this field. Therefore, it is probable that the late 1970's will see the beginning of another long-term program to double the amount of space per family. Whether at that time they will still think in terms of apartment houses or have shifted to private homes remains to be seen.

INDUSTRIAL TARGETS

Industry in 1970 is planned to produce two and one-half times as much as in 1960, and to exceed by nearly one-third the level

This will be the most typical sight in the Soviet Union for another twenty years

of 1963 in the United States. Actually, by 1960, according to an American study* the Soviet industries that govern future growth were already operating at levels equal to or higher than American ones. The industries manufacturing machinery and shaping metals were running at 98 per cent to 109 per cent of the U.S. figures, and the production of mineral construction materials was 55 per cent higher than the American. However, because the output of consumer goods, chemicals, and combined fuel-and-power production were so much lower than in the United States, total Soviet industry was at only three-fifths the level of American.

In 1980, the U.S.S.R. hopes to produce six times as much, over-all, as in 1960. In evaluating the possibility that this goal will be attained, two facts should be borne in mind. One is that output in 1962 was equal to the *combined total* for the thirteen years of industrialization, 1928–1940. Secondly, Soviet industry did grow fivefold in the fifteen years after the end of World War II. Therefore, a further sixfold rise in twenty years is not out of the question.

It is planned to link the entire vast country from Leningrad to the Pacific in a single power network to enable electricity to be sent instantaneously wherever it is most needed. By 1963, over half the electricity in the U.S.S.R. was routed by one control panel in Moscow. Other countries transmit long-range power by alternating current, which is limited by losses in transmission; Soviet engineers have solved the problem of transmission by direct current, and in 1962 put into operation an 800,000-volt line of that nature. Secretary of the Interior Udall, who inspected the line and the Soviet dams that are the world's greatest individual power producers, believes that this type of transmission could solve the problem of providing California with seasonal peak power from the Bonneville Dam on the Columbia River, which could provide power far exceeding the needs of Oregon and Washington.

PROPOSED SOCIAL REFORMS

Mitchell Wilson, author of *Meeting at a Far Meridian* and other novels translated into Russian, recently lived in the Soviet Union for six months on his ruble royalties. He was a welcome guest in the homes of Soviet writers, scientists, and theatre people. He found that it was they, not the political leaders or managerial people, who had the country's highest incomes. Yet of forty homes he visited, the most spacious was an apartment of four large rooms. A Nobel Prize winner, Professor Semyonoff, who is also a member

* Tarn and Campbell, *American Economic Review,* September, 1962.

of the Academy of Sciences, had three small rooms. He describes his hosts' summer cottages as "modestly middle class" by American standards. They employ maids, and they own cars comparable to American compacts.

Wilson cites royalty figures to show that a best-selling novelist earns only one-eighth as much as an American writer of equal popularity measured in numbers of books sold. Thus, the Soviet's highest income groups live much more modestly than do landowners, merchants, bankers, and industrialists in very much poorer countries in Latin America and Asia. The lowest income groups in the U.S.S.R. certainly do not go hungry; they have adequate clothing, essentially free medical care, assurance of jobs, education, and radio, movies, and amusement parks.

But there is still a substantial difference between the "modestly middle class" family and the peasant family. That is the difference in income levels that exists in the U.S.S.R. The Party Program contains a promise to triple the real income of people in the minimum-wage bracket by 1970, which would bring these lowest earners up to about 20 per cent above what the average Russian today regards as a satisfactory living. Meanwhile, it is planned almost to double the earnings of the person of average income. The spread of 3 to 1 that now exists between average and minimum earnings would thus be narrowed to 2 to 1 in ten years.

It is expected that collective farmers' incomes will rise more rapidly than city incomes because of faster increase in productivity, through mechanization and basic changes in farming methods. While city incomes twenty years from now are planned to be more than three times as high as today, farm income is to be more than four times as high. Considering the present difference between town and country living, this means that the farmer of 1980 would still not be living quite as well as his cousin in town.

Though full communism is expected to come after 1980, one-half of the income level of that year is to be not in the form of money, but in free goods or services. The free items are foreseen as: (1) full-time boarding schools for children of those parents who wish to raise their children this way (the government hopes all will, and is budgeting tremendous sums for this); (2) all other education; (3) public support of all who are unable to work (in 1964, collective farmers were brought under this umbrella for the first time in the history of the U.S.S.R.); (4) medical care including drugs and sanatorium treatment (drugs, although cheap, and part of sanatorium costs, must be paid for at present); (5)

Farm laborers' club room

housing in apartments; (6) partially free vacation resorts and
other facilities; (7) larger and more inclusive benefit payments of
all kinds (higher student scholarships for living costs, for example);
and (8) a full midday meal at work or in school.

Leisure is expected to increase greatly. The average work week
in the U.S.S.R. today is thirty-nine hours. This is probably the
lowest average for full-time employment anywhere, but the Soviet
person wastes a great deal of time because of inadequate shopping
facilities. The program pledges elimination of this nuisance, and
contains a promise of a thirty-five-to-thirty-six hour work week by
1970, with thirty hours for underground and harmful jobs. The
minimum paid vacation is to be increased to three and subsequently
to four weeks. Actually, many people already have vacations of
that length. Collective farmers are also to get paid vacations. Night

shifts are to be abolished except in service occupations (public transportation, hospitals) and continuous-process operations.

For leisure, "there are to be more libraries, lecture halls, and reading rooms, theatres, clubs, houses of culture, and movies." Formal education is to be expanded at all levels, and noncredit courses are to be developed on a large scale. "A large network of scientific and technical laboratories and of art and movie studios will be provided for the use of all who have the inclination and ability."

It is promised that such facilities will be distributed uniformly throughout the country for the benefit of rural people and the populations of the cities now being built in Siberia and east of the Volga.

The over-all picture of the future planned for 1980 is of modest comfort for the entire population by American middle-class standards of today. There would be just enough housing space for quiet reading, conversation, or listening at home. There would be little distraction by children, thanks to boarding-school upbringing of children, with parents free to participate or to take over, to whatever degree they desire. Educational opportunity is to be unlimited, with enough colleges for all who wish to attend. Jobs are to be physically undemanding and work interesting in a progressively automated technology, and leisure is to be ample for pleasure, self-development, and participation in public affairs. This is the plan. Measured against the Soviets' previous rates of progress, it is cautious, not visionary. The 50 per cent rise in crops, and 100 per cent in livestock farming since 1953, indicate that when enough money is put into agriculture, they get results there as well. Of course, the whole plan becomes meaningless if there is war.

INTERNATIONAL ASPECTS

The Program is cautious in its international as in its internal aspects. The future living standard is calculated entirely upon what Soviet resources themselves can provide with further development of present levels of industry, farming, science, and skills. If the world situation improves to permit resumption of unrestricted trade, Russia will gain by a faster improvement in living standards, just as her trading partners will benefit by the acquisition of an enlarged world market. But she is not counting on this in her planning, although a more varied diet is already resulting from commerce with Asia, Latin America, and Africa. Yet the Program does say that a tense world will mean a slower rise in living stand-

Moscow University

ards, while a quicker improvement will occur if disarmament is agreed upon.

This was demonstrated by the Soviet purchase of almost a billion dollars' worth of grain in 1963. The domestic crop was actually no lower than in 1959, which had been an excellent year by previous standards. But at that time the Cold War was raging, and Moscow did not dare spend its precious gold hoard abroad for food. In 1963, the bomb-test treaty had been signed, the U.S. and U.S.S.R. had pledged not to put bombs in orbit, and Khrushchev felt free to maintain the improved living standard by purchases abroad.

The very idea of a Twenty-Year Plan in the atomic age assumes a world at peace. The tremendous sums expended in gathering the data on which to base such a long-term plan for so vast a country, the training of an enormous personnel for this planning, the building and allocation of costly computers to make the necessary calculations, all indicate a serious intent. If nothing else, the great undertakings in progress that any tourist may see—the rebuilding of the large cities—would be senseless if the Soviet leaders expected them to be destroyed in a nuclear war. The U.S.S.R. has presented the United Nations with a sculpture entitled: *Let Us Beat Our Swords into Plowshares*. Commented Soviet leader Mikoyan: "We are not put out by the fact that these words are taken from the Biblical prophet Isaiah."

MORAL CODE

The ethics of the communist way of life are spelled out in the Party Program of 1961 in a moral code that roused great interest in the Soviet Union, judging by letters to the press between the publication of the draft and the adoption of the new program in final form. Here are selections:

Conscientious labor for the good of society—he who does not work, neither shall he eat. [Compare the Bible, 2 Thessalonians 3 : 10 "For even when we were with you, this we commanded you, that if any would not work, neither should he eat."]

Concern on the part of everyone for the preservation and growth of the public wealth; collectivism and comradely mutual assistance: one for all and all for one; humane relations and mutual respect between individuals—man is to man a friend, comrade, and brother; honesty and truthfulness, moral purity, modesty and openness in public and private life; mutual respect in the family, and concern for the upbringing of children; an uncompromising attitude toward injustice, parasitism, dishonesty, and careerism; intolerance of national and racial hatred.

The discussion of this code in letters to the press showed no cynicism, but a desire to plug loopholes by which individuals or organizations avoid their moral responsibilities. A woman construction foreman wanted the Program to state that Party organizations have the duty to help build a new family life based on this code of morals. She said the Party had not been concerning itself with anything but increasing industrial output, and with public affairs. Clearly, she regards the organization as being like a religious order. Far from wanting it to keep out of personal life, she believes it to be failing in its duty by not entering it.

A pensioner wanted the moral code to include its "irreconcilability to profit-making," indicating that temptation is still there. A woman county-government head complained that few women were in high positions. She wrote that men prevented this by a prejudiced attitude and then took a condescending attitude toward women who did occupy responsible posts. On the farms, she protested, men took the office jobs and relegated women to the hard physical labor. Since the war, she reported, women had become so accustomed to this that some of them even objected to the advancement of members of their own sex. Therefore, she proposed that the code also include the following: "Assistance in raising women's position in public affairs, irreconcilability to manifestations of an uncomradely attitude and to attempts to infringe upon woman's dignity and role as an active builder of socialism."

A woman from Turkmenia, which is just north of Iran and has a Mohammedan cultural background said that there are thirty-five Turkmen women managing industrial enterprises, nineteen heading collective farms, 280 holding the office of vice-chairmen of collective farms, 109 holding paid Party positions, and 288 in government administration. The entire Turkmen nationality numbers about a million. She agreed that "some Party and government agencies are still dragging their feet in the promotion of women and, when they do promote them, give them inadequate assistance." There can be no doubt that the sending of Valentina Tereshkova into space in June, 1963, was a tremendous boost to women's morale and to the average earthbound man's respect for women's abilities and courage.

All in all, the letters to the editor give the impression that Soviet people regard the moral code as desirable, possible of achievement, but not yet the normal standard of conduct by far.

PARTICIPATION IN PUBLIC LIFE

One of the factors contributing to the dictatorial aspects of Soviet government has been that, in the past, the common man had neither the time nor the education to participate actively and in an informed manner. He has some of both today, and by 1980 is expected to be working much shorter hours. He will then have,

San Francisco–Moscow peace walker of 1961 with Mrs. Khrushchev

as a minimum, high-school education equal to junior college by present American standards. On this basis, the Program sets the objective "that work on government staffs eventually cease to constitute a profession."

The present picture is strangely mixed. On the one hand, there is a real effort to carry out the promise "always to consult the working people on the major questions of home and foreign policy, to make these questions an object of nation-wide discussion." On the other hand, there is flat violation of the letter and spirit of this promise, as in 1962 when the entire structure of Party and government were suddenly split on agricultural-industrial lines with no advance public discussion. No word of disagreement among Soviet citizens with foreign-policy concepts or tactics has yet been allowed to appear in any of the newspapers or magazines available to correspondents in Moscow or received abroad. The Chinese Communists, by publishing the statements of both sides in the deep policy split in the Communist world, compelled Moscow to do so also, and this contributed greatly to freedom of discussion in the U.S.S.R.

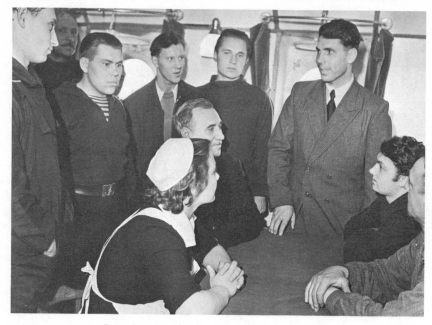

Longshoreman congressman with constituents—
crew of ship based in district

I know of at least one Soviet citizen who disagrees with foreign policy (obviously there are more) for I saw him conduct a one-man picket line for a Tolstoian-Gandhian peace policy in the lobby of the Moscow Hotel in 1962. This action had no precedent in thirty-five years.

The Program repeats the standard formula of the desirability of "criticism and self-criticism" and condemns the "cult of the individual." Yet not one word criticizing Khrushchev has appeared in all his years in power, and it is rare for a formal speech by anyone on any subject whatever not to credit him for one thing or another. On the other hand, Khrushchev condemned praise of himself in his striking closing speech at the 1961 Party Congress. Today, no town or institution any longer bears his name or that of any other living Soviet political figure.

The press has, however, published demands by ordinary citizens for rights beyond those promised in the quotations above. For example, the Program states: "The principle of electivity and accountability to representative bodies and to the electorate will gradually be extended to all the leading officials of government bodies." Officials now appointive are to become elective.

The Program also calls for an apparatus by which the people can monitor the operation of government bodies. A long letter in *Trud* rejoined that the unions ought to have this function and that, in any case, these monitoring bodies should be elective. Further, the writer wanted the regional heads of all business activities (chairmen of councils of the national economy) to be elective. He wasn't satisfied with the fact that the Program calls for an end to bureaucracy, but asked why there should be any at all forty-four years after the Revolution, and demanded that, in its final form, the Program carry an explanation of this. His demand was not met.

The debate on all aspects of life continues. A new Constitution of the Union of Soviet Socialist Republics is slowly being drafted for the purpose of writing new liberties in a fresh framework. When the draft is completed, a formal point-by-point national discussion will begin anew. Apparently, the doors that have been opened are not to be closed again.

14: East–West Points of
Contact—Sports, Arts, Trade

Peaceful competition, competitive coexistence, peaceful coexistence—call it what you will—between Americans and Russians in sports has been going on since the 1952 Olympic Games, the first in which the Soviet Union participated. The Americans won the Olympics of 1952, and all the men's dual track-and-field meets now held annually with the U.S.S.R. The Soviets won the 1956 and 1960 Olympics, and all the women's events in the dual track meets. Sometimes Russians take over events in which Americans have traditionally excelled—the high jump, the broad jump—and sometimes it is the other way around, particularly in certain women's events. But in the dozens of encounters that have by now taken place in all sports, in the United States, in the Soviet Union, and elsewhere in multinational meets, the athletes have always gotten along in a manner the diplomats could take lessons from. This has been true even in sports like ice hockey, in which bruising body contact and stick play are part of the game.

The press, radio, and television have brought the good will surrounding these encounters to the people at large. Here is *Trud* on April 26, 1958, describing the preliminaries at the first visit of an American basketball team to Russia:

228

Flags of the United States and of the Soviet Union hung over the stands. Friendly words of greeting in both English and Russian were hung above one of the stands. . . . The American and Soviet basketball players paraded onto the court to stormy applause. . . . Then the President of the Amateur Athletic Union, Mr. Kellum Johnson, took the floor. . . . He said: "Dear friends of the Soviet Union. We are very glad to visit your country and are sure the games here will promote friendship among our athletes. We also are sure that your sportsmen in the United States will receive the same kind of hospitality. We have a high regard for Soviet athletes. Long live friendship between our people." These words of Mr. Johnson were drowned by a stormy ovation in the hall.

On another occasion, *The New York Times* opened a story from Moscow: "Russians Applaud as U.S. Crew Wins. . . . Hundreds of fans and dozens of husky Soviet women oarsmen who train at the club ran to the dock to congratulate the Americans."

Russian courtesy has been reciprocated when Soviet athletes have visited the United States: the AAU canceled the usual band music during competition at the 1961 championships, in which Russians participated, because they were not used to this and found it "distracting, disturbing, and irritating."

Soviet sports contacts have expanded enormously. The number of teams going abroad increased from forty-nine in 1951 to 455 in 1961, and the number of countries visited rose from fifteen to fifty-one. The figures for foreign teams visiting the U.S.S.R. were almost exactly the same.

The tremendous improvement in Russian athletes reflects better training, of course, more facilities, more leisure time, but above all else, the vast numbers of participants from whom international competitors are drawn. In preparation for the 1960 Olympics (where the point score was U.S.S.R. 807½, U.S.A. 564½) twenty million people participated in the Third U.S.S.R. Games of 1959. That figure rose to forty million in 1963 (one-sixth of the population!), when the preliminary meets were held at 300,000 industries, institutions, educational establishments, collective and state farms. Thus, the Soviets are approaching their goal of interesting practically every able-bodied person in participating in what they call physical culture. They also conducted national high-school championship meets for the first time in 1963, including track-and-field, swimming and diving, basketball, and gymnastics.

Russian sports interests differ from American to some degree. Baseball is unknown, as is golf. The most popular mass-participation sport is track-and-field, followed by skiing, soccer, wrestling, boxing, and rowing, in that order. Like most Continental Europeans, Russians value stamina most in running, and their interest in the sprints is low. Skiing to them is a cross-country sport, and lift facilities for downhill skiing are very few. There are many jumping hills, however. Girls do not take part in soccer, wrestling, or boxing, but they row in all classes of boats, particularly the eight-oar shells.

Purely recreational sport—the kind you see at a picnic—favors volleyball, played hard and fast, in the summer. In winter, skating becomes a universal recreation for young and old, and miles of park pathways are flooded for freezing. The ice show is a very new thing in the Soviet Union, but with the Russian love for skating and ballet, they have created an extraordinarily fine company in just a few years.

Basketball, virtually unknown in the U.S.S.R. before World War II, today ranks second only to volleyball as recreation among youth. There are tens of thousands of courts, and Soviet teams are at or near the top in the world championships. Soccer is now third as a pick-up game.

On a summer Sunday, I have seen the great network of canals and reservoirs outside Moscow swarming with sailboat regattas. Most of the boats are club property, although increasing numbers of people are now building their own.

While horse racing at tracks is on the decline, a variety of saddle sports is part of the way of life of the Russo-Ukrainian Cossacks, the Georgian mountaineers, the Kazakh and Kirghiz plainsmen of Asia, and the Turkmenian counterparts of the Bedouin of the desert. They practice straight racing—often for extreme distances—and primitive native polo, lacrosse, and pushball on horseback. The northern minorities race reindeer teams.

Russian country boys—and country-born city folk—enjoy a stick-throwing game on the bowling principle. The sticks are heavy, and the game requires great strength. A traditional competition in the villages is to see how many times a seventy-five-pound iron ball with a handle can be lifted straight-armed above one's head, which explains why Soviet youth took to the bar-bells like ducks to water.

There's nothing in the United States quite like the ambition among Soviet boys and girls to win an all-round athlete pin. The requirements aren't easy: a half-mile swim, cross-country skiing, cross-country running, exercises showing co-ordination and strength, and tests of speed, agility, and endurance. Forty million wear the pin! This figure includes adults who won it in their youth.

CULTURE

The story of the gangling twenty-three-year-old from Texas who won the Tschaikovsky piano competition in Moscow is one of the great tales of this generation. But Van Cliburn has been followed by a steady stream of young pianists, cellists, and violinists, from the United States and all the world, who go to Moscow to be judged by international juries of the great masters of these instruments. Some Americans have won prizes, some have not, but the contact with young people—Chinese and Japanese as well as Israeli and English—equally devoted to music, has resulted in personal friendships and mutual understanding.

It has become expected that American audiences will be warmer to Russian performers, and Russian to American, than to people of other citizenships, in each case. There is little doubt that this reflects, on both sides, an attempt by the common man in the audience—box seats or balcony—to express in his own way the hope that the two peoples never meet on more hostile ground than this. And when Ed Sullivan puts the Moiseyev dancers on television screens throughout America, and Benny Goodman is heard on every radio set in Russia, certainly a blow is dealt to the "we will bury you" image of Russians, and the "aggressive imperialist" picture of Americans.

Cultural exchange represents something more positive than merely live and let live. It means that each people recognizes that there is some benefit to be obtained, some healthy human pleasure to be gained, and—particularly in science—something to be learned from the other. When American and Soviet physicists at a conference in the United States both speak of the enormous benefits to be reaped by probing new sources of energy with atom-smashers that can only be built at the cost of billions of dollars, they know that they are advancing the cause of disarmament, because not even countries as wealthy as these can afford both such vast expenditures on science and a continued arms race. And when these scientists say to each other: Why come together just once a year to exchange ideas when we could fertilize each other's work that much more easily by working side-by-side; why limit ourselves to the high-energy machines our governments can afford individually when so much more could be learned from more powerful machines jointly financed?—they push their countries toward a more civilized, and a safer, existence.

When the Russians ask Jan Peerce to stay in Moscow to train opera singers, and when the ambition of every girl working seriously at a ballet-bar in Portland, Oregon or Maine, is to study with the Bolshoi Ballet, hopes for human survival have become just a little bit higher.

An American exhibition in Moscow spurs Russians to set their sights for a living standard higher than they had aimed, and sooner. Russian exhibitions in the United States have caused Americans to want more substantial education for their children and better provision for preschool care.

The Russian woman is excited by American home appliances to help her have as much free time as her husband, and the American woman is excited by the Russian's opportunity to do anything open to a man, including flight in outer space.

When "Sixteen Tons" becomes the rage with Soviet teenagers, and "Midnight in Moscow" stays near the top of the hit parade for weeks in the United States, the listeners in each country can't feel very belligerent toward the other. The disappearance of the feeling of mystery that would result if the present student exchanges were extended to the high-school level is suggested by the following observations of the fifteen-year-old son of *The New York Times* correspondent in Moscow, after two years in a Soviet school: *

Although there are the expected differences between Soviet and American youths, their interests are practically the same—girls, music, cars. . . . Boys wait a month between haircuts, but otherwise they are well-groomed. They usually have one or two heavy sports jackets for everyday wear, and one good suit, or sports jacket and slacks, for school dances. . . . There will probably be about twenty school dances this year. They are held before each of the four vacations and on some Saturday evenings. . . . Recently there was a variety show organized by the Komsomol (Communist Youth League). . . . The Komsomol also supplied a jazz quintet. . . . Their dance to fast music is what is called the Mashed Potato in the United States.

[At a party at his house, they] danced a little and played spin-the-bottle. This game is just as well known here as in the United States.

My friends and I go to the movies quite often, once in a while with girls. The boys also watch a lot of television. . . .

We have gone on two hikes into the forest about twenty miles out-

* *The New York Times,* June 11, 1963.

At a factory club

side Moscow, both for two days. . . . Both hikes were organized by the kids themselves. . . . The eighth-grade boys gathered firewood, the eleventh-grade boys put up the tents, and the girls prepared the meals: sandwiches, borscht, and meat mixed with mashed potatoes. After we ate, we sat down around the fire, singing songs and telling jokes. . . . I managed to get about three hours' sleep, which my friends say is doing well on a hike.

Boys start smoking at about fifteen, without their parents' knowledge, of course. (They are quite independent and do not see their parents much.) During recess, the older boys go into the school washroom to smoke. . . .

My friends express interest in visiting foreign countries, especially the United States. As they say, "we want to find out and see new, interesting things."

As this is written, only about twenty American high-school students per year visit the Soviet Union, under a program organized by the Choate School at Wallingford, Connecticut. No Soviet teenagers visit the United States, except for an occasional diplomat's child.

On February 9, 1963, *The New York Times* printed an editorial that represented a sharp change in its attitude on an important area of possible contact with the U.S.S.R.:

TRADING WITH MOSCOW

In the past few days Moscow has successfully concluded new trade agreements with France and Japan, in further expansion of the already appreciable Soviet commerce with these major industrialized free world nations. These agreements fall into the general pattern of the past decade, which has seen sharp increases in Soviet commerce with most of the countries of Western Europe and Japan.

The great exception to this pattern is of course the United States. Soviet-American trade remains relatively minuscule. . . . A great many goods the Russians would like to buy here—notably advanced production machinery in many fields—are barred to them by our stringent system of strategic trade controls. Those controls are far tighter in the United States than they are elsewhere. Moscow claims it can buy in Western Europe and Japan many items denied it here.

A great deal has happened in the world since the United States first imposed strategic trade controls. In those far-off days the Soviet Union was weak, and there was perhaps then some basis for hope that if the West refused to aid Moscow's economic development the Soviet Union would remain weak. Any such hopes have been blasted by events. Moreover, when the original policy was created, this country had no balance of payments problem of any consequence and there were no worries about our losses of gold. Today this situation is substantially altered too. It is time for a serious re-examination of an embargo policy that contrasts sharply with the attitude taken by many of America's allies.

Until Canada's immense half-billion-dollar grain sale in 1963, West Germany did more business with the Soviet Union ($400 million per year) than any other NATO country. The firm most active in promoting this is the great Krupp combine, providing a striking example of conversion from armaments to peacetime manufacture. France will be doing just about the same amount of business with Moscow as Germany under the three-year Franco-Soviet agreement of 1963, providing for an increase of 10 to 15 per cent. Britain is close behind with $330 million. By an offer to sell Britain machine tools that England now buys from the United States, the Soviet Union told Washington indirectly that America could have the U.S.S.R. either as a customer or as a competitor, but could no longer ignore her in world commerce. A London

"Big Inch" pipeline

Chamber of Commerce representative said of this machinery that it was at least the equal of the American product currently being imported into Britain.

The new pact with Japan referred to in the editorial provides for a 50 per cent jump in trade with Russia within three years. All these countries, plus very small ones like Finland, and underdeveloped lands like India and Brazil, do more trade with the U.S.S.R. than did the United States, until the $250–$375 million grain sale of 1963. Of course, the Communist countries, with East Germany in the lead, do more business with the U.S.S.R. than do Western nations, but that is another story.

Large numbers, in dollars or anything else, are not very meaningful to most of us. Let's look at this trade in terms of the items sold. In 1962, Japan, the world's greatest shipbuilding power, received the largest foreign order in its history from the Soviet Union: twelve 35,000-ton tankers, five 12,000-ton freighters, and twenty-eight other ships and floating harbor equipment. France is selling the U.S.S.R. entire factories for making electronic equipment and for processing foods. One British company sold Moscow

Cubans in Moscow

a complete nylon factory, and another a complete tire works, regarded as the world's most modern. In 1961, Italy, which ranks lower in total Soviet commerce than the other NATO powers listed, sold Russia complete plants to make methanol, ammonia, and other chemicals; complete equipment for a very large paper-pulp mill; a whole tire-cord factory; automation and remote control equipment; oil pipeline equipment; and rayon.

Soviet sales to France include petroleum and petroleum products, hard coal, manganese and chromium for steel-making, watches, and machine equipment. Other products sold to developed countries include lumber, grain in normal crop years, and vegetable oil. What the U.S.S.R. sells to underdeveloped countries may be illustrated by the list in their treaty with Brazil: oil-drilling, mining, foundry, and electronic equipment; planes, helicopters, tractors, trucks, watches, fertilizers, gasoline, chemicals, newsprint, cellulose, medical instruments, oil, and wheat. From Brazil the U.S.S.R. buys coffee, fruit juices, guitars, movies.

The seriousness with which European business regards the Soviet market is indicated by the fact that seven hundred British companies exhibited their products at a special British Trade Fair in

Moscow in 1961, and in 1964 Britain arranged in that city the first agricultural show it has ever organized abroad, to spur trade in farm products.

Russia has aided many underdeveloped countries in the form of loans at 2 or 2½ per cent interest, with no repayment due until a year after she has delivered the complete plant under the agreement. The purpose of the delay is to enable the countries to repay out of the profits of these new enterprises. Total Soviet nonmilitary credits and grants outside of the Communist bloc were over five billion dollars by the end of 1962. The major impact of these commitments has yet to be felt, because only one-quarter of this sum had been drawn upon by the recipients by that time. For example, India, the largest non-Communist beneficiary, was given a billion dollars in credits by Moscow for economic aid and technical assistance. She had been able to make use of less than one-quarter billion by mid-1962, but had already built with it a large steel mill, machinery plants, and mines. The Aswan Dam in Egypt, which is being built with Soviet equipment, plans, and engineers, involves seventeen times as much rock work as the Great Pyramid of Cheops.

The Russians believe there is room for both East and West in the industrialization of the formerly colonial countries. A leading Soviet economist, Professor Rubinstein, writes:

The simultaneous construction of steel mills in India by the Soviet Union, Britain, and West Germany may be mentioned as an illustration. It is, however, necessary to increase substantially the technical assistance to the underdeveloped countries from the United Nations Fund. Much could be accomplished through bilateral and multilateral co-operation.

Before World War II, the U.S.S.R., third in population, was only sixteenth in world trade. Since then its foreign commerce has multiplied twenty times over, and now ranks fifth, after the U.S., West Germany, Britain, and France. Inasmuch as the U.S.S.R. is second in production, its share in the world market can be expected to increase. Three-quarters of its business is with its allies, one-quarter with the West and with neutral countries on all continents. Trade with the West doubled in the five years from 1956 through 1961. With Asia and Africa it tripled. The U.S.S.R. does business now with eighty countries, twice as many as at the end of World War II. In the words of John F. Kennedy:*

* Speech at the American University, June 10, 1963.

We must deal with the world as it is, and not as it might have been had the history of the last eighteen years been different. . . . Let us re-examine our attitude toward the Soviet Union. . . . Almost unique among the major world powers, we have never been at war with each other. . . . Both the United States and its allies, and the Soviet Union and its allies, have a mutually deep interest in a just and genuine peace and in halting the arms race. . . . We are willing and able to engage in peaceful competition with any people on earth.

Four months later, announcing the 1,700,000-ton sale of wheat and cattle feed to the U.S.S.R., the late President said that this "will benefit our balance of payments and gold reserves and substantially strengthen the economic outlook for those employed in producing, transporting, handling, and loading farm products." He called it "one more hopeful sign that a more peaceful world is both possible and beneficial to us all."

Index

Abramov, Fyodor, 200
Academy of Sciences, 16, 182ff., 190; Siberian Center of the, 92
Adenauer, Konrad, 42
Afghanistan, 3, 61
Agriculture, before 1917, 14–15, 18, 51; and collective farms, 7, 24f., 26, 28, 29–30, 38f., 40, 50, 59, 75, 79, 115–20, 121, 123–24, 127, 135, 220; growth of, 48, 51–52, 54, 60–61, 121–23, 124f., 127–28; and land-reclaiming projects, 4–5, 6, 39, 61f., 101, 120f., 147; reorganization of, 43, 140; and state farms, 120–21. *See also* Labor, Management
Aksenov, V., 199
Aleuts, 65
Alexander II, 18
Allies, Western, 23
Alma-Ata, 62f.
Alphabet, 16
Alyoshin, Samuel, quoted, 203
American Relief Administration, 25
Antarctica, Treaty on, 191
Anti-Bolsheviks, 66
"Anti-Comintern Pact" (Japanese-German-Italian alliance of 1936), 31f.
Anti-Semitism, 44, 66ff., 211. *See also* Jews, Judaism
Apsheron Peninsula, 54
Archangel, 23f.
Architecture, 5, 55, 57f., 60, 62, 194
Arctic regions, 32, 64–65, 182–83, 186
Armed forces, 20, 34, 36, 40, 67, 70. *See also* Red Army
Armenia, 8
Armenian Gregorian Church, 86
Armenians, 53–54, 85f.
Artists Union, 213
Arts, plastic, 30–31, 44, 114, 194, 206–09, 213
Artsimovich, Lev A., 187
Ashkenazy, Viktor, 211
Atheism, 8, 83f.
Atkinson, Brooks, quoted, 13, 204, 208
Attlee, Sir Clement, 35
Aurora, 22
Austria, 6
Autonomous republics, government of, 63–64
Azerbaijan, 8, 54

"Babi Yar," 44, 68, 211
Baku, 7, 20, 54f., 144

Ballet, 53f., 63f., 194, 197, 211f., 232
Baltic States, 7–8, 33, 55–57, 86
Banks, nationalization of, 22
Bashkirs, 63
Baumgartner, Dr. Leona, quoted, 129–30
"Believers," 81–86
Belorussia (White Russia), 8, 33, 50–53, 83, 165
Belyutin, Eli, 206
Berestov, Vladimir, 200
Bergelson, David, 68
Beria, Lavrenti P., 39
Berlin, 37; East, 38
Bessarabia, 33
Black Hundreds, 20
Blok, Alexander, 194
Blokhin, Dr. Nikolai, 132
"Bloody Sunday," 19
Boarding schools, 89, 93, 219
Bolotnikov, Ivan, revolt of, 15
Bolsheviks, 66
Bondarev, Yuri, 199
Books, 31, 67–68, 94–95. *See also* Literature
Borodino, battle of, 17
Brezhnev, Leonid I., 181
Britain. *See* Great Britain
Buddhism, 86
Bulganin, Nikolai A., 139
Bulgaria, 36
Byedny, Demyan, 194
Bykovsky, Valery, 188f.
Byzantium, 14

Calendar, 16
Capitalism, 11–12, 74
Caucasus, 7f., 23, 53–55
Central Asia, 8, 23, 28, 53, 55, 57–62
Central Asia, University of, 59
Central Committee, Communist Party, 26ff., 39, 41, 43f., 125, 139–40, 145, 147, 185–86. *See also* Presidium
Chabukiani, Vakhtang, 53, 197
Chiang Kai-shek, 38
Children, and parents, 93–94; and out-of-school activities, 94–97
Chinese Communists, 38, 225
Christianity, 8, 14, 22, 43, 55, 87, 81–84, 85–86
Chukchi, 64–65
Chukhrai, Gregory, 202
Churchill, Sir Winston, 23; quoted, 33f.
Citizen organizations, 166–67